Larry Kramer is a writer and AIDS activist.

In 1981 with five friends he cofounded Gay Men's Health Crisis, the world's first provider of services to people with HIV. In 1987, he founded ACT UP, the worldwide advocacy and protest organization.

After receiving his B.A. from Yale University in 1957, he entered the film industry, becoming Assistant to the President of, first, Columbia Pictures, and then United Artists.

With the arrival of the plague of HIV in 1981, Kramer turned full-time to his activist work, writing plays, articles, and speeches, as well as becoming deeply committed to ACT UP.

He is the first creative artist and the first gay person to be honored by a Public Service Award from Common Cause. He is also a recipient of the Award in Literature from the American Academy of Arts and Letters.

In the year 2000 one of his most cherished dreams came true with the establishment of the Larry Kramer Initiative for Lesbian and Gay Studies at Yale.

Kramer was born in Connecticut, grew up in Washington, D.C., lived in London from 1961 to 1970, and now lives in New York and Connecticut with his lover, architect/designer David Webster. He is working on a long novel about the plague, *The American People*.

Susan Sontag said this about him: "Larry Kramer is one of America's most valuable troublemakers. I hope he never lowers his voice."

By Larry Kramer

Fiction
Faggots

Plays
Sissies' Scrapbook
A Minor Dark Age
The Normal Heart
Just Say No
The Destiny of Me

Screenplay
Women in Love

Nonfiction
Reports from the holocaust: the story of an AIDS activist

Women in Love

and

Other Dramatic Writings

by Larry Kramer

Women in Love: The Screenplay
Sissies' Scrapbook
A Minor Dark Age
Just Say No
The Farce in Just Saying No: An Essay

With a Foreword by Frank Rich

Grove Press
New York

For Tom Erhardt, David Picker,
and Will Schwalbe

Foreword

The first time I met Larry Kramer was in the early 1970s, when he was in the movie business and I was a fledgling movie critic. The place was Lillian Hellman's home on the Upper East Side of Manhattan. Hellman was not there, but the friend who was throwing the dinner party had access to the grand old dame's apartment, a drab repository for the furniture and knickknacks she had salvaged for personal use from the sets of her Broadway productions. Kramer was not yet involved in the theater. Nor was I. He was certainly not involved in politics. But in retrospect it's clear that Hellman's home was a prescient setting for the artist and activist he would become. Perhaps no American playwright since Hellman, including Arthur Miller, has had Larry Kramer's determination for juggling a career in the theater with no-holds-barred political advocacy, carried out in his case to enormous effect on the front lines of one of the transformative battlefronts of late-twentieth-century America.

The trouble for an artist who swings between art and front-page political activity is that the art sometimes is ignored or short-changed by audiences and critics who want to see a writer's work through a single lens. Larry Kramer wrote only one play that was expressly about his crusade to awaken the world to AIDS, *The Normal Heart*. It is a powerful play that is constantly revived, but it is far from the sum of his career as a writer, any more than *Watch on the Rhine* is the sum of Hellman's. In this volume, the reader will find a collection of some of the less well known products of his writing life from its inception to its maturity, including one play, *A Minor Dark Age,* that has never been previously published or produced. Through them, and through the funny and candid essays that accompany them, one can assemble the biography of a writer who cannot be pigeonholed in either style or substance by his performance on stage and off during the era of AIDS and *The Normal Heart.*

That biography begins with the movies. When I first met Kramer, he had already written his adaptation of *Women in Love,* an early directorial effort of Ken Russell, the English filmmaker whose name would eventually become a synonym for florid cinematic overkill. In his introduction to his screenplay, Kramer lets us in on the idiocies, indignities, and heartaches of being a lowly screenwriter up against the moneymen and revolving-door directors—a story in this instance that includes not just Russell but pungent cameos by such then notables in the industry as Sam Jaffe, David Picker, and Oliver Reed. "The realities of the movie business are very cruel," Kramer writes, and indeed his portrait of his adventures in the screen trade seems a run-up to his later-in-life dissections of governmental, political, and medical bureaucracies. In the case of *Women in Love,* the patient lived—the movie was an art-house hit— but not without a price. Kramer's loving reconstruction here of the scenario as he originally conceived it in the Lawrence spirit, before it was Ken Russellized, is in itself a lesson in the vagaries of commercial filmmaking, especially if read in conjunction with watching a video of the film that was actually released.

The plays that follow are fascinating on many levels, offering clues to the development of Kramer's novel *Faggots,* as well as to both of his more openly autobiographical plays, *The Destiny of Me* and *The Normal Heart.* In his first work for the stage, *Sissies' Scrapbook,* Kramer gives a view of sexuality, gay and straight, in the New York of the early 1970s that is as much a time capsule for its era as *Faggots* would be for later in the decade and *The Normal Heart* would be for the mid-1980s. At the same time, *Sissies' Scrapbook* is also a snapshot of the burgeoning theatrical experimentation of its day, combining the rock-ribbed social detail that is in all of Kramer's work with an explicit presentation of sex and sexuality as well as some playful flights of decidedly nonnaturalistic stagecraft. Some of the experimentation would be flattened out along with the title when *Sissies' Scrapbook* was revised as *Four Friends* for a disastrous, one-night commercial run at the Theater de Lys (now the Lucille Lortel, where *The Destiny of Me* would play two decades later). Kramer's description of his play's path from its initial airing in 1973 at the original Playwrights Horizons, run by Robert Moss in an old gym at 53rd Street and Eighth Avenue, to its ignominious opening night downtown in 1975 is an archetypal portrait of the vicissitudes of life in the do-or-die New York theater. "You must be a masochist to work in the theater and a sadist to succeed on its stages," Kramer has written. Here the masochism knows few bounds, and I will not dispute his account of a *New York Times* drama critic who sealed the production's fate by arriving at the premiere a half hour late in a state of, shall we say, less than keen mental acuity.

The ugly demise of *Sissies' Scrapbook* kept Kramer away from the stage until *The Normal Heart.* The lack of takers for the never-staged *A Minor Dark Age* is the theater's loss. It's without question an unwieldy script, as are most plays that haven't had the opportunity for revision and cutting that rehearsal and performance afford. But the dreamlike quality of the writing is haunting and so is the protagonist, a searching young man, written for the actor Brad Davis, who is far less sure of himself and far more vulnerable than Ned Weeks, the Kramer alter ego whom Davis would later make famous. Kramer's use of language, an underrated quality in his work, here often has a poetic sheen (but never pretentiously so), though many of the themes he touches upon, including the difference between sex and passion, are staples of his entire output.

Just Say No could not be more violently different. It's a cry of anger from the depths of the Reagan era—it was first produced in 1988—in which Kramer goes after political nemeses big and small with all the anger that coursed through *The Normal Heart* but in the far different style of flat-out farce. I have never seen this play on stage; critics who did in New York and Chicago were hostile toward it. What's clear from the page is that Kramer was intent on making a true theatrical departure by writing in a wholly new language. In an afterword, Kramer writes, not without reason, that "theater today is polite and boring." Though *Just Say No* may be hard to realize on stage—and, like all satire, destined to lose some of its bloom as the topical references start to fade—it is never polite and never boring. It's the work of a playwright who, for all his travails in the theater, is addicted to the stage as a platform for the freest imaginable artistic exploration.

As the reader completes the journey from *Women in Love* to *Just Say No,* it's hard to believe that all the works in this volume are from the same writer, such are the many moods and strategies of Kramer's literary voice. And yet there are strands that unite his entire canon (including a preoccupation with medicine and disease, which surfaces through a cancer-stricken character in *A Minor Dark Age*). Long before Kramer had a specific news story to write about, his plays were almost journalistic in their observation of the fine-grained documentary details of American life, from the social politics of Yalies to the way that money is made to the class distinctions of modern New York and its environs. Yet his aim is never to be journalistic; his greatest calling is to plumb the normal heart. He is a student equally of men in love, women in love, and families in love. The fathers and sons and brothers are as persistent in his work as they are in Arthur Miller's.

"Open yourself up to whatever is bottled up inside you," says Andrew to Alicia in *A Minor Dark Age*. That line is the perennial Kramer imperative. Whether sorrowful or angry or funny, whether illuminating the public arena of contemporary America or the private realm of the bedroom, he is trying to cut to the truth of who people really are. In this collection, as in all his writing, Larry Kramer ruthlessly strips his characters of their poses and lies and agendas until the passions bottled up within can come pouring out, in drama that may well prove timeless.

Frank Rich
May 2002

Women in Love

Screenplay adaptation of the novel by D. H. Lawrence, with annotations on the making of the film

It is, I have discovered, an arduous task to relive a part of your life, particularly the creation of a piece of work from that past. That is what I found myself doing when I agreed to prepare a book version of my screenplay adaptation of *Women in Love*. It has taken me much too long to prepare this: I found I could work on it only a few hours a day without collapsing under the weight of memory and the pressure to return to my creations of the present.

I had not even seen the film in many years; I can't recall how many. You see it so many times during its making that you think that should be enough to last you for your lifetime. It must be like a parent who at some point says about the kid: Let him grow up on his own already. I've always had a few videos of it around various places I've lived, but they all remained unwrapped. I am not certain why this lack of desire to look at it lasted so long. It represents an achievement I am proud of. It wasn't the happiest time of my life, personally, and the making of the movie was very hard on my spirit. Perhaps that's the reason. I was certain when I saw it I would remember what drama was going on just out of the camera's range on every shot, and I still remembered most of them without having to see the actual movie to remind me. When I finally came to look at the movie as the first step in assembling this book, I was actually quite impressed. Not a bad job for a young man of thirty-three or so, an ambitious young man to be sure, who, at twenty-five, had bet the group in the Columbia Pictures training program, of which he had been one, that he would produce his first feature film by the age of thirty.

Preparing a "final" version of any screenplay is a myth. There is no final version. After the writer finishes, the director fiddles and actors sneak in stuff during dubbing and the editor slices out this and that and music or sound effects drown out that and this and then a production script is prepared (or was in the days of this film) by a bunch of secretary types working over machines that allow them to count footage and convert it into seconds and reels and indicate exactly what mouths are saying and sounds are heard. This is used for making foreign versions. It is a very unromantic and unatmospheric and undramatic and forbidding thing, the final production script. It bears little resemblance to the romance and mystery that created the "project" in the first place and excited not only the writer and director and actors to participate, but the money people to put up the financing.

And printing up my final draft leaves questions and gaps to anyone who sees the movie and wants to read the screenplay. What happened to that? In the movie, so and so says such and such: you don't have such and such. It's almost a cheat to print up a screenplay and call it the script of the film.

What I have tried to do here is something I haven't seen done before. I took my final draft, and I took the production script, and I took my earlier drafts, and I took the novel itself, and I tried to put together a faithful version of what is on the screen, pausing here and there to indicate what should have been here and what was taken away from there and what or who had changed this or that and displeased the screenwriter, whose back was momentarily turned. I try to explain reasons for some of the choices and try to indicate some instances of how a movie is created, often inadvertently, by many people and is the sum of many accidents and intentions, not all of them necessarily out of fidelity to the original great novel that is this particular movie's source. I try to show how personalities and relationships off-camera affect what is being shot. And of course the complicated relationship between the director and the screenwriter and the producer, which since the beginning of cinema has been never less than terribly fraught. I must say that I was impressed how, in one way or another, perhaps because I was producer as well as screenwriter, what is on the screen represents what my final draft represents and indeed what the seven or eight drafts preceding it represented.

I am grateful to my old friend Sandy Lieberson, who has produced many films and run many film companies and now teaches film students all over the world how to prepare their own ideas for presentation, for the notion of presenting my adaptation in this fashion. He says that students want to know why and how along the way.

In adapting an indisputably great novel, a great book, one faces additional problems and overwhelming responsibilities to its readers, to its author, to the work itself. One cannot take liberties, or rather one cannot take just any old liberty. One of the several directors who was connected with *Women in Love* along its long journey to the screen wanted outrageous changes, including allowing Gerald Crich to live at the end. It is an indication of how powerful his word was over mine to the financier's ears and how desperate I was by this time to get the film made that I even considered this suggestion, telling myself I don't know what about how I would deal with this fight later.

A screenplay usually goes through many drafts, many of them unnecessary, most of them written because of some reason other than getting the movie actually made. A studio can't make up its mind so asks for another draft (when they can't even verbalize what's wrong with the present one); a new director shows an interest but he or she wants "a few changes." A star might consider playing so and so if the part were bigger, or funnier, or more sympathetic, or or or. Another writer is called in, then another; then the original writer is called back to clean up the mess. None of this, you realize, has anything to do with "writing," with "art," though these words are freely bandied about.

Women in Love suffered some of these stalling tactics. But fortunately the producer never had to fire the screenwriter or deal with another screenwriter. It has been my experience from years of being both a story editor and a screenwriter that most often the first draft's initial impulses, when one looks back at them, were the most correct (and that all further drafts reflect a decline in energy and imagination) and that if more films were made from the first writer's first draft, I'll bet there would have been a lot more better movies. Because I started out as the producer, and never lost control of the rights to the "property," I was able to wield a bit more control over things than your usual writer-for-hire. Directors don't usually like to work for writer-producers; indeed, directors today usually form their own companies and place their own producers in charge. This does not result in better movies. It results in directors being allowed to get away with things that a good creative sounding board who can say no and make it stick can provide to a director who has too many things to be in charge of anyway and is often unable to see all of them very clearly as it is.

If the relationship between the director and the writer is the most important one in the making of a film, it is a well-kept secret from the public and the critics. The director winds up with all the attention, and the writer is usually treated badly from beginning to end by everyone from the director to the producer to the financing entity to the press. The only one anyone pays any attention to or gives any credit to is the director. Period. If the movie's any good, he or she is applauded. If it isn't, the script is usually blamed. The process in the theater is just the reverse: the writer is king, and the director is there to serve the writer. Perhaps that is why I came to write fewer screenplays and began to write plays. I began to feel dirty writing movies, writing for this cast of characters for whom I was only a means to an end.

There were five directors considered for *Women in Love*. The first was Silvio Narizzano, who brought the book to me. The second was Jack Clayton, who, famous for taking a long time to make up his mind, did truly that, eventually turning it down. Next was Peter Brook, who was in Paris during this time of student revolt, so we could not get a script to him. The fourth was Stanley Kubrick, and I cannot recall what happened with him. We were acquainted well enough that he would have read the script had I asked him to, but I am not certain it came to that. The final director was Ken Russell.

I had met Ken at about the same time I had met Silvio, in the early 1960s, shortly after arriving in London from New York to take up my job as a story editor for the Columbia Pictures production outpost there. I was only about twenty-six years old, and it was a wonderful job, a wonderful time, a wonderful opportunity for an ambitious kid with a lot of energy and curiosity and nerve. Not only was it my job to find good stories and writers for our movies, but I had been encouraged to keep an eye out for possible new directors. One of my earliest ideas was to develop a group of extremely low budget films by young British television directors and writers, and both Silvio and Ken were doing exceptional work in television drama. Silvio had received much praise for adaptations of Arthur Miller and Tennessee Williams. Ken was doing extraordinary docudrama-biographical pieces for BBC-TV's Monitor program. I had brought each of them into my office. Ken and I discussed doing a film about the world of fashion; he had been a fashion photographer, and that world fascinated me. We never got anywhere, but our meetings were pleasant. Silvio and I hit it off immediately. Though Canadian, he had a New York sense of humor and energy and spunk, an unusual mix in London. A young television writer, Julian Bond, was commissioned to write an original screenplay idea of his called *Another Day Tomorrow*. It was budgeted at some ridiculously low amount. The film was not made. First there were a few of those delaying tactics I describe above, mainly by my boss, who could not make up his mind; low-budget movies often take longer to get a green light than big-budget ones, and he had too many of these on his mind. Then Silvio got an offer to direct something else. In preparation for making *Another Day Tomorrow*, Columbia had given him a multipicture contract. While waiting, he had already made one movie, *Die! Die! My Darling!* with Tallulah Bankhead, which I had put together for the Hammer Films horror movie folks, who released through Columbia. Then, with still no go-ahead forthcoming for our little film, he directed *Georgy Girl*, which became a huge international success. After that, there was no way he was going to come back and do our modest movie. He was hot, as they say, and big offers were coming in, and he intended to capitalize on them. Who could blame him?

We stayed friends, and I was with him when he left his wife (a television story editor and also my friend) to live with a young man. I left London to return to New York to be assistant to the president of United Artists, David Picker, a job I did not like, nor did I enjoy being back in New York. I somehow got David to send me back to London as associate producer on a film called *Here We Go Round the Mulberry Bush* (which would be a huge hit there, with music by Stevie Winwood and Spencer Davis). I was back in London in six months and was with Silvio and his new young lover when

Silvio left to direct a western in Utah with Terence Stamp called *Blue.*

The one movie Silvio wanted to make more than anything was *Women in Love.* (Looking back, I can certainly see that it reflects many of the problems he was having in his own life.) He had told this to Sam Jaffe, an American producer living in London (and formerly one of the most powerful agents in Hollywood), and Sam had indicated he would produce it, even though he was nervous about the book's bold sexual content. "I'm an old man, and I don't know if I have it in me to fight these battles," he said to me somewhere along the line. Like most of the Americans in London in the sixties working in movies—we had quite a colony—Sam and I were friends. His son-in-law, John Kohn, was a young Columbia producer, for whom I'd found *The Collector,* which became a film the great William Wyler directed for us.

I'd never read *Women in Love.* Knowing of my impatience to do something on my own, Silvio suggested I read it while he was away and if I liked it to take it over from Sam (Sam had no objection), and he would agree to my producing it. He said this was his thank-you for putting him on the path of *Georgy Girl.* Getting a commitment from a hot director was a generous gift indeed. Needless to say, I hastened to read the novel.

I read it and I didn't understand it, and then I fell in love with a man named Giorgio who lived in Milan whom I was trying to get to move to London. He came to London, hated it, and gave me the flu before he went home, and I was stuck in bed with nothing to read. I reread *Women in Love* and realized what a great work of art I was holding in my hands. Silvio in Utah was also having love problems, but far more dire. The young man had not wanted to leave England and join him in America. Silvio insisted. He was lonely. The young man finally relented. One day while driving to visit

Silvio on the set, the young man was killed in an automobile accident. Silvio, already behind schedule on his first big-budget film, was overcome by guilt. The movie spiraled out of control, costwise. It was that year's *Heaven's Gate,* and Silvio was a hot director no more. The film companies I had already dangled *Women in Love* in front of were no longer interested.

I had commissioned a screenplay from a well-known British writer of that era, David Mercer, who was from Yorkshire and the coal mines area of England, akin to D. H. Lawrence. I'd used every last penny I had to option the book and pay Mercer's first draft fee. He'd turned in a terrible script. It was more a Marxist tract (most of the young good liberal writers were passionate Marxists, something this unpolitical American fellow knew next to nothing about), with so little connection to the novel that even his agent, the great Peggy Ramsay, who was also my friend, tried to get me to take Mercer's payment back. "David has been shameful and shameless," she said, which was generous of her but did not get me a usable screenplay. It was Silvio who suggested I try to write it myself, just before his own life fell apart. I had no choice but to try.

I had done rewriting on *Mulberry Bush,* but I had never done a whole screenplay before. I'd always wanted to be a writer, and a great deal of my psychoanalysis (another reason I wanted to get back to London: I missed my shrink) was spent trying to figure out why I was so afraid of trying to be one. Well, there is nothing like having your back against the wall in a situation like mine to make you try. No script, no movie. No movie, no job. No job, no future; I'd have to go back to New York. I sat down and got to work on the screenplay for *Women in Love.* The first thing I did was to read every critical assessment of the novel and of Lawrence I could find. (I had been an English major at Yale.) This served a great double purpose. It made me understand a very difficult novel better, and it made me realize, even more, what a great, great gift and opportunity I now had. Next I got in my car and headed north. I wanted to see where this man had lived and had written about. I stayed in small inns and cheap hotels and talked to people in pubs and drove for hours in Sherwood Forest and the Derbyshire Dales and became familiar with all the tiny towns that dot the unbelievably beautiful landscape of the Midlands part of England, Nottinghamshire, Derbyshire. (When Ken came on, I was able to show him where much of the novel had actually happened.) Then I came home and started my screenplay.

Until Silvio became persona non grata at every single studio, I would send him what I was writing, and his reactions were terrific. When I next saw David Picker on one of his trips to London (I'd hoped to make my deal with UA because they gave producers 50 percent of the profits, more than any other studio), he told me he still was interested but he would no longer take Silvio. The realities of the movie business are very cruel. *Georgy Girl*'s success was forgotten; all that counted now was that *Blue* was a disaster and Silvio was unemployable. He came back and we sat down and he told me that I was writing a fine script, that I had done all the work on getting the film made, and that I must not stop trying to get the film made, and he knew this could no longer happen with him. He named a price for me to buy him out, and I agreed. It was a painful and sad meeting and my first personal experience of these harsh film world realities. (But we stayed friends.) Before Picker left London, I took David Mercer's script and fifty pages of mine and gave them to him without telling him which was which. "One of these is by a famous British writer and the other one is by an unknown writer I've found." He called me up a few days later. "The famous writer is David Mercer and his script is terrible and you're the unknown writer and yours is terrific and let's make a deal and start looking for another director." He even gave me some money to live on while I finished writing the script.

Ken Russell, who proved to be a good choice, really got the job because of a famous producer of that time, Harry Saltzman (he coproduced the first James Bond films, among many others), who had a deal with UA and who also had Ken Russell under contract, with nothing for him to do at the moment. Ken had made *Billion Dollar Brain* for him and it was a flop, which coming after two previous film failures meant that he badly needed a success or he would never do anything but television. One reason he was more or less "controllable"—he had a bad temper and Paddy Chayefsky, for whom Ken would direct *Altered States,* always maintained that Ken gave him the heart attack that almost killed him (one would shortly come along and finish the job)—was that he knew if he struck out on *Women in Love,* that was it.

He was a strange man. We did not like each other, and he did not like Martin Rosen, who was my co-producer. I don't think he liked Americans in general, certainly not American film people. He certainly did not like an American who was not only his producer but the author of the screenplay he would have preferred writing himself. Much of my energy (I'll indicate several examples as we go along) was spent trying to keep him from slipping in his rewrites behind my back. We weren't shooting very long before I realized it was essential to me and my script and the movie that I be on the set every single moment. I have always been someone who would accept good ideas to make anything I'm involved in better, if I believed they were better. But Ken's ideas were not better. They were awful and usually off-the-wall. Anyone who has seen some of his later movies and TV work, filled with naked nuns on altars and other harsh images, will know what I mean. The more eccentric and extreme the actor and the image, the more florid would become his style. I had to concentrate on getting the most out of the young Ken Russell who had impressed me originally: the man with one of the best visual eyes in Britain, who could shoot that country and its landscape and its architecture and place figures in these images so that all looked gorgeous, and related to these characters, to the story they were a part of, and to D. H. Lawrence. *Women in Love* was to be his best work.

Ken was not a verbal man. He didn't talk much, and the dialogue he would write and try to sneak in had no feel for how people talk. Indeed, he wasn't good at conveying what he wanted to anyone, cast or crew. Actors like Glenda Jackson and Oliver Reed, who did what they wanted to anyway (Oliver had little range to do much else), flourished, and neither was ever as good in anything as each was in *Women in Love.* But actors who liked to discuss things, like Alan Bates, and poor Jennie Linden, who had been cast only days before shooting began and who'd had no time to prepare or research her role (which was based on Freda Lawrence), were out of luck as far as getting help from Ken was concerned.

Because his visual precision demanded much of the crew, his biggest communication problem was with the crew, who came to hate him and make jokes about him behind his back. This only made him egg them on further and harder. By the end of shooting he was dressing à la Erich von Stroheim in military jodhpurs, high leather riding boots, while thwacking a riding crop against his thigh. Several times he actually prodded crew members or extras until Martin told him this was forbidden. He was afraid of Martin. I believe it was because Martin and I went out of our way to befriend them that no one on the crew quit or they did not "work to rule." Remember, when you are on a very tight budget, as we were, an unhappy crew can totally destroy you. A happy crew will work their asses off if they like you. We honored our crew and their industry and their artistry at every opportunity, with parties, special dinners, beer blasts, and champagne every one-hundred "takes." They were grateful to us. We were shooting most of our film on location. Our shooting schedule was some sixteen weeks away from homes, families, even England. (Indeed, romances flourished, and a few marriages broke up.) Over thirty years later, I still get Christmas cards and recently not a few calls from old crew members worried about the state of my health.

While I did not like him, I could tell with my own eyes from what he was shooting that he was doing a good job and that he was strangely right for the film. I suspect because he was a person almost without sentiment and with little sense of humor, and he was a director obsessed with rigidly controlled images, that this balanced the Laurentian language, which was so often over-the-top. Ken's style worked somehow as a brake on too much gush. Indeed, it allowed the script to be more faithful to what Lawrence had his characters saying.

Alan Bates had come to me the minute he heard I'd optioned the book. He wanted to play Birkin. That was fine with me. Excellent indeed. He had just starred in a major film, *The Fixer,* for which he had received an Oscar nomination. So I knew I had one "name" to bargain with when I went to the studios.

Getting the rest of the three leading roles cast was not so easy. United Artists suggested Oliver Reed because they were about to release an expensive film, *Hannibal Brooks,* about schlepping some elephants across the Alps or some such, with Oliver as star. They were banking on it turning him into a big international star. I didn't want him. I'd never seen him good in anything, and he was completely wrong physically for what Lawrence described, a glacial, blond, cold man. I wanted Edward Fox, who would play the lead in

The Day of the Jackal. But Ken had worked with Oliver on several of his TV docudramas, and Oliver was acceptable to him. From the very beginning, I wanted Glenda Jackson for Gudrun. I had seen her on the stage and could see how good she was. She was a major talent ready to explode. But UA did not want her: she had no name, and she was not attractive. And Ken did not warm to her originally. She had terrible varicose veins on her legs and needed dental work to straighten her teeth. When she agreed to attend to those, and I agreed to accept Oliver, UA relented. (And by the time Vidal Sassoon, then a young man, refashioned her hair and Shirley Russell, Ken's phenomenally talented wife, costumed her, she was quite beautiful.)

Casting Ursula was all that remained. No name actress would take the part once Glenda was cast. They knew she would dominate the screen. We were only days away from shooting, and Nathan's, where the costumes were made, told us if we didn't come up with an Ursula quickly, she would have nothing to wear when we started. By chance my assistant, Tom Erhardt, had seen a screen test of an unknown actress with Peter O'Toole for a role in *The Lion in Winter.* She looked interesting. Her agent told us that she had retired to have a baby. We rushed to Reading, where she was nursing, and met Jennie Linden for the first time. Yes, she would be fine. Jennie had the hardest job of all: acting with all these names and so unprepared. She was not quite right for the part, and she was not what Ken wanted, which often made him rather short with her, but she held her own.

And so we approached our first day of shooting, outside of Sheffield. The night before, Oliver had arrived drunk at the hotel where we were all staying. I was lying on a sofa after dinner, with a few of our folks. He walked up to my sofa and upended it and me, so that I tumbled to the floor. Then he announced that he wanted my suite, that he did not like his suite, and that if he could not have my suite, he would leave the movie. I had to think fast on this one, my first true test of how a producer deals with a difficult star. "My suite is your suite," I said, and went upstairs to start moving. Roy Baird, our associate producer, came up shortly thereafter and said that Oliver had decided to stay where he was. I guess I somehow passed his test because, contrary to what I feared would happen, he was extremely easy for me to deal with after this, whether he was drunk or sober, whether he was there with his wife or his mistress. He was rumored always to have had affairs with his leading ladies, and he'd made it known that he considered Glenda unattractive; so we were worried how they would get on. The first day they acted together, she was so dazzling that somehow he rose to the challenge of being impressed enough to respond and to do some good acting for a change himself.

Indeed, as we worked more and more on the making of the movie, everyone got caught up in the book's greatness. We all wanted to do it justice.

And now to the screenplay.

INT. BRANGWEN SITTING ROOM. DAY

The BRANGWEN *family home in Beldover, a small, ugly colliery town in the Midlands. It is small and compact, two stories, a row-house. The year is 1920.* URSULA, *twenty-six, and* GUDRUN, *twenty-five,* BRANGWEN *are sisters.* "GUDRUN *was beautiful, passive, soft-skinned, soft-limbed. She wore a dress of dark blue silky stuff, with ruches of blue and green linen lace in the neck and sleeves; and she had emerald green stockings. Her look of confidence and diffidence contrasted with* URSULA'*s sensitive expectancy." Both cannot wait to escape from the provincial life of their town, although* GUDRUN *is just back from spending several years in London, where she studied art. She regrets bitterly that she has come home. They come down from upstairs and start out of the house.* MRS. BRANGWEN *is laying the table, and* MR. BRANGWEN *is hammering a piece of leather work.*

GUDRUN: We're going to see that wedding.

MR. BRANGWEN: But you haven't been home five minutes.

URSULA: You don't have a wedding every day, do you?

MRS. BRANGWEN: Now look, Gudrun, your aunt Jessie is coming to lunch and you haven't seen her for two years. Why don't you want to stay?

GUDRUN: Well, two more days won't make much difference, now will it? Come on. . . .

URSULA: It's a Crich wedding, Mum!

EXT. BRANGWEN HOME. DAY

URSULA *and* GUDRUN *come out of the house.* GUDRUN *closes the door and they walk down the steps.*

GUDRUN: Ursula, do you really not want to get married?

URSULA: I don't know. It depends how you mean.

GUDRUN: It usually means one thing. But wouldn't you be in a better
  position if you were married?

EXT. BELDOVER. VARIOUS. DAY

As URSULA *and* GUDRUN *come out of their house and walk down their own respectable street . . . down a steep hill into the misery and poverty of the town . . . through the miners' slum back-to-backs, where a group of miners' wives stare at the well-dressed girls in their stylish clothes and bright stockings . . . past the overpowering and threatening colliery . . . to the tram station and then finally onto the tram, which takes them into the country. People waiting for and riding the tram include miners and blind and wounded soldiers. Over above:*

URSULA: I might be. I'm not sure, really.

GUDRUN: You don't think one needs the experience of having been
  married?

URSULA: Oh, Gudrun, do you really think it need be an experience?

GUDRUN: It's bound to be. Possibly undesirable but bound to be an
  experience of some sort.

URSULA: Not really. More likely to be the end of experience.

GUDRUN: Yes, of course, there is that to consider.

(*They walk in the direction of a country church, with wedding guests streaming toward it.*)

EXT. LUPTON'S HOUSE. DAY

RUPERT BIRKIN, *in formal dress, comes running out of the comfortable country house toward a waiting carriage, pulling on his coat and urging someone still inside to hurry.* BIRKIN, *about thirty, is intense, intellectual, proud, lonely.*

BIRKIN: Hurry, Tibby! We really are late!

(LUPTON, *a handsome young man in naval uniform, runs and jumps in the carriage as it starts off.*)

EXT. WILLEY WATER CHURCH. DAY

An obviously important wedding is about to take place. Well-dressed guests arrive, some in automobiles, and mingle with the crowd. Standing most impatiently looking up the road is GERALD CRICH, *perhaps thirty, exceptionally handsome, but rather cold and unyielding.* "But about him also was the strange, guarded look, the unconscious glisten, as if he did not belong to the same creation as the people around him. GUDRUN [will light] on him at once. His gleaming beauty, maleness, like a young, good-humoured, smiling wolf, did not blind her to the significant, sinister stillness in his bearing, the lurking danger of his unsubdued temper." HERMIONE RODDICE, *proud, imperious, the daughter of a Derbyshire baronet, and thought to be one of the most remarkable women in the Midlands, comes to stand by* GERALD. *She is "full of intellectuality, and heavy, nerve-worn with consciousness. She was passionately interested in reform, her soul was given up to the public cause. . . . She had various intimacies of mind and soul with various men of capacity." Now she is interested in* BIRKIN, *the local schools inspector. But "he fought her off, he always fought her off. The more she strove to bring him to her, the more he battled her back. And they had been lovers for years*

*now. . . . She knew he was trying to break away from her finally. . . . " She
too looks up the road.*

HERMIONE: Where is Birkin?

GERALD: With the groom. They're late.

> (*A carriage pulls up with* WINIFRED, *Gerald's younger sister, and his
> mother,* MRS. CRICH, *a queerly unkempt and inattentive elderly lady
> in dark clothing who seems to lean forward from her yellowish face.*
> GERALD *helps them down, kissing his mother, who turns her cheek
> away.*)

GERALD: Winifred. Hello, Mother.

[The following was not used:

MRS. CRICH: I don't know half the people here.

GERALD: Most of them are yours, Mother. Your daughters. . . .

MRS. CRICH: Now Laura is getting married there will be another one
I don't know. I know just what he will say. "How are you,
Mother?" I ought to say, "I am not your mother in any sense."
What's the use, Gerald. (*As if suddenly realizing she's talking to
him.*) Gerald. You are the most wanting of them all. I should
like you to have a friend. You have never had a friend. Where
is your sister who is being married? You cannot organize a
wedding as you do the mines.]

EXT. WILLEY WATER CHURCH. DAY

URSULA *and* GUDRUN *walk from the bank of the water to stand beneath a
huge tree, from which they can watch but not be seen.*

EXT. COUNTRY ROAD. DAY

BIRKIN *and* LUPTON *riding in a carriage, the horses urged on by the driver.*

BIRKIN: It's such bad form for the groom to be late. Gerald will be furious.

LUPTON: Oh, don't worry about it. Something unconventional will do that family good. Laura's not going to run away, you know. They'll just have to wait.

EXT. WILLEY WATER CHURCH. DAY

LAURA CRICH, *the bride, and the ailing and infirm* MR. CRICH, *a proud man who is dying, arrive in an open carriage.*

GERALD: Father . . . Hello, Laura.

(BIRKIN *and* LUPTON *can be seen pulling up. Before his carriage stops,* LUPTON *jumps out and runs after* LAURA, *who sees him . . .*

LAURA: Tibby!

. . . and runs toward the church. GERALD *looks on grimly.* BIRKIN *laughs.* HERMIONE *joins* BIRKIN *and tries to put her arm through his as they walk toward the entrance. But* BIRKIN *holds back. He watches* LAURA *and* LUPTON *standing on the church steps, kissing.* LAURA *finally breaks free and runs inside, followed by* LUPTON.)

GERALD: What a spectacle!

BIRKIN: Does it hurt your sense of family pride?

GERALD: It does rather. Do a thing properly or don't do it at all.

BIRKIN: But it's a masterpiece of good form! It's the hardest thing in the world to act spontaneously on one's impulses, and it's the only gentlemanly thing to do—provided you're fit enough to do it.

GERALD: You don't expect me to take you seriously, do you?

BIRKIN: Yes, Gerald, you're one of the very few people that I do expect that of.

(GERALD *heads into the church.* HERMIONE *stands waiting for* BIRKIN.)

BIRKIN: Hello, Hermione.

HERMIONE: What made you late?

BIRKIN: The groom would talk about the immortality of the soul and he hadn't got a button hook.

HERMIONE: The immortality of the soul? More appropriate for an execution, I would have thought, than a wedding.

(*They enter the church. They are the last to do so.*)

EXT. WILLEY WATER CHURCH. DAY

URSULA *and* GUDRUN *sit and lie on the tombstones in the church's graveyard.*

GUDRUN: Perhaps it would be nice if a man came along. I mean, I wouldn't go out of my way to look for him. But if there did happen to come along a highly attractive individual of sufficient means ... well ... Oh, don't you find yourself getting bored? Don't you find that things fail to materialize? Nothing mate-rializes! Everything withers in the bud. Everything.

URSULA: It is frightening. Do you hope to get anywhere by just marrying?

GUDRUN: It seems the inevitable next step.

URSULA: But you see ... it's just impossible. The man makes it impossible.

(LAURA *and* LUPTON *emerge from the church and run through the canopy of crossed swords made by a group of Tibby's naval chums. Confetti.*

A photographer has posed the entire group for a shot and explodes his camera's puffs. The church bells are pealing loudly. Somehow through the crowd GUDRUN *and* GERALD *exchange eye contact. The same is true for* URSULA *and* BIRKIN. HERMIONE *comes and once again puts her arm through* BIRKIN's.)

INT. URSULA'S CLASSROOM. LATE AFTERNOON

URSULA *is teaching catkins to her class of some fifteen children, all about twelve years old. (Intercut with this scene are shots of* URSULA *at the wedding observing* BIRKIN, *and* HERMIONE *conducting him away.*)

URSULA: Now sometimes catkins are called lambs' tails. Don't you think they look like them? So lovely, and tiny, and soft?

(BIRKIN *has entered the room quietly.* URSULA *does not notice his arrival and is startled when she sees him.*)

BIRKIN: Sorry. Did I startle you? I thought you'd heard me come in.

URSULA: (*Faltering.*) No ...

BIRKIN: You're doing catkins ... Are they as far out as this already? I hadn't noticed them this year. Give them crayons. It's the fact you want to emphasize, not the impression. And what's the fact? Red little spiky stigmas of the female flower, dangling yellow male catkin, yellow pollen flying from one to the other. Make a pictorial record of the fact, as you do when drawing a face. (*At the blackboard.*) Two eyes . . . a nose . . . mouth with teeth . . .

(*The children laugh.* HERMIONE *enters. No one sees her, so she switches on the light.*)

HERMIONE: I've been waiting for you for so long, Rupert, I thought I'd come and see what a schools inspector does when he's on duty. (*To* URSULA.) How do you do, Miss Brangwen. Do you mind my coming in?

URSULA: Oh, no.

HERMIONE: You sure? (*Turning to* BIRKIN, *who is bending over a girl at her desk.*) What are you doing?

BIRKIN: Catkins.

HERMIONE: Really? What do you learn about them?

BIRKIN: Well, from these little red bits the nuts come, if they receive pollen from these long danglers.

HERMIONE: (*Looking at the small buds.*) Little red flames. Little red flames. Aren't they beautiful? I think they're so beautiful.

BIRKIN: Had you never noticed them before?

HERMIONE: No. Never before.

BIRKIN: And now you will always see them.

HERMIONE: Now I shall always see them. Thank you so much for showing me. I think they're so beautiful. Little red flames. Little red flames. (*To* URSULA.) [Your sister has come home?

URSULA: Yes.

HERMIONE: And does she like being back in Beldover?

URSULA: No.

HERMIONE: No, I wonder she can bear it. It takes all my strength, to bear the ugliness of this district, when I stay here. Won't you and your sister come and stay with me at Breadalby for a few days.... Do ... I think your sister is wonderful. I think some of her work is wonderful. I have two water-wagtails, carved in wood. Little things seem to be so subtle to her. Rupert, Rupert ... Are little things more subtle than big things?

BIRKIN: Dunno.

URSULA: I hate subtleties. I think they are a sign of weakness.]

[This is a perfect example, of which there could be hundreds, of wonderful exchanges that there simply was no time to include if we were not to have a movie of inordinate length. This became more and more of a problem—this time factor—as we proceeded to shoot and became insurmountable with the Soho bohemian adventures of Birkin and Gerald, which we'll get to shortly. It becomes evident very early on how fast a film can be shot and how long a director needs to establish his style without rushing, and it becomes equally evident fairly early on that something is going to have to go. Film financing being what it was (and is) for young producers, it's best to discover the director's pace as early as possible so that what money there is to shoot the film doesn't run out too fast.]

(URSULA *picks up and energetically rings the bell on her desk, and the children jump up and rush to leave.* URSULA *watches* BIRKIN *leave with* HERMIONE. *"She had spoken with him once or twice. ... She thought he seemed to acknowledge some kinship between her and him. . . . But there had been no time for the understanding to develop. She wanted to know him more. . . . And something kept her from him, as well as attracted her to him. There was a certain hostility, a hidden ultimate reserve in him, cold and inaccessible.")*

EXT. LAKE. DAY

GERALD, *naked, runs through the tall grass and onto a jetty, from which he dives into the lake and starts swimming out.*
 GUDRUN *and* URSULA *are climbing up the hill on a walk.*

GUDRUN: Fancy her barging into your classroom like that. What a liberty!

URSULA: Oh, Hermione loves to dominate everyone. She'd like to dominate us, I think.

GUDRUN: Oh, so that's why she's invited us for the weekend.

 (*They pause in their climb and look back toward the lake.* GERALD *waves.*)

GERALD: Hello!

URSULA: It's Gerald Crich!

GUDRUN: (*Turning away from the lake.*) I know.

[URSULA: You know Gerald accidentally killed his brother? I thought you knew. Oh, when they were boys. They were playing together with an old gun. He told his brother to look down the gun and it blew the top of his head off.

GUDRUN: Isn't it horrible for such a thing to happen to one when one is a child, and having to carry the responsibility of it all through one's life.

URSULA: Perhaps there was an unconscious will behind it. This playing at killing has some primitive desire for killing in it, don't you think?

GUDRUN: (*Angry.*) But I cannot see how that applies to a couple of boys playing together. Oh, damn the thing.]

[I have no idea why this important passage was not filmed. Perhaps it was cut so as not to load the deck so much against Gerald, as compared to the others. This passage does appear in my early drafts (there were some fifteen altogether) but disappears, as often happens, as you refine and condense from draft to draft, often overlooking the original source itself.]

(*Carries on walking.*) So Gerald's in charge of the mines now?

URSULA: Making all kinds of "latest improvements." They hate him for it. He takes them all by the scruff of the neck and fairly flings them along. He'll have to die soon, when he's made all the possible improvements and there's nothing more to improve. He's got "go" anyhow.

GUDRUN: Certainly he's got "go." I've never seen a man that's showed signs of so much. The unfortunate thing is, where does his "go" go to?

(*The sisters both laugh and put their arms around each other.*)

[In the novel, Birkin and Gerald take the train to London and have a rather orgiastic weekend there. On the train, and at Halliday's flat, they exchange much of Lawrence's philosophy about the possibility of love and commitment to another person, the finality of love, which has been dispersed in the screenplay into a number of other scenes.

This train ride appears to have had a troubled genesis. The one that Lawrence uses, finally, seems rather patched together and indeed perhaps rewritten yet again for this insertion after the bulk of the novel had been completed. Here we see Birkin and Gerald meet on the train to London by chance and decide to spend the weekend together after Birkin tells him what it will include, which intrigues Gerald. Even after the wedding, where we have seen them as friends (after all, why would Birkin be a groomsman if they were not?), they are now presented as if they are relative strangers getting to know each other. Of more interest is a discarded beginning to *Women in Love,* which is published in one of the Phoenix anthologies of Lawrence's unpublished writings, in which Birkin and Gerald go away on a trip to Switzerland and become lovers. There is no question that all the jockeyings between Birkin and Gerald in the published novel, and thus in the script, are attempts by Birkin to tell Gerald how much he loves him and wants him. There is also no question that this is an issue that has rarely been critically discussed, even acknowledged by generations of critics afraid to confront all this, even to this day. As someone once said to me, the novel really should be called *Men in Love.*]

[INT. JULIUS HALLIDAY'S SOHO FLAT. NIGHT

The last remnants of a wild party. The flat is large, heavily draped, and ornately furnished in the esoteric moods of the moment. Layers of smoke hang over the remaining guests: a few showgirls, society slummers, bearded artists, dancers scantily dressed and hardly moving to some distant rhythm. Empty champagne bottles everywhere and empty glasses being filled by HASAN, *an Arabic-looking servant in clothes much too big for him. In a corner, an artist with palette and brush is painting the body of a nude model as if she were a canvas. No one pays them any notice. An aesthetic-looking young poet with flowing hair and velvet jacket kneels at the legs of a statuesque showgirl, pulling out the feathers in which she seems mainly to be clothed, one by one.*

YOUNG POET: (*In French.*) She loves me. She loves me not.

(GERALD *stands looking at a lovely and delicate blonde with large, innocent eyes. She is surrounded by several men. She knows* GERALD *is watching her. Her name is* MINETTE. BIRKIN *is standing on the side of the room. A voice comes up from a deeply cushioned chair below him. He looks down and sees a waiflike girl.*)

WAIF: Are you someone important? If I know who you are, then I know how to act. I'm very adaptable.

BIRKIN: You seem too intelligent to be so adaptable.

WAIF: The last thing a girl should do is think.

(*A man in a clown costume, with a monkey on his shoulder, rushes in.*)

CLOWN: (*Confiding to the room.*) There's hashish in the loo!

(GERALD *is about to go when* MINETTE *leaves her group.* BIRKIN *is confronted by a lady wearing large, intellectual-type glasses.*)

WOMAN IN GLASSES: I don't know why everyone takes drugs these days. It's because they have nothing to believe in. I believe in God.

(MINETTE *and* GERALD *both come to* BIRKIN, *from opposite directions.*)

MINETTE: You hawdly come and stay here anymore, Wupert.

BIRKIN: There's always somebody else in my bed. I guess all the decent rebels are now fighting somewhere else.

MINETTE: Julius is howwid to me now. First he makes me live here and then he thwows me out. I'm going to have his baby. He wants me to hide in the country. It's ten weeks old.

(*Two young men enter:* JULIUS HALLIDAY *is swarthy, slender, with long black hair, handsome but without any animal vitality; the other is* MAXIM, *a dark-skinned Russian with black, oily hair, always with* HALLIDAY, *who rarely speaks.* HASAN *immediately gets to* HALLIDAY.)

HALLIDAY: Want more money! More money! I take you in from the streets and give you another man's clothing and now you want your own? (*To* MAXIM.) Give him a shilling. Minette, what are *you* doing here? Why have you come back? I told you not to come back.

BIRKIN: She comes as she likes, Halliday. You know you wanted her to, so sit down.

HALLIDAY: (*Sitting down.*) I won't sit down with Minette.

BIRKIN: It's late. I'm going to bed. Gerald, ring me up in the morning. (*Goes into one of the bedrooms.*)

HALLIDAY: (*To* GERALD.) I say, won't you stay here. Oh, do.

MINETTE: But there are only two rooms, now Wupert's here.

MAXIM: Julius and I will share one room.

(MINETTE *goes out of the room.*)

MINETTE: (*Coldly.*) Good night.

MAXIM: (*To* GERALD.) That's all right. You're all right.

GERALD: *I'm* all right, then?

MAXIM: Yes! Yes! You're all right.

MINETTE: (*Reappearing.*) (*To* HALLIDAY.) I know you want to catch me out. But I don't care. I don't care how much you catch me out.

INT. BEDROOM AT JULIUS HALLIDAY'S SOHO FLAT. MORNING

MINETTE *is still asleep.* GERALD, *beside her, wakes up and looks down at her. Both of them are naked, having had a wild night of sex to judge by the disheveled linens. Then he gets up and goes into the living room.*

INT. LIVING ROOM

HALLIDAY *and* MAXIM, *both completely naked, are studying with deep concentration a piece of African sculpture—the carved figure of a savage woman in labor, her nude protuberant body crouched.* HALLIDAY *looks up. He is not so friendly toward* GERALD *this morning.*

HALLIDAY: Good morning. Oh, did you want towels? (*Strides to a cupboard and pulls out a towel for* GERALD.) How perfectly splendid it must be to be in a climate where one could do without clothing altogether.

GERALD: Yes, if there weren't so many things that don't sting and bite.

(BIRKIN *appears.*)

BIRKIN: There's the bathroom now, if you want it.

GERALD: What do you think of that figure there?

(GERALD *looks at the two naked men looking at this naked woman.*)]

[It is a pity we could not shoot this bohemian weekend. Ken had wonderful ideas for doing part of it as a ball, all in black and white.]

EXT. SWIMMING POOL. BREADALBY. DAY

Breadalby is the imposing Roddice family home in Derbyshire.

  HERMIONE *and* BIRKIN *are reclining on a canopied chaise longue beside the pool.* BIRKIN *is reading a newspaper with the headline* MINERS' RIOTS.

  On the far side of the pool, two of Hermione's "artistic" friends, SALSIE *and the* CONTESSA, *dance in their bathing costumes.* GUDNUFSKY, *a young Russian, is on a chaise longue.*

HERMIONE: Dreadful. Dreadful. All this strife and dissension. If we could only realize that in the spirit we are all one, all equal in spirit, all brothers ... the rest wouldn't matter ... there'd be no more of this carping ... envy ... and all this struggle for power which destroys, only destroys.

  (BIRKIN *pours himself some champagne.*)

BIRKIN: It's just the opposite, Hermione. It's just the contrary. The minute you begin to compare, one man is seen to be far better than another. All the inequality in the world that you can imagine is there by nature. I want every man to have his fair share of the world's goods, so that I can be rid of his importunity! So that I can say to him: "Now you've got what you want. You've got your fair share of the world's gear. Now you mind yourself and don't obstruct me!"

HERMIONE: (*Laughing.*) It sounds like megalomania, Rupert.

  (*He spills some champagne. He laughs and puts his glass down. His laugh stops as* HERMIONE *licks the champagne from his shoulder. She pulls him closer and tries to kiss him passionately. He pulls away, and she turns away, and then gets up.*)

I must go and dress for lunch. Don't be late, Rupert.

(*She walks past a hammock in which* LAURA *and* LUPTON, *the young newlyweds, are sleeping in each other's arms.*)

EXT. BREADALBY. DAY

GUDRUN *and* URSULA *are being driven in an open touring car. The front of the imposing mansion can be seen.*

URSULA: So this is Hermione's "country cottage."

GUDRUN: Well, there's one reason Rupert's attracted to her.

URSULA: Oh, do you think so? I don't think so.

(GUDRUN *is helped by the driver out of the car, which has now stopped at the front entrance.*)

GUDRUN: Lovers would sell their souls for less, my dear.

[We shot all of the Breadalby scenes at and in Kedleston Hall, the magnificent eighteenth-century masterpiece of Robert Adam. It was too grand for Hermione's, but we had the opportunity to shoot there and we just couldn't turn it down. Our extraordinarily persuasive location manager, Lee Bolon, whose job it was to find locations where we might shoot scenes, had somehow hit upon Kedleston and struck up a friendship with Lord Scarsdale (the Scarsdales have lived in Kedleston since the 1760s), a dapper old gent with a twinkle in his eye who took a fancy to all the pretty girls we had with us. Originally we were permitted only to shoot outside, but as Lord Scarsdale took more and more interest in the film, we were given access to the historic interior rooms you'll see. Lady Scarsdale (there appeared to be just the two of them living in this huge place) regaled us with her experiences in America when she visited Scarsdale, New York, and went through I can't recall how many pairs of gloves shaking every-one's hands.]

EXT. GARDEN. BREADALBY. DAY

A luncheon party is in progress at a table set up under a huge tree. Waiters are serving everyone and replenishing wineglasses.

HERMIONE: At least here you will have an opportunity to observe Nature.

BIRKIN: Gudrun Brangwen. Gerald Crich. Tibby and Laura Lupton. Rupert Birkin. Rupert Birkin. Peculiar names we all have. Do you think we've all been singled out for some extraordinary moment in life, or are we all cursed with the mark of Cain?

URSULA: I'm afraid Ursula was a martyred saint. It's been rather difficult to live up to.

(BIRKIN *laughs.*)

GERALD: And who is Gudrun?

GUDRUN: In a Norse myth, Gudrun was a sinner who murdered her husband.

GERALD: And will you live up to that?

GUDRUN: Which would you prefer me to live up to, Mr. Crich? The sinner or the murderer?

BIRKIN: Ah, I see that the perpetual struggle has begun. Oh, we all struggle so, don't we.

(HERMIONE *is ignoring him, devoting all her attention to eating a fig.* BIRKIN *rings a silver bell to attract attention.*)

The proper way to eat a fig in society . . .

(*He will illustrate with a fig. Various reaction shots.* GERALD *is embarrassed, the newlyweds smile at each other.*)

. . . is to split it in four, holding it by the stump, and open it so that it is a glittering, rosy, moist, honeyed heavy-petalled flower. Then you throw away the skin after you have taken off the blossom with your lips. But the vulgar way is just to put your mouth to the crack and take out the flesh in one bite . . . (*Which is exactly what* HERMIONE *is gracelessly doing.*) The fig is a very secretive fruit. The Italians vulgarly say it stands for the female part . . . the fig fruit . . . the fissure . . . the yoni . . . the wonderful moist conductivity towards the center . . . involved . . . in-turned . . . One small way of access only, and this close-curtained from the light . . . Sap that smells strange on your fingers, so that even goats won't taste it. . . . And when the fig has kept her secret long enough . . . so it explodes, and you see through the fissure the scarlet . . . and the fig is finished, the year is over. That's how the fig dies, showing her crimson through the purple slit . . . like a wound, the exposure of her secret on the open day. . . . Like a prostitute, the bursten fig makes a show of her secret. (*Looking at* HERMIONE.) That's how women die, too.

[This poem is not in the novel but is a poem by D. H. Lawrence and included in his *Collected Poems*. Ken discovered it, and including it here and the way he directed it and Alan delivered it were brilliant.]

HERMIONE: (*At length.*) Would you like to come for a walk? Would you like to come for a walk? The dahlias are so pretty. Will you come for a walk, Rupert?

BIRKIN: No, Hermione.

HERMIONE: Are you sure?

BIRKIN: Quite sure.

HERMIONE: And why not?

BIRKIN: Because I don't like trooping off in a gang.

HERMIONE: But the dahlias are so pretty.

BIRKIN: I've seen them.

HERMIONE: Then we'll leave a little boy behind, if he's sulky. Good-bye . . . good-bye, little boy.

(*She leads the guests away, leaving* BIRKIN *and* GERALD *alone, still seated at the luncheon table.*)

BIRKIN: Good-bye.

HERMIONE: (*Off.*) This way! This way!

BIRKIN: Impudent hag!

GERALD: Have you ever really loved anybody?

BIRKIN: Yes, and no.

GERALD: But not finally?

BIRKIN: Finally . . . no.

GERALD: Nor I.

BIRKIN: Do you want to?

GERALD: I don't know.

BIRKIN: I do. I want the finality of love.

GERALD: Just one woman?

BIRKIN: Just one woman.

GERALD: I don't believe a woman—and nothing but a woman—will ever make my life.

BIRKIN: You don't? Then what do you live for, Gerald?

GERALD: I suppose I live for my work. And other than that, I live . . . because I'm living.

BIRKIN: I find that one needs one single pure activity. I would call love a single pure activity. But I don't really love anybody. Not now.

GERALD: You mean that if there isn't a woman, then there's nothing?

BIRKIN: More or less that. Seeing there's no God.

GERALD: Rupert, what is it you really want?

BIRKIN: I want to sit with my beloved in a field, with daisies growing all around us.

(BIRKIN *smiles.* GERALD *stares at him.*)

INT. BREADALBY. NIGHT

HERMIONE *claps her hands to get attention. She stands in a large and impos-ing marble rotunda, with* URSULA *and* GUDRUN. *All are wearing exagger-ated heavy makeup and costumes.* GUDNUFSKY *sits at a grand piano. The* CONTESSA *leans against it.* LAURA *and* LUPTON *seat themselves on a couch.* GERALD *and* BIRKIN *move from a portico to be closer.*

HERMIONE: We have devised an entertainment for you in the style of the Russian ballet.

GERALD: (*To* BIRKIN.) Who are those two Brangwen girls?

BIRKIN: Teachers in the Grammar School. Gudrun pretends she's an artist as well.

GERALD: And what's their father?

BIRKIN: Handicrafts Instructor in the Grammar School.

GERALD: Really!

BIRKIN: Class barriers are breaking down.

GERALD: That their father teaches handcraft in school, what does it matter to me?

[GERALD: How is it Hermione has them here?

BIRKIN: She knew Gudrun in London. I knew her there as well. She'll know about Minette and Halliday, though she wasn't quite their set. More conventional, I suppose.

GERALD: Is her work any good?

BIRKIN: I think sometimes they are marvelously good. Hermione has two wagtails in her boudoir carved and painted in wood.

GERALD: She might be a well-known artist someday?

BIRKIN: I think she might. But she is a restless bird, gone in a week or two to heaven knows where. Her contrariness prevents her taking anything seriously. And she won't give herself away. She's always on the defensive. That's what I can't stand about her.]

(*The piano music starts.*)

HERMIONE: I shall be Orpah, a vivid sensational widow. I am only just a widow, and I slowly dance the death of my husband before returning to my former life. And Gudrun . . . her husband too has just died. She weeps with me, and laments. And Ursula will be the mother-in-law, Naomi.

(*This is news to* URSULA.)

Our husbands were her sons. Her own husband died years ago. Thus all her men are dead. She stands alone, demanding nothing. And the Contessa will be the wheat fields rippling in the evening air. And Birkin will turn the pages for the maestro.

(*And so begins a most free-form ballet, in the style of Isadora Duncan, with much waving of hands and scarves and awkward poses of the body. The music will become more frantic as the women become energized dervishes, particularly* HERMIONE, *who is completely caught up in her drama, so much so that she entwines herself sinuously around one column after another, then grabs a large fringed shawl, which she twirls and waves and raises high as she comes toward* BIRKIN *to envelop him with it. He won't allow it and she spins past him.* BIRKIN *whispers into* GUDNUFSKY's *ear, and he immediately switches to playing ragtime.* HERMIONE, *forced to stop dancing, can't believe her ears or her eyes as* BIRKIN *grabs* URSULA *and starts to dance with her, joined by* GERALD *and* GUDRUN, *and* LAURA *and* LUPTON. HERMIONE *is livid. She returns to confront* URSULA.)

Little tart!

BIRKIN: Madame!

(*Hermione marches out.*)

INT. BREADALBY DRAWING ROOM. NIGHT

HERMIONE *sits pouting on a long couch.* BIRKIN *comes in and sits on the other end.* BIRKIN *is a little drunk.*

BIRKIN: I'm sorry if I spoiled your ... dance. It was an act of pure spontaneity.

HERMIONE: My arse.

BIRKIN: You can't bear anything to be spontaneous, can you? Because then it's no longer in your power. You must clutch things and have them in your power. And why? Because you haven't got any real body—any dark, sensual body of life. All you've got is your will and your lust for power!

HERMIONE: How can you not think me sensual?

BIRKIN: All you want is pornography ... looking at yourself in mirrors, watching your naked animal actions in mirrors, keeping it all mental. If one cracked your skull, maybe one could get a spontaneous, passionate woman out of you, with real sensuality.

(*He has walked around the room and slumped down again into the sofa. She has been standing by a desk, her hand playing with a heavy glass paperweight. She suddenly swings around and strikes him with it. She tries to do it again, but he manages to ward off her blow. They continue their struggle. Blood trickles down his head. Finally* BIRKIN *breaks away.*)

No, you don't, Hermione! I don't let you.

(*He runs out of the house, down the magnificent curving stone staircase of its entrance, and out to the trees beyond.*)

INT. BRACKEN, TREES, WOODS. NIGHT INTO DAY

As BIRKIN *runs farther and deeper into the forest, yanking off his shirt, ripping off his clothing, grabbing needles and branches from the bracken, the trees become small fir trees, no taller than he, and he rubs himself with them, wiping himself clean, being one with the beauty of nature. He wants "to touch them all, to saturate himself with the touch of them all." He is naked, his feet among the primroses. He lies down, "letting them touch his belly, his breasts," and looks up at the sky.)*

EXT. PARK IN BELDOVER. DAY

A brass band playing, a small crowd singing "Jerusalem," awaiting a minister to unveil a statue of a bronze soldier holding a bayonet. URSULA *is seen standing in the back of the crowd.*

MINISTER: And Jesus Christ our Lord hath said that greater love hath no man than he who lays down his life for his brother. And no greater love hath man than the love of man for man and brother for brother. We shall now move forward into an uninterrupted age of brotherhood and love. For love is the greatest thing the world has ever known or shall ever come to know.

(BIRKIN *is seen working his way through the crowd to stand beside* URSULA. *He relieves her of some of the parcels she is carrying.*)

BIRKIN: He might as well say that hate is the greatest thing. . . . What people want is hate . . . hate and nothing but hate. (*Starts making his way back through the crowd.*) In the name of righteousness and love ye shall have hate. . . . Out of love ye shall throw down nitroglycerine bombs and ye shall kill your brother. It's the lie that kills. Ah, if people want hate let them have it. Death, torture, murder, violent destruction, let's have it. But not in the name of love.

(He pushes his way through, followed by URSULA *who looks apologetically at the people he jostles.)*

URSULA: Sorry . . .

BIRKIN: Oh, I abhor humanity. I wish it were swept away. It could go and there would be no absolute loss if every human being perished tomorrow.

URSULA: *(To someone.)* I beg your pardon. *(To* BIRKIN.*)* So you want everybody in the world destroyed?

BIRKIN: Yes! Absolutely! You yourself—don't you think it's a wonderful and clear idea, a world empty of people, just uninterrupted grass and a rabbit sitting in it?

URSULA: You don't seem to see much love in humanity. What about individual love?

BIRKIN: I don't believe in love, any more than I believe in hate or grief. Love is an emotion you feel or you don't feel according to your circumstances.

URSULA: If you don't believe in love, what do you believe in? Just in the end of the world, and rabbits?

BIRKIN: The point about L-O-V-E is that we hate the word, because we've vulgarized it. It should be taboo, forbidden from utterance for many years till we find a new and better idea.

URSULA: Well . . . *(She stops walking and takes her parcels back from Birkin.)* . . . I shall just have to leave it to you to send your new and better ideas down from the holy altar. When you think the world is ready, of course.

(Brass band starts to play. URSULA *walks away, and* BIRKIN *looks after her.)*

EXT. BELDOVER RAILWAY CROSSING. DAY

A locomotive approaching full speed. GERALD *on his mare races the train, whipping his horse more and more.* URSULA, *carrying books, and* GUDRUN *are walking home from school. He nods to the sisters. The train is now upon* GERALD; *and the horse, rigidly held in position frighteningly near to it, begins to panic.* GERALD *responds by pressing his spurred boots even harder into the animal. The wail of the engine sends the horse up almost verti-cally, so that it appears* GERALD *might be thrown. With a steely control and icy determination and no sense of panic whatsoever, he leans forward and brings the mare down to all fours, not stopping their speed for a moment.* GUDRUN *is watching all this with spellbound fascination bordering on excitement.* URSULA *is appalled by* GERALD's *cruelty, even more so when* GERALD *rams his spurs even harder into the mare's already bleeding flanks.*

URSULA: Gerald! Oh, don't!

> (*The mare, trying to get away from the train, is rearing and plunging, and* GERALD *continues to flog her.* GUDRUN *shakes* URSULA *by the shoulders to quiet her. The last coal car passes and* GERALD *forces his mare forward and they gallop away across the field.*)

GUDRUN: (*Screaming after him.*) I should think you're proud! (*The sound of Gerald laughing.*)

INT. THE CRICH COAL MINES. DAY

Coal tubs run along rails and tip out their coal. GERALD *shoves one along. He is as dirty with coal dust as his men.*

A high shot of the sorting room where lines of men, women, and chil-dren are sorting out slate from the coal as it moves on a conveyor belt down chutes. GERALD *comes down the stairs and moves toward the sorting table, where* BARBER, *an elderly miner, is struggling to move a large piece of slate.* GERALD *picks up the slate and throws it on the floor.*

GERALD: Report to the office.

> (*Barber walks away silently. The river of coal continues moving.*)

INT. THE CRICH OFFICE AT THE MINES. DAY

MR. CRICH *is surreptitiously handing* BARBER *a ten-shilling note from his own wallet.* GERALD *comes in and sees this. He pours water in a basin and washes his hands.*

MR. CRICH: Can't you keep him on a little longer?

GERALD: I've already replaced him, Father. Don't you think his pension will be sufficient?

BARBER: 'Tis not the pension, it's the work. I still have a few more years' work left in me.

GERALD: Not the sort of work I want.

> (*Both* BARBER *and* MR. CRICH *lower their eyes rather than look at each other.*)

EXT. THE CRICH COAL MINES. DAY

Coal trucks rattling past. GERALD *wheels his father in his wheelchair. Miners, leaving, raise their caps as they pass.*

MR. CRICH: They hate you. I'm glad I won't have to see it much longer.

GERALD: Their hate is better than your love. You made a fortune exploiting them, and now you try to ease your guilt by slipping them a few coins. At least I give them a fair salary, if they can do the work.

MR. CRICH: They'll be few of them left to pay soon. You and your new machines.

GERALD: Yes. Me and my new machines.

MR. CRICH: They say you've stopped the widows' coals. We've always allowed all the widows of men who worked for the firm a load of coal every three months.

(*They stop beside a Rolls-Royce. A uniformed chauffeur sits behind the wheel.* GERALD *helps his father into the car.*)

GERALD: Well, they'll have to pay cost price from now on. The firm's not the charitable institution you seem to think it is, Father. (*To the chauffeur.*) Will you take us home, please.

(*High shot of miners pouring out of the gates and the white Rolls-Royce in the middle of them, moving forward.*)

EXT. ALLEYWAY. EVENING

GUDRUN *walks down a narrow alley separating miners' back-to-back houses. Men are washing up in their backyards and turn and stare at her as she walks by them, her umbrella up.*

MINER ONE: What price that, eh? She'll do, won't she?

MINER TWO: Boy, I'd give my week's wages for five minutes with her, just five minutes.

MINER ONE: Your missus'd have summat to say to you.

MINER TWO: Hey, you're first class, you are!

MINER ONE: D'you think she'd be worth a week's wages, eh?

MINER TWO: Do I? I'd bloody well put 'em down this second.

(GUDRUN *continues walking, smiling to herself.*)

EXT. RAILWAY ARCH. NIGHT

GUDRUN *walking underneath the overhead line. We can dimly see couples as they stand against the wall, kissing.*

EXT. PUB AND MARKET. NIGHT

Two whores stand outside a pub. Lighted windows and much rowdy commotion inside. GUDRUN *passes them by. Two men stagger out of the pub, fighting, one of them breaking a bottle over the other's head.* GUDRUN *stares at them.* PALMER, *a miner, staggers out. One of the whores grabs him. He kisses her, then pushes her aside and goes to join* GUDRUN.

[Palmer is the incorrect name to have used. Gudrun in fact was dating a young and uninteresting and proper electrician by the name of Palmer. This would certainly not have been he.]

PALMER: You be wanting company?

(GUDRUN *stares at him silently and then starts walking. The market stalls are all lit with flares.*)

PALMER: Sure you do. You'd be wanting a little company.

GUDRUN: Who be you then?

PALMER: A man.

GUDRUN: What work?

PALMER: Miner. Good enough for you? Why'd you ask all these
questions?

GUDRUN: How are your thighs?

PALMER: My thighs?

GUDRUN: How are they? Are they strong? Because I want to drown
in flesh. Hot, physical, naked flesh.

PALMER: Flesh.

(GUDRUN *moves forward, laughing.* PALMER *follows her. He pushes
her into the doorway of another pub and embraces her. She tries to shrink
away from him.*)

Come here. You're dying for it, aren't you?

(GUDRUN *kicks him.*)

Ow!

GUDRUN: You are hideous and ridiculous like all the rest.

PALMER: Come here, you silly bitch!

(*He tries to hold on to her and they struggle. The door of the pub opens
and* GERALD *stands there.*)

GERALD: Good evening, Miss Brangwen.

(PALMER *lets go of* GUDRUN *and backs away.*)

Anything wrong, Palmer?

PALMER: Mr. Crich . . . No offense, Mr. Crich.

(*Two whores are with* GERALD *and he follows them, smiling, as he
passes* GUDRUN.)

GUDRUN: (*Shouting after him.*) I was born here and I'll die here, until I fly away!

GERALD: (*Calling back.*) Well, don't fly away till you come to our picnic.

(*He puts his arms around the whores and moves through the market stalls, lit by torches into the distance as far as the eye can see.*)

EXT. SHORTLANDS. DAY

Shortlands is the CRICH *estate, on Willey Water. The grounds are filling with crowds arriving for the annual picnic. Brass bands play. Carriages drive into shot to discharge their passengers. Miners and their families in their best clothing wander about. People on foot line up at the gates in a steady stream to hand their cards to policemen, who let them in.* MR. *and* MRS. BRANGWEN, *followed by* URSULA *and* GUDRUN, *stand in line, moving forward.*

GUDRUN: Did you imagine yourself in the midst of all this, my dear?

URSULA: It does look rather awful.

GUDRUN: Imagine what it'll be like.

URSULA: I suppose we can get away from it all.

GUDRUN: (*Handing her invitation to a* POLICEMAN.) Police to keep you in. The Criches are afraid you're going to run off with the silver. (*To* POLICEMAN.) Good afternoon.

POLICEMAN: Good afternoon.

(*At the far end of the lawn, his back to a window in his house,* MR. CRICH *sits with young* WINIFRED *on his knee. He holds a tankard of beer.*)

WINIFRED: Please, Father, may I have just a little bit of beer?

(MRS. CRICH *stands on the other side of the window, looking out at everything disapprovingly.*)

MR. CRICH: No, no, no . . .

WINIFRED: Please!

MR. CRICH: Well, you can have just a little.

(MRS. CRICH *shakes her head in displeasure.* LAURA *runs over and stoops to kiss* MR. CRICH.)

LAURA: We're going for a dip, Father.

LUPTON: (*Arriving.*) You drinking, Winifred?

MR. CRICH: (*As* LAURA *and* LUPTON *start off.*) Be sure not to stay in the water too long.

(*People are dancing on the grass, including* GERALD *waltzing with* HERMIONE. *Children play on a roundabout.* BIRKIN *is throwing balls at a coconut. The* BRANGWENS *are walking over the grass toward* BIRKIN.)

URSULA: This is Mr. Birkin, Father.

(BIRKIN, *hearing his name, swings around.*)

MR. BRANGWEN: How do you do? I hope you're keeping well.

BIRKIN: Yes, thank you. I'm fit. Hello, Mrs. Brangwen. I know Gudrun and Ursula quite well.

MRS. BRANGWEN: Yes, I've heard them talk about you often enough.

GERALD: (*Joining them.*) Mr. and Mrs. Brangwen? I'm so glad you could come to our picnic. How do you do?

MR. BRANGWEN: You forgot our invitation last year.

BIRKIN: Tea!

GERALD: Yes. Would you like tea here, or would you rather go and have it in the house?

URSULA: Oh, can't we have a rowing boat and get out?

GERALD: Get out?

GUDRUN: Well, you see, we know hardly anyone here. We're almost complete strangers.

GERALD: Oh, I'll see to it that you're set up with a few acquaintances.

GUDRUN: Oh, you know what I mean. Can't we go over there and explore?

(GUDRUN *runs through the dancers, followed by* GERALD *and* URSULA, *to the jetty on the lake, still with a few boats.*)

The light is so perfect, perhaps we could bathe. It reminds one of the Upper Reaches of the Nile. Well, as one imagines the Nile. . . .

(LUPTON *arrives and pushes a skiff off, then jumps into it.*)

LUPTON: Hello!

GUDRUN: Hello.

GERALD: Do you think it's far enough off? Yes, I suppose you could go there. Unfortunately we don't seem to have any more boats. They're all out now.

URSULA: Oh, it would be so lovely.

GERALD: Do you handle a boat pretty well?

GUDRUN: Pretty well.

URSULA: Yes, we both row like water spiders.

GERALD: Then there's a small light canoe of mine I didn't bring out for fear somebody would drown themselves. Do you think you'd be safe in that? You see, I'm responsible for this water.

GUDRUN: I had a canoe at Arundel. I can assure you I'm perfectly safe.

GERALD: Then I shall see to it that you're given a tea basket, and you can have a picnic all to yourselves. That is the idea, isn't it?

GUDRUN: How fearfully good. How frightfully kind of you.

EXT. WILLEY WATER LAKE. AFTERNOON

GUDRUN *paddles the canoe. They are moving farther away from the shore, Shortlands receding in the distance, the sounds of music and festivities dimmer, though still to be heard.*

LUPTON *and* LAURA, *both naked, creep down to the water's edge and drop into the water. They embrace and start swimming out.*

EXT. THE FAR SHORE OF THE LAKE. LATE AFTERNOON

URSULA, *now naked, is swimming.*

URSULA: Are you happy, Prune?

GUDRUN: (*Also swimming naked.*) Ursula, I am utterly, utterly happy!

URSULA: So am I!

(GUDRUN *and* URSULA, *now dressed, are enjoying their picnic basket.* GUDRUN *lies back and puts her head in her sister's lap.* URSULA *sings a song.* GUDRUN *gets up and dances to the song, running among the low-hanging branches and embracing the trees. She runs up a hill and suddenly looks startled.* URSULA, *from where she is, jumps to her feet and runs to her sister's side. A herd of horned Highland cattle is slowly approaching.*)

GUDRUN: Aren't they charming, Ursula?

URSULA: Charming! Won't they do anything to us?

GUDRUN: Oh, I'm sure they won't.

URSULA: I'm frightened.

GUDRUN: Keep singing.

(GUDRUN, *with her arms outspread and her face uplifted, goes into a strange pulsating dance toward the cattle, thrusting her body toward them as if in a spell, her arms and wrists and hands stretching out to the herd, then pulling back, her breasts thrust forward toward the cattle. . . . She seems carried away, in some sort of ecstasy. As she drifts closer and closer toward them, they do not move. They stare at her as she comes even closer, almost to touching them.* URSULA, *spellbound, keeps up her thin, irrelevant song, which pierces the fading light as evening slowly approaches.*

Suddenly one of the cattle snorts, ducks its head, and backs away. Others follow. GUDRUN *is in triumph and runs after them as the herd turns and starts to stampede away.*

GERALD *and* BIRKIN, *having beached their boat, come running up the hill,* GERALD *yelling.*)

GERALD: What do you think you were doing?

URSULA: I think we've all gone mad.

BIRKIN: (*Doing a little jumping dance.*) It's a pity we aren't madder!

(GUDRUN *is running back to the group.* GERALD *seizes her and stops her.*)

GUDRUN: Why have you come?

GERALD: And why do you want to drive them mad?

(GUDRUN *starts laughing and falls to the ground.*)

GERALD: They're nasty when they turn.

GUDRUN: Turn where?

GERALD: Turn against you.

GUDRUN: Turn against me?

GERALD: Anyway, they gored one of the farmer's cows to death the other day.

GUDRUN: What do I care?

GERALD: I care, seeing they're my cattle.

GUDRUN: How are they yours? You haven't swallowed them. Give me one of them now.

(*She holds out her hands.*)

GERALD: You know where they are.

GUDRUN: You think I'm frightened of you and your cattle, don't you?

GERALD: Why should I think that?

(She leans forward and swings round her arm, catching him a light blow on the face with the back of her hand.)

GUDRUN: That's why.

GERALD: You have struck the first blow.

GUDRUN: And I shall strike the last.

(She runs from him and leans against the trunk of an enormous tree.)

GERALD: Why are you behaving in this impossible and ridiculous fashion?

GUDRUN: You make me behave like this.

GERALD: Me? How?

GUDRUN: Don't be angry with me.

GERALD: I'm not angry with you. I'm in love with you.

GUDRUN: That's one way of putting it.

GERALD: *(Standing behind her.)* It's all right, then?

GUDRUN: *(Softly, as if drugged.)* Yes, it's all right.

(Farther along the lake's edge, URSULA is walking with BIRKIN.)

URSULA: I must be going home now.

BIRKIN: Must you? How sad.

URSULA: Are you really sad?

BIRKIN: Yes. I could go on walking like this forever.

EXT. WILLEY WATER. EVENING

The lighted lanterns in their canoe are reflected in the water. BIRKIN *and* URSULA *float along.* URSULA *puts out her hands to cup the red-and-gold lantern, close to her face.*

BIRKIN: There is a golden light in you which I wish that you would give me.

URSULA: I always think I'm going to be loved, and then I'm let down.

(*On another part of the lake,* LUPTON *and* LAURA *are bobbing up and down, disappearing then reappearing, smiling, laughing, calling to each other, trying to find each other's locations.*)

LAURA: Tibby!

LUPTON: Laura? (*He swims in the direction of* LAURA, *looking around for her, still calling.*) Laura? Laura! Where are you! Laura! (*He dives under. Coming up, coughing.*) Oh God. Help me please. Help! Help me, someone! (*He dives underwater to try again.*)

(BIRKIN, *paddling rapidly, with* URSULA, *moves toward the cry. Another canoe approaches with great speed, with* GERALD *and* GUDRUN. GERALD *dives into the water, fully clothed.*)

GERALD: (*Shouting.*) Laura! Lupton! My God . . . Where are they?

URSULA: (*Shouting.*) I don't know!

GERALD: I've got to find them!

(BIRKIN *grabs for* GERALD.)

BIRKIN: You can't!

GERALD: Why should you interfere?

BIRKIN: You can't see. (*To* URSULA.) Try to keep the boat still. (*Trying to lean over and get a hold on* GERALD.)

URSULA: I'm trying.

BIRKIN: Get out!

(GERALD *disappears from view under the water.*)

Gerald! Are you all right!

(*As* GERALD *surfaces.*)

Hang on!

(*On the shore,* MR. CRICH *and a group of miners hurry to the water's edge.* URSULA *is banking the canoe.* BIRKIN *helps* GERALD *from the water to the land.* GUDRUN, *still in her canoe at the bank, watches.*)

GERALD: We shan't save them, Father. There's no knowing where they are. And there's a current as cold as hell.

MR. CRICH: Go home and look to yourself! (*Issuing orders to the miners.*) We'll let the water out. Rupert, you go to the north sluice. . . .

GERALD: There's room in that water there for thousands.

(GUDRUN *approaches with* GERALD's *blazer, which she puts around his shoulders.*)

GUDRUN: Two is enough.

GERALD: There's one thing about our family, you know. Once anything goes wrong it can never be put right. Not with us.

EXT. SLUICE GATES. NIGHT

BIRKIN *and a* GATEMAN *are turning handles. Beneath them the water is pouring through.*

EXT. WOODS NEAR SLUICE GATE. NIGHT

URSULA: Do you think they're dead?

BIRKIN: (*Arriving.*) Yes.

URSULA: Isn't it horrible! Do you mind very much?

BIRKIN: I don't mind about the dead. The worst of it is they cling to the living and won't let go.

URSULA: I'm afraid of death.

BIRKIN: Death's all right. Nothing better.

URSULA: But you don't want to die?

BIRKIN: I would like to die from our kind of life ... be born again through a love that is like sleep, with new air round one that no one's ever breathed before.

URSULA: I thought love wasn't good enough for you.

BIRKIN: Oh, I don't want love. I don't want to know you. I want to be gone out of myself, and you to be lost to yourself, so we are found different. Oh, we shouldn't talk when we're tired and wretched.

URSULA: Say you love me. Say "my love" to me.

BIRKIN: Oh, I love you right enough. I just want it to be something else.

URSULA: Why? Why? Why isn't it enough?

BIRKIN: Because we can go one better.

URSULA: We can't. We can only say we love each other. Say "my love" to me. Say it. Say it. (*She stops and turns to face him.*)

BIRKIN: Yes. "My love." Yes, "my love." Let love be enough then. I love you then. I'm bored by the rest.

(*He continues walking. She seizes him and turns him around to face her, putting her arms around his neck. They kiss. He slips off his jacket, she helps him. He sinks to his knees and pulls her down to him. Soon she is lying on her back, with* BIRKIN *on top of her, caressing her, pushing up her skirt and petticoats, and yanking down her drawers.*)

URSULA: Say it! Oh, say it.

(*He tears off his shirt and unfastens his trousers, pushing them below his waist. Her hands are gripping his shoulders, his back.*)

I do love you. I do.

(URSULA, *her eyes closed,* BIRKIN *kissing her, entangle with each other in an awkward, uncomfortable coming together.*)

[This would appear to be the first time in the novel that Ursula and Birkin, for all their talk, actually make love, although this is not perfectly clear. If it is making love, it is very quick, this wham-bam, over in a few brief paragraphs of solid Laurentian sex-prose. Perhaps that is the point. In Birkin's mind, Ursula has not agreed to the terms of what he seeks; nor has he for her. It is interesting that this coupling, whatever it entails, is placed in the novel just as the bodies of two lovers are about to be discovered.

It is also interesting to compare the various passages where it seems Ursula and Birkin are making love and where they may very well not be. She comes to him several times at his Mill House, and they also go on an "excurse" to a country inn, in the novel after the "three rings" scene in the wheat fields. With this last there is no doubt they make love. For a change, the point of view is hers: the description of her passion is forefront. Again, perhaps this is Lawrence's point in progressing through these scenes, going from the less precise to the undeniable. She loves him now, as he does her. Previously they both waffled too much for both of them or one or the other of them. If they had made love earlier, then, it was not truly satisfactory, in the Laurentian sense.

It is worth remembering, for much of it is between-the-lines sort of stuff that you are likely to forget, and which few critics ever remind us of, that both Birkin and Gerald are quite sexually experienced. Birkin appears to have favored the occasional trip up to London and Soho and shacking up with a bohemian crowd of friends. Gerald's experiences sound to have been more of the lost weekend orgy with strangers sort of thing. He does not like to deal with the same woman for very long and then likes to pay them so he is under no obligation.]

EXT. MUDDY BED OF WILLEY WATER LAKE. DAWN

The naked bodies of the drowned LAURA *and* LUPTON *lie in the mud, clasped in each other's arms.* GERALD *walks through the mud toward them, slipping in the ooze, then standing and looking down at them.*

[In the novel, the dead bodies are of Diana, yet another Crich daughter, and of her unnamed beau. In opting to make them those of Laura and Lupton, characters we have come to care about, Ken and I perhaps took too much license. It did, and still does, seem to have been worth it.]

EXT. WOODS. EARLY MORNING

URSULA *and* BIRKIN *lying in the same position as the drowned lovers. They stir, he rolls over onto his back, and she turns on her side, her back toward him, her eyes filled with tears.*

BIRKIN: Must it be like this?

EXT. WOODLAND PATH. EARLY MORNING

BIRKIN *and* URSULA *come out from the trees, both dressed, walking slowly. Miners are walking carrying two stretchers.* GERALD *walks beside the first stretcher.* MR. CRICH *and* HERMIONE *follow.* GERALD *pauses before* BIRKIN.

GERALD: She killed him.

(*He walks on.* BIRKIN *stops* HERMIONE.)

BIRKIN: What did he mean?

HERMIONE: Perhaps it's better to die than live mechanically a life that's a repetition of repetitions.

(*She continues to follow the procession.* BIRKIN *goes with her.* GUDRUN *appears, and* URSULA, *still crying, is embraced by her sister. They walk away together, following the others.*)

[This has been quite a sequence, a sustained piece of narrative, the longest in the film, some fifteen pages, traversing from bright day to deep night to the following morning and encompassing every possible action and emotion and all our leading players. The earliest part, of the crowds arriving and pouring onto the grounds, took the longest to shoot, perhaps because Ken wanted long tracking shots that were hard to coordinate with the hundreds of extras and the horses and carriages. The Highland cattle, believe it or not, were relatively docile and obedient. The shots before their arrival and after their departure, mostly of Gudrun photographed in long shot against the water, dancing among the trees, are for me among the most beautiful in the film. Night shooting had additional difficulties: the temperature of the water was very cold, and those who had to be in it were shivering mightily between takes. Lawrence's novel is not known for its narrative power, nor is this film, both of which have so much obligatory philosophy to impart. Ken (and cinematographer Billy Williams, of course) did a splendid job pulling all of this together and making it all relevant and allowing us to care for these complicated people.]

EXT. LIBRARY. SHORTLANDS. DAY

A large paneled room with an enormous fireplace. GERALD *is facing the fire and* BIRKIN *is making a drink.*

GERALD: By God, I'd just come to the conclusion that nothing in the world mattered except somebody to take the edge off one's being alone. The right somebody.

BIRKIN: Meaning the right woman, I suppose?

GERALD: Yes, of course. Failing that, an amusing man.

BIRKIN: Well, if you're bored, why not try hitting something?

GERALD: Perhaps. So long as it was something worth hitting. Did you ever do any boxing?

BIRKIN: No. So you think you might as well hit me?

GERALD: You? Well. Perhaps! In a friendly kind of way, of course.

BIRKIN: Oh, quite. I never learned the gentlemanly art.

GERALD: You know, I've got the feeling that if I don't watch myself, I shall do something silly.

BIRKIN: Why not do it? I used to do some Japanese-style wrestling once. I was never any good at it. Those things don't interest me.

GERALD: Don't they? Well, they do me. How do we start?

BIRKIN: Well . . . You can't do much in a stuffed shirt.

GERALD: All right. Let's strip, and do it properly. (*Gerald takes off his coat . . .*

BIRKIN: Very good.

> *. . . as does* BIRKIN, *who then drags aside the bearskin rug he's been lying on. They strip off their clothing.*)

BIRKIN: Now you come at me any way you want, and I'll try and get out of it.

GERALD: Admirable. (*Gerald turns the key in the door.*)

> (*"So they wrestled swiftly, rapturously, intent and mindless at last, two essential white figures working into a tighter, closer oneness of struggle, with a strange, octopus-like knotting and flashing of limbs in the sub-dued light of the room; a tense white knot of flesh gripped in silence between the walls of old brown books. Now and again came a gasp of breath, or a sound like a sigh, then the rapid thudding of movement on*

the thickly-carpeted floor, then the strange sound of flesh escaping under flesh. Often, in the white interlaced knot of violent living being that swayed silently, there was no head to be seen, only the swift, tight limbs, the solid white backs, the physical junction of two bodies clinched into oneness. Then would appear the gleaming, ruffled head of GERALD, *as the struggle changed, then for a moment the dun-colored, shadowlike head of the other man would lift up from the conflict, the eyes wide and dreadful and sightless.*

"At length GERALD *lay back inert on the carpet, his breast rising in great slow panting, whilst* BIRKIN *kneeled over him, almost unconscious.* BIRKIN *was much more exhausted. He caught little, short breaths, he could scarcely breathe any more. The earth seemed to tilt and sway and a complete darkness was coming over his mind. He did not know what happened. He slid forward quite unconscious over* GERALD, *and* GERALD *did not notice. Then he was half conscious again, aware only of the strange tilting and sliding of the world, everything was sliding into the darkness. And he was sliding, everything was sliding off into the darkness. And he was sliding, endlessly, endlessly away.*

*"*GERALD, *however, was still less conscious than* BIRKIN. *They waited dimly, in a sort of not-being, for many uncounted, unknown minutes."*)

GERALD: Was it too much for you?

BIRKIN: No. No. One ought to wrestle and strive to be physically close. It makes one sane.

GERALD: You do think so?

BIRKIN: I do. Do you?

GERALD: Yes.

BIRKIN: We are mentally and spiritually close. Therefore we should be physically close too. It's more complete. You know how the old German knights used to swear blood brotherhood?

GERALD: Yes. Make wounds in their arms and run blood into each other's cuts.

BIRKIN: Yes. And swear to be true to each other with one blood all their lives. Well, that's what we ought to do. Well . . . no wounds, I mean that's obsolete. But we ought to swear to love each other, you and I. Implicitly, perfectly, finally. Without any possibility of ever going back on it. Shall we swear to each other one day?

GERALD: We'll wait till I understand it better.

BIRKIN: Well, at any rate one feels freer and more open now. And that's what we want.

GERALD: Certainly.

BIRKIN: In a way, that's what I want with Ursula. Single, clear, yet balanced.

(*He gets up and walks to his clothing on a chair. He puts on his trousers.*)

But they're all the same, women. Lust for passion, greed for self-importance in love. I should think Gudrun is even worse. You see her lately?

(GERALD *puts on his trousers and his shirt.*)

GERALD: She's coming over next week. Hermione suggested she teach Winifred to draw. The child hasn't been the same since her sister . . . since the drowning. Are you fond of Ursula?

BIRKIN: I think I love her. I suppose the next step's an engagement, then marriage.

GERALD: You know, I always believed in love, in true love. But where do you find it nowadays?

BIRKIN: (*Picking up his shirt.*) I don't know. Life has all kinds of things. There isn't only one road.

GERALD: I don't care how it is with me, as long as . . . well, as I feel that I've loved. I don't care how long it is as long as I can feel that.

BIRKIN: Fulfilled.

GERALD: Yes. I suppose it could be fulfilled. I don't use the same words as you.

BIRKIN: Well, it's the same.

GERALD: Would you like a bath?

BIRKIN: Mmm.

(*"There was a pause of strange enmity between the two men that was very close to love. It was always the same between them; always their talk brought them into a deadly nearness of contact, a strange, perilous intimacy which was either hate or love, or both. . . . Yet the heart of each burned for the other. They burned with each other, inwardly. This they would never admit. They intended to keep their relationship a casual free-and-easy friendship, they were not going to be so unmanly and unnatural as to allow any heart-burning between them. They had not the faintest belief in deep relationship between men and men, and their disbelief prevented any development of their powerful but suppressed friendliness."*)

[The above scene, perhaps one of the most famous in the book (where the chapter is entitled "Gladiatorial") and certainly the one that the film is most remembered for (we came to call it "the wrestling scene"), presented us, from the beginning, we knew, with our biggest challenge. No British or American studio–financed film had ever released something like this. What came to be known as "full-frontal male nudity" was not allowed. What came to be known as "homoeroticism" had never been shown to such a marked degree. I was determined that somehow we would get on the screen, un-scathed, what Lawrence had written and we had filmed.

Our opposition to achieving this goal existed, mightily, in the person of one Lord John Trevelyan, the British government's offi-cial film censor. Censorship was legal, and John was not known for leniency. A script had dutifully been sent to his office before we be-gan shooting, and his comments were dutifully returned to us before we began filming—in other words, with enough time to rewrite and do something about correcting them. He told us in no uncertain terms that this scene would present an insurmountable roadblock to the film's release, as would, as presently constituted, the Birkin-Ursula wham-bam sex scene after the Water Party and a later scene between Gerald and Gudrun, in Switzerland, what we came to call the "revenge fuck" scene. His final decision rested, of course, he hastened to assure us, on the taste with which Ken handled all of this, though, he also hastened to assure us, he did not see how Ken, or anyone, could get around the insurmountable problems of the wrestling scene.

It should be emphasized that as the producer I had signed a contract with United Artists that in order to get their money I was legally obligated to deliver unto them a film that had passed the censor. This was standard procedure in those days. If John didn't give us a certificate and Ken and I refused to change anything, then United Artists took control of the film and could cut it any way they wanted to.

We decided to play it straight, so to speak, to film exactly what was said and described on the printed page of a novel that had been in print since 1921 without provoking undue excitement or any lessening of public morals. The set was made to look like the one the novel describes, and every bit of action that we could duplicate we did. Alan Bates and Oliver Reed spent many hours working with a fight choreographer to find movements that corresponded to what Lawrence was describing. The dialogue, as I said, is word for word from the book. When we came to show the film to John, we pointed out our utter fidelity. We stressed over and over again that the book had been in print since 1921. He gave in, finally, but only after Ken appeased him by agreeing to snip out a few feet of waving cocks, seen dimly in long shot, of which we had put in too much of to be prepared for just such a compromise.

It was a difficult scene to shoot. Neither actor was happy about displaying it all. Oliver would disappear for a few moments before each take, we later discovered, so that he could make his penis look bigger, which on the closest of inspections it appears to be, though in reality Alan's was. Both actors, who were not the best of chums, would take hefty shots of spirits to overcome their apprehensions. Oliver, on the first day of shooting this scene, arrived with a letter from his doctor saying he had injured his shoulder and a body double would have to be used. Ken, who had worked with Oliver before, would have none of this and was not afraid to tell him so. (Oliver was a heavy drinker, to put it mildly, and a bully, and people were afraid of him.) He not only insisted that Oliver appear, but at the last minute he yanked the padding out from underneath the large rugs (the indentation of the bodies when they fell on it bothered him) so that the men were wrestling, in effect, on very hard stone flooring.

An interesting problem had been Oliver's weight. He drank an awful amount, and it varied considerably; but as we approached the days for shooting the wrestling scene and he was more bloated than ever, I went up to him and said, rather courageously, I thought: "Oliver, you are going to be seen naked by your millions of fans after we shoot this scene, and you are too fat." He stared at me silently for a long time. I thought he might actually be considering slugging me. The next day, I threw in another reminder when passing him: "Your millions of fans, Oliver . . ." By the day of shooting, which was only a few days distant, he showed up having completely slimmed down. Evidently he and his stand-in had spent the entire nights in the tiny sauna box in the basement of the Derby hotel where we were staying. As soon as the scene was shot, it would not be so long before he was his hefty self again. If you look at him closely throughout the film you will see how much his weight varies. He was not a happy camper, Oliver. He talked often to me of wanting to go away and live on a desert island and be a poet.]

EXT. SHORTLANDS. DAY

MRS. CRICH *is looking out her window again, and again not liking what she sees, which this time is a group of miners walking up the front drive and toward the house.*

GUDRUN, *carrying a large sketchbook, is walking up the drive behind the miners.*

MRS. CRICH *comes out of the house followed by three Dobermans, whom she lets loose.*

MRS. CRICH: Get 'em! Drive them away!

(*The dogs attack the miners, who try to fend them off.*)

[Again, I do not believe for a moment that Mrs. Crich would unleash a group of Dobermans on the miners, or on anyone, or would even have Dobermans. Ken and I had a fight over this one. He won, but I got fewer Dobermans and less mayhem. But this is a good example of how differing ideas of a character can cause friction. The actress playing Mrs. Crich was no help. She was ready to play Medea.]

EXT. GARDENS. SHORTLANDS. DAY

GERALD *and* WINIFRED *are pushing* MR. CRICH *in his wheelchair.* GERALD *reacts to the commotion and runs to investigate.*

EXT. SHORTLANDS. DAY

The dogs are viciously attacking the miners. The GROOM *and the* BUTLER *run out and try to stop the dogs.*

GROOM: Ranger! Here, boy!

> (GUDRUN *stands back as the dogs continue their savage attacks. The miners are now on the ground.* GERALD *reaches* GUDRUN.)

GERALD: Are you all right?

GROOM: Heel! Heel!

GERALD: Who the hell let these dogs in the drive?

> (MRS. CRICH *slashes down with a leash she is holding.*)

Take them back! Here, come on, heel, boy. Take them back to the kennel.

> (WINIFRED *pushes* MR. CRICH *to confront* MRS. CRICH.)

MR. CRICH: Have you taken leave of your senses, Christiana? How many times must I tell you? No one is ever turned away from my door.

MRS. CRICH: Oh, yes, I know. I know. Love thy neighbor. And you love your neighbor more than your own family. Why don't you turn me and the children out and keep open house for them.

MR. CRICH: If it wasn't for them, you wouldn't have this house. Now if they're in trouble, it's my duty to help them.

MRS. CRICH: You think it's your duty to invite all the rats in the world to come and gnaw at your bones.

GERALD: Let's go inside, Mother.

MRS. CRICH: Mr. Crich can't see you. You think you can come here whenever you like? Go away. There's nothing for you here.

(GERALD *leads a reluctant* MRS. CRICH *back to the house. She continues to look at the miners over her shoulders.*)

[This was one of two disagreements with Ken that I lost. (I will tell you about the second later.) I believe Mrs. Crich is meant to be a lost, rather scattered, vacant, unhappy, dissatisfied woman, in no way vicious to this degree. She no longer understands the world around her, or her family or her husband, or his ownership of the mines. All she knows is that none of it has brought her contentment of any sort. I believe the novel's text bears this out, and I believe the dialogue Lawrence provided for her does as well.]

EXT. SUMMER HOUSE. SHORTLANDS. DAY

GUDRUN *walks out onto the balcony of a small summer house. She bends to take a rabbit from* WINIFRED, *who is climbing onto the balcony.* WINIFRED *is an odd, sensitive child, quite detached. Her father adores her.*

GUDRUN: Give him to me.

WINIFRED: Thank you. Gerald says, if you like it, we could have it all to ourselves as a studio.

GUDRUN: Oh.

WINIFRED: Of course, we'll mend the windows and have it decorated. But Gerald says it all depends on you, so . . . do you like it?

GUDRUN: It's remarkable.

WINIFRED: Oh good! Gerald!

(GERALD *is walking nearby.*)

Come on, let's go and see Gerald. Come on, Bismarck.

(WINIFRED *takes the rabbit and climbs quickly down to her brother.* GUDRUN *stands alone on the balcony.* GERALD *stands below her, looking up.* WINIFRED *with her rabbit are beside him.* GERALD *takes the rabbit from her and strokes it.*)

GERALD: Winifred seems to have taken to you. Will you come again?

GUDRUN: I feel very drawn to her. Yes, I can come again.

WINIFRED: Oh, Gerald, isn't it wonderful? We're going to draw Bismarck. Isn't he beautiful? Isn't he strong? (*Her hand now stroking the rabbit, too.*) Let its mother stroke its fur then, darling. Because it's so mysterious.

EXT. WHEAT FIELD. DAY

*A beautiful day. The fields are tall with golden waving wheat stretching far
into the distance.* URSULA *sits, almost lost in it all.* BIRKIN *is seated beside
her. He throws a small package to her.*

[As I recall, this was the first scene we shot. Jennie Linden, who was
naturally quite nervous working with such well-known fellow players, was being thrown right into the thick of things quickly. Alan, a
great gentleman, worked with her and befriended her mightily
throughout the film.]

BIRKIN: Look what I bought.

> (URSULA *unwraps the package, revealing three rings.*)

URSULA: How lovely. How perfectly lovely. But why did you give
them to me?

BIRKIN: I wanted to. Am I called on to find reasons?

URSULA: Opals are unlucky, aren't they?

BIRKIN: I prefer unlucky things. Luck is vulgar. Who wants what luck
would bring? I don't. They can be made a little bigger.

URSULA: Yes.

> (*She places her hand on his arm and then lays her head against his
> shoulder.*)

I'm glad you bought them. Won't it be lovely going home in
the dark?

BIRKIN: Well, I promised to go to Shortlands tonight to have dinner
with Gerald.

URSULA: Well, it doesn't matter. You can go tomorrow.

BIRKIN: Hermione's there. She's going away in a couple of days. I suppose I ought to say good-bye to her. You don't mind, do you?

URSULA: No, I don't mind. Why should I? Why should I mind?

BIRKIN: Well, that's what I asked myself. Why should you mind? But you seem to.

URSULA: I assure you I don't mind in the least. If that's where you feel you belong, then ... that's where you must go.

BIRKIN: Oh you are a fool with your 'that's where you belong.' It's all finished between Hermione and me. Well, she seems to mean much more to you than she does to me.

URSULA: I'm not taken in by your word twisting. If you still feel you belong to Hermione, then you do, that's all. You don't belong to me.

BIRKIN: If you weren't such a fool you'd know that one could be decent even when one is wrong. It was wrong of me to go on all that time with her. It was a deathly process. But after all, one can have a little human decency. But now, you must tear my soul out with your jealousy at the very mention of her name.

URSULA: I? Jealous? She means nothing to me, not that! (*Snapping her fingers.*) It's what she stands for that I hate her. . . . Her . . . her . . . lies! And her falseness. It's death. But you want it, don't you? You can't help yourself. Well then you ... you go out and get it, that's what I say. But don't come to me! I've got nothing to do with it!

BIRKIN: Oh, you're a fool!

URSULA: Yes. Yes, I am a fool. And thank God for it.

(*She has started gathering her things, and he is repacking the picnic basket.*)

URSULA: And too big a fool to swallow your cleverness. You go to your women, your spiritual brides. Or aren't they common and fleshy enough? No . . . no, you're not satisfied, are you? You'd marry me for your everyday use. And keep your spiritual brides for tripping off into the beyond. Oh yes, yes. I know your dirty little games. You think I'm not as spiritual as Hermione. Well, Hermione's a fishwife—a fishwife! So you go to her, that's what I say, go to her! In her soul she's as common as dirt! And all the rest is just pretense, but you love it. Do you think I don't know of the foulness of your sex life and hers? Well I do, and it's that foulness that you want. You liar! Well, have it! Have it! Have it! You're such a liar.

(*She has slapped him and fallen against a tree, sobbing.*)

BIRKIN: There's a bicycle coming.

URSULA: I don't care.

(*A* MAN *approaches riding a bicycle and continues on.*)

MAN: Afternoon.

BIRKIN: Good afternoon. (*After he disappears.*) Maybe it's true. Lies, dirt, and all. But Hermione's spiritual intimacy is no rottener than your emotional jealous intimacy.

URSULA: I am not jealous. What I say, I say because it's true. You're false and a foul liar. That's what I say, and you hear it.

BIRKIN: Very good. The only hopeless thing's a fool.

(URSULA *throws her rings to the ground.*)

URSULA: Yes, quite right. So you take back your rings and buy yourself a female elsewhere. I'm sure there'll be plenty of women who'd be quite willing to share in your spiritual nest.

(URSULA *stalks off.* BIRKIN *picks up the rings. He starts walking to the road where a motorcycle with sidecar is parked.* URSULA *puts a flower into his hand.*)

URSULA: See what a flower I've found you?

BIRKIN: (*Kissing her.*) Pretty.

URSULA: Did I abuse you?

BIRKIN: Wait. I shall have my own back.

EXT. FIELDS. DAY

As they ride on his motorcycle, she in the sidecar.

EXT. MILL HOUSE. DAY

An old stone cottage on a running stream, deep in the countryside. They drive up and get off the cycle.

INT. MILL HOUSE. DAY

URSULA *and* BIRKIN *enter. The place is sparsely but essentially furnished.*

URSULA: So this is where you've been living all the time. Oh, what a perfectly lovely, noble place. So warm and cozy.

BIRKIN: I'm thinking we must get out of our responsibilities as quick as we can. We must drop our jobs like a shot. We must say . . . we must write . . . "Dear Sir, I would be very grateful if you would liberate me as soon as possible . . .

URSULA: ... from my post as schoolmistress of the Beldover Grammar School, without waiting for the usual month's notice." Oh, I could be so happy here.

BIRKIN: No, we'll wander a bit first. We'll get married straight away and we'll wander a bit. We'll never go apart.

URSULA: No, because we love each other.

> (*"They threw off their clothes, and he gathered her to him, and found her, found the pure lambent reality of her forever invisible flesh. Quenched, inhuman, his fingers upon her unrevealed nudity were the fingers of silence upon silence, the body of mysterious night upon the body of mysterious night, the night masculine and feminine, never to be seen with the eye, or known with the mind, only known as a palpable revelation of living otherness.*
>
> *"She had her desire of him, she touched, she received the maximum of unspeakable communication in touch, dark, subtle, positively silent, a magnificent gift and give again, a perfect acceptance and yielding, a mystery, the reality of that which can never be known, vital, sensual reality that can never be transmuted into mind content, but remains outside, living body of darkness and silence and subtlety, the mystic body of reality. She had her desire fulfilled. He had his desire fulfilled. For she was to him what he was to her, the immemorial magnificence of mystic, palpable, real otherness."*)

[The visualization of this was not successful, at least so I thought at the time and continue to believe. We were all racking our imaginations trying to come up with a new and interesting and unclichéd way of portraying the culmination of such a love. Who hit upon filming it sideways, Ursula and Birkin floating as it were through ecstasy and space, whether it was Ken (most likely) or Billy Williams, I can't remember. But the device did not set the cinema world on fire. It looked a bit corny then, and so it remains. Originally I had scripted voice-over narration by each of the lovers, extolling the Laurentian philosophy we have by now had much of (and are yet to have even more of), but it seemed that would not be what two lovers would be thinking of in quite this situation. And voice-over narration still would not solve what visuals were to accompany the words.]

INT. MR. CRICH'S BEDROOM. SHORTLANDS. EVENING

INT. BILLIARDS ROOM. SHORTLANDS. EVENING

Intercut WINIFRED *reading to the sick* MR. CRICH, *a nurse attending to him, with* GERALD *playing billiards and speaking to someone, who will be seen to be* GUDRUN.

[There are several short sequences in the film where scenes are intercut with each other. These are a good example of devices not scripted but created very much out of collaboration, in this case between Ken and his editor, Mike Bradsell, with whom he'd worked on much of his Monitor work.]

WINIFRED: "And the third Angel poured out his vial on the river and the fountains of water. And they became blood."

GERALD: After Laura's death . . .

WINIFRED: "For they had shed the blood of the Saints and Prophets and thou has given them blood to drink, for they are worthy."

GERALD: . . . Father's world collapsed. We haven't had much illness in the house, either. Not until Father. It's something you don't reckon with until it's there. And . . .

WINIFRED: "And I heard another out of the altar say . . . 'Even so the Lord God Almighty . . . '"

GERALD: . . . you realize it was there all the time. It was always there. The possibility of this incurable illness, this creeping death. There's nothing left. Do you understand what I mean? You seem to be reaching at the void, then you realize that you're a void yourself. You can't go on holding up the roof forever. You know that sooner or later you've got to let go. So you don't know what to do.

GUDRUN: You must. If I can help you . . . ?

GERALD: I don't want your help because there's nothing to be done. I just want to talk to somebody, sympathetically.

(*Both react to the door opening.* MRS. CRICH *stands there.*)

Ah, Mother! How nice of you to come down. How are you? You know Miss Brangwen, of course, don't you?

MRS. CRICH: Yes. Winifred tells me the doctor has something to say about your father. What is it?

GERALD: Oh, it's that his pulse is very weak and it misses altogether on occasions and he might not last the night out.

MRS. CRICH: You're not getting into a state, are you? You're not letting it make you hysterical?

GERALD: No, I don't think so, Mother. It's just that somebody's got to see it through.

MRS. CRICH: Oh, have they? Have they? And why should you take it on yourself? What have you got to do with seeing it through? It'll see itself through. You're not needed.

GERALD: No, I don't suppose there is much I can do. It's just how it affects us, you see.

MRS. CRICH: You like to be affected, don't you? It's quite a treat for you. You would have to be important. You've no need to stop at home. Why don't you go away? You're as weak as a cat, really. Always were. [You are inclined to take too much on yourself, Gerald.]

(*She walks slowly to the door, "as if she were unaccustomed to walking."* GERALD *walks with her.*)

[Don't come any further with me. I don't want you any further.]

GERALD: A strange lady, my mother.

GUDRUN: Yes.

GERALD: [She has her own thoughts.] With ideas of her own.

GUDRUN: Yes.

GERALD: You want to go? I'll see to it that the car's brought round.

GUDRUN: No, I want to walk.

GERALD: You might just as well drive.

GUDRUN: But I'd much rather walk.

GERALD: You would! Then I shall come with you.

EXT. UNDER RAILWAY ARCH. NIGHT

GERALD *and* GUDRUN *are kissing. Another couple is doing the same nearby.*

GERALD: You help me so much.

GUDRUN: I can't believe it.

GERALD: Why? Why can't you believe it? It's true. It's as true as . . . as we stand here.

GUDRUN: You are so beautiful. And I must go. No. Let me go alone.

(GUDRUN *walks into the distance.*)

INT. MR. CRICH'S BEDROOM. NIGHT

MR. CRICH, *lying in bed, his eyes closed. Suddenly he opens them and looks up.*

MR. CRICH: How much more water leaked into the pit?

(GERALD, *sitting in a chair by his bedside, jumps up.*)

GERALD: Some more. We'll have to run off the lake.

(MR. CRICH *starts coughing and choking and hemorrhaging blood from his mouth.*)

EXT. CEMETERY. DAY

A brass band is playing a dirge. WINIFRED *is sobbing bitterly. A trowel is thrown down on the coffin.* MRS. CRICH *is giggling.* GERALD *looks at her.*

[Yet again! Mrs. Crich would not giggle at her husband's funeral. This woman has become a strange hysteric, totally out of keeping with Lawrence's Mrs. Crich. You can see how much this came to bother me. A chance for a heartbreaking character study had been thrown away in exchange for a morbid caricature.]

INT. BILLIARDS ROOM. SHORTLANDS. NIGHT

GERALD *by the fireplace, glass in hand. He is pacing about, then smashes the glass into the fireplace. He walks out.*

EXT. CEMETERY. NIGHT

GERALD *walking through the mud until he reaches his father's grave, which is covered with wreaths. He lies on top of it. His hand digs for some earth, which he lifts to his face and then throws down. He stands and walks away.*

EXT. BRANGWEN HOME. NIGHT

GERALD *walks quickly, then runs up the steps to the front door. He turns the doorknob.*

INT. HALL. BRANGWEN HOME. NIGHT

GERALD *entering.* MR. BRANGWEN *can be seen asleep in a chair in the living room.* GERALD *walks up the stairs.*

INT. UPPER LANDING. NIGHT

GERALD *reaches it and opens a door, then walks into the room, closing the door behind him.*

INT. GUDRUN'S BEDROOM. NIGHT

GUDRUN *is asleep but the sound of the door wakes her up.*

GUDRUN: Ursula?

GERALD: No, it's me. Gerald.

(*She switches on a light, gets out of bed, walks to him, locks the door.*)

GUDRUN: You're very muddy.

GERALD: I was walking in the dark.

(*She sits on the bed.*)

GUDRUN: What do you want from me?

GERALD: I came because I must. . . . Why do you ask?

GUDRUN: I must ask.

GERALD: There is no answer.

> (*She removes her nightdress and switches out the light.* GERALD *sits and removes his boots and clothes. He puts his face in her lap, then his head between her breasts. She caresses him.*
>
> *Sounds and then shots of* MRS. CRICH *laughing at the burial site are intercut with* GERALD *and* GUDRUN *making love.* GERALD *is not a gentle lovemaker and* GUDRUN *appears to respond to this.*)

INT. GUDRUN'S BEDROOM. MORNING

GUDRUN *is awake.*

GUDRUN: You must go, my love. It's getting late.

> (GERALD *stirs and then embraces* GUDRUN.)

GERALD: No . . . no, not for a minute.

GUDRUN: Yes, you must go. I'm afraid if you stay any longer.

> (GERALD *kisses her, then climbs out of bed.* GUDRUN *huddles with the sheet around her.*)

EXT. BRANGWEN HOME. EARLY MORNING

GERALD *opens the front door,* GUDRUN *behind him. They kiss. Then* GERALD *leaves. The* MILKMAN *is making his deliveries. From behind the half-closed door* GUDRUN *looks after* GERALD, *before closing it.*

INT. GERALD'S STUDY. SHORTLANDS. DAY

GERALD: Shall Gudrun and I rush into marriage along with you?

BIRKIN: If I were you, I wouldn't marry. But ask Gudrun, not me. I mean, you're not marrying me, are you?

GERALD: I thought you were dead nuts on marriage.

BIRKIN: There are all kinds of marriages, and there are all kinds of noses. Snub and otherwise.

GERALD: And you think that if I marry it'll be snub? What's the alternative?

BIRKIN: Well, if you don't know, don't do it. Marriage in the old sense seems to me to be repulsive—the whole world in couples—each couple in its own little house, watching its own little interests, stewing in its own little privacies. It's the most repulsive thing on earth.

GERALD: Yes, I quite agree. There's something inferior about it. But there again, what's the alternative?

BIRKIN: We've got to find one. I do believe in a permanent union between a man and a woman. Shopping about is merely an exhaustive process. But a permanent relationship between a man and a woman isn't the last word. It certainly isn't.

GERALD: Quite.

BIRKIN: We've got to take down this love-and-marriage ideal from its pedestal. We want something broader. I believe in the additional perfect relationship between man and man. Additional to marriage.

GERALD: Well, I don't see how they can be the same.

BIRKIN: They're not the same, but equally important, equally creative, equally sacred, if you like.

GERALD: I know you believe something like that, only I don't feel it, do you see?

EXT. MILL HOUSE. DAY

URSULA *is hanging wash out to dry on a line. The stream is rushing by beneath her and* BIRKIN, *who sits on the bank.*

URSULA: Gudrun might rush into marriage like we have. Wouldn't that be nice?

BIRKIN: Rubbish! Gudrun is a born mistress, just as Gerald is a born lover. If all women are either wives or mistresses, then Gudrun is a mistress.

URSULA: Then all men are either lovers or husbands. Why not both?

BIRKIN: No, no, the one excludes the other.

URSULA: (*Puts her arms around him.*) And I want a lover.

BIRKIN: Oh, no you don't.

URSULA: Oh, yes I do.

EXT. MARKET. DAY

URSULA *and* BIRKIN *are rummaging through the secondhand furniture for sale at a crowded outdoor market.* BIRKIN *is considering a chair.*

BIRKIN: How much is it?

STALLHOLDER: Ten shillings.

URSULA: Oh, no, I don't like that. We can have furniture from the house.

BIRKIN: It's so beautiful.

URSULA: What!

BIRKIN: So pure.

URSULA: Oh! Well, then I'm only going to give you five shillings.

STALLHOLDER: Right.

>   (*She pays him.* BIRKIN *carries the chair through the crowd,* URSULA *following, stopping to inspect items . . .*)

BIRKIN: It almost breaks my heart, my beloved country. It had something to express, even when it made this chair. Now all we can do is to fish amongst rubbish heaps for remnants of the old expressions. There's no production in us anymore. Just sordid and foul mechanicalness.

URSULA: Well, I hate your past. I'm sick of it.

BIRKIN: Not as sick as I am of the accursed present.

URSULA: Well, I don't want the past to take its place. I don't want old things.

BIRKIN: The truth is, we don't want things at all. The thought of a house and furniture of my own is hateful to me. (*To a couple behind him.*) Madam. Madam, it's yours. There. (*Gives man the chair.*) There, I hope you will both be very, very happy together.

URSULA: We must live somewhere.

BIRKIN: No, not somewhere. Anywhere. Not have a definite place. Just you and me and a few others. Where we needn't wear any clothes. Where we can be ourselves without any bother.

(*They continue walking through the market.* URSULA *puts her arm through his arm.*)

URSULA: Rupert, whatever did you mean: you, me, and a few other people? You've got me.

BIRKIN: Well, I always imagined our being happy with a few other people.

URSULA: Why should we be?

BIRKIN: I don't know. One has a hankering after a sort of fellowship.

URSULA: Why? Why should you hanker after other people? Why should you need them?

BIRKIN: Mmm. Don't you need them? Or does it just end with us two, then?

URSULA: Yes. What more do you want? If people care to come along, we'll let them. But it must *happen.* You can't do anything about it with your will. You always seem to think you can force the flowers to come out. People must love us because they love us. You can't make them.

BIRKIN: I know. (*He has walked ahead, letting go of her hand.*) But must one just go on as if one's alone in the world?

URSULA: (*Coming up beside him and kissing his cheek.*) You've got me. Why should you need others? You must learn to be alone.

(*They have arrived at a tea stall.*)

BIRKIN: Two teas, please.

INT. GUDRUN'S STUDIO. DAY

GUDRUN *is working on a model of* GERALD's *head.* URSULA *is seated by an electric fire, toasting bread.*

GUDRUN: Did you know that Gerald Crich has suggested we all go away together at Christmas?

URSULA: Yes, he's spoken to Rupert about it.

GUDRUN: Well, don't you think it's amazingly cool?

URSULA: I rather like him for it.

GUDRUN: And what did Rupert say, do you know?

URSULA: Mmm. He said it would be most awfully jolly. (*Scraping the toast, which she will proceed to butter and eat.*) Well, don't you think it would be?

GUDRUN: I think it might be awfully jolly as you say, but ... don't you think it was an unpardonable liberty to speak to Rupert like that? Well, you see what I mean, Ursula, they could have been two men arranging an outing with some little type they picked up.

URSULA: Oh, no, no. Nothing like that. Oh, no. No, I think the friendship between Rupert and Gerald is really rather beautiful.

They're so simple. They just say anything to each other, like brothers. There's something I love about Gerald. He's really much more lovable than I thought him. Oh, he's free, Gudrun. He really is.

GUDRUN: Do you know where he proposes to go?

URSULA: Mmm. Near Zermatt. I don't know where exactly, but . . . Oh, it would be rather lovely, don't you think? High up in the perfect snow.

GUDRUN: Very lovely.

URSULA: Of course I think that Gerald spoke to Rupert about it so that it shouldn't seem like an outing with a . . . "type."

GUDRUN: I know of course that he does quite commonly take up with that sort.

(*The sound of a motorbike's engine has been heard and now its horn beeping.*)

URSULA: Does he? How do you know? (*She looks out the window.*)

GUDRUN: I know of a model in Chelsea.

EXT. GUDRUN'S STUDIO. DAY

BIRKIN, *on his motorbike, points to the seat in his sidecar.*

INT. GUDRUN'S STUDIO. DAY

URSULA *kisses her sister good-bye.*

URSULA: Well, let's hope he had a good time with her. I must go, Prune. Rupert's waiting.

(*She leaves.* GUDRUN *sticks her modeling knife into* GERALD'S *head.*)

EXT. APPROACH TO LODGE. SWITZERLAND. DAY

The lodge is high up in the Alps, above Zermatt. The day is bright, cold, icy white. A horse-drawn sleigh carrying our two couples comes up the hill and toward the hotel. The Matterhorn comes into view.

EXT. SWISS LODGE. DAY

A small rustic hotel. A few guests can be seen. GERALD *climbs out of the sleigh and helps* GUDRUN, *who runs out to face the majestic mountain. She throws her arms up, outstretched to the peak.*

GUDRUN: The minute I set foot on foreign soil I am transported! I am a new creature, stepping into life!

[I am uncertain where the above lines come from. I cannot find them in the novel. They sound more Glenda than Gudrun, although she was less a culprit in this area than Ken, who never stopped trying every gambit he could think of to sneak new lines into the script. Gudrun is actually quite apprehensive upon arrival. If anything, this journey begins her withdrawal from this life.

Actors as well as directors are known to do things like rewrite their lines, often quite flagrantly after the writer is no longer around. Well, this screenwriter, who was also the producer, was on the set every single moment. If I was not and someone tried to quickly insert and film new lines, our continuity person, Angela Allen, who was an old friend of mine, would quickly dispatch a gofer to "go get Larry, quick!"

By the time we got to the Swiss sequences we had been shooting for some three months, all over England. While we all knew one another much better, we were also beginning to get, if not tired, then a bit peevish. Actors, director, screenwriter, feel more proprietary about their parts and their movie the longer they are participating in it. This ownership has to be made to work for the whole, not rend it apart. Putting your foot down and saying "No, you can't do that!" is less effective than it would have been in the early weeks.

In the end, much is based on compromise, although since we were following Lawrence's dialogue so closely, not so much in our case as some may have wanted. So all in all, and in the end, my adaptation fared quite faithfully, even if the producer, when the filming was completed, had something of a nervous breakdown from expending all the energy required to protect it!]

(*Gerald joins her and they embrace.*)

GERALD: It's never quite the same in England. One's . . . one's afraid to let go. Afraid what'll happen if . . . everyone else lets go.

(BIRKIN *is also running free.*)

BIRKIN: We're all out of it. So let's all let go together.

(*He and* URSULA *begin an exchange of snowballs, joined by* GERALD *and* GUDRUN.)

INT. LODGE. NIGHT

The rustic lobby is filled with dancers doing a polka. GERALD *and* GUDRUN *dance, as do* URSULA *and* BIRKIN. *On the heavy wooden staircase leading upstairs, two men,* LOERKE *and* LEITNER, *the former older than the other, are watching.* LEITNER *is handsome in a soft way.* LOERKE *is "a thin, dark-skinned man with full eyes, an odd creature, like a child, and like a troll, quick, detached," with fine black hair that reminds* GUDRUN *of a bat.* LOERKE *watches* GUDRUN.

(*Another dance ends.*)

GUDRUN: Oh, how romantic it all is.

LEITNER: (*Approaching her.*) *Wollen Sie tanzen, gnädige Frau?*

(*They dance off.* GERALD *turns and bows to a rosy-cheeked young woman,* KRISTINA.)

GERALD: Shall we dance?

(*And they dance off too.* LOERKE *watches for a while and then approaches* LEITNER *on the dance floor, indicating that they should leave; he bows to* GUDRUN *and leaves with* LOERKE. *She walks off the dance floor.* GERALD *and* KRISTINA *are dancing with more and more spirit.*)

GUDRUN: (*Passing* GERALD.) What a fine game you're playing. She's in love with you. Oh dear me, she's in love with you.

INT. GERALD AND GUDRUN'S BEDROOM. THE LODGE. NIGHT

GUDRUN *is brushing her hair.* GERALD *comes in and puts his hand on her shoulder; she kisses it. He bends to kiss her neck. They then kiss each other.*

INT. BIRKIN AND URSULA'S BEDROOM. THE LODGE. NIGHT

They are in bed together.

URSULA: Do you love me?

BIRKIN: Far too much. I couldn't bear this cold eternal place without you.

URSULA: Why, do you hate it then?

BIRKIN: Mmm. If you weren't here, it would kill the very quick of my life.

URSULA: It's good that we're warm and together.

EXT. TOBOGGAN SLOPES. DAY

The two couples prepare to toboggan down the slope.

URSULA: I want a go.

BIRKIN: All right then, have a go.

(GERALD *is now seated on a toboggan.* GUDRUN *climbs on behind him.*)

GERALD: Now push!

(URSULA *and* BIRKIN *push.* BIRKIN *falls forward into the snow.*
        BIRKIN *now lying on a toboggan.* URSULA *stands beside him, putting on her goggles.*)

URSULA: Wait. I'll have to put on my goggles.

BIRKIN: Okay?

URSULA: (*Lying on top of* BIRKIN.) Ready. I'm not on! I'm on now.

(*They go swiftly, passing* GERALD *and* GUDRUN *before tumbling off. Now* GERALD *and* GUDRUN *pass them. Much laughter and yelling by all.*)

GERALD: We're going to come off! We're going to come off!

(*They tumble, falling back.* GERALD *falls beside her.*)

[If you look closely, you might notice that Glenda's costumes have become quite baggy. She had told us a month or so earlier that she was several months pregnant, and she was now beginning to show it. Ken, always the consummate picture maker, was rather annoyed that his leading lady could not be so physically agile from now on, and of course Shirley's costumes for her had to be swiftly altered. Jennie had been nursing when we cast her. This explains why both of our ladies had such full breasts and nipples (a question often asked me, believe it or not).]

GERALD: It wasn't too much for you?

GUDRUN: No. Oh! It was the most complete moment of my life.

[This is another hyperbolic line out of Gudrun's mouth that I can't seem to locate in the novel or screenplay drafts. Like Gudrun's salutation to the Alps upon arrival, it seems more Glenda, or Ken, than Lawrence. This is more Gudrun: "Gerald . . . convince me of the perfect moments. Oh, convince me, I need it."]

(GERALD *laughs. He puts his arms around her and lifts her up. They embrace each other.* BIRKIN *and* URSULA, *pulling their toboggan, walk past them.*)

BIRKIN: See you down there.

(LOERKE *and* LEITNER *ski past as* GERALD *and* GUDRUN *go by, walking their toboggan.* URSULA *and* BIRKIN *continue on, tobogganing.*)

INT. LODGE. DAY

GUDRUN *enters and heads up the staircase.* URSULA, *seated at a table, has been talking with* LOERKE, *who is drinking and smoking a cigar.*

[Ken had Loerke sitting on a windowsill, with his feet on the table where Ursula is eating a creamy dessert, while he changes his socks and puts on his boots. Then, while smoking, he tips his ash into her ice cream. As far as I was concerned this was more of the Mrs. Crich and the Dobermans. I hated it. I also hated the actor who played Loerke, but we had truly been unable to cast anyone else in the part. Both Ken and I had agreed on Klaus Kinski, but he asked an exorbitant price. In actuality, the actor and the performance, seen today, are not that off the mark from the novel. Originally I had hoped to feel some understanding of what drew Gudrun to Loerke, believing it was physical, something this actor could never make me feel. But if one reads the following passage, it appears that it could be the childish silliness and vulnerability that appeals to Gudrun, not the highfalutin stuff about strange games and sinister goings-on in Munich, an interpretation that had not occurred to me then.]

> (*"There was the look of a little wastrel about him that intrigued her, and an old man's look that interested her, and then, beside this, an uncanny singleness, a quality of being by himself, not in contact with anybody else, that marked out an artist to her. He was a chatterer, a magpie, a maker of mischievous word-jokes, that were sometimes very clever, but which often were not. And she could see in his brown, gnome's eyes the black look of inorganic misery which lay behind all his small buffoonery."*)

URSULA: (*To* GUDRUN.) Prune, isn't it interesting. Herr Loerke is doing a great frieze for a factory in Cologne. Oh, is it for the outside? Mmm, the outside, the street.

GUDRUN: (*From the stairway.*) So you are an artist. I knew it.

LOERKE: You know, I think that the machinery, the … er … (*Stamping his feet on the table in frustration at not knowing the English.*) … the acts of labor, are extremely beautiful. The … the factory of today must be the Parthenon.

GUDRUN: Oh, do you believe Art should serve Industry?

LOERKE: Ah, art should interpret industry, *ich glaube*. As art once interpreted religion.

URSULA: Gudrun is an artist as well, you know.

LOERKE: Oh? What do you do?

GUDRUN: I'm a sculptress.

LOERKE: And what do you sculpt?

GUDRUN: Animals, birds.

LOERKE: Knickknacks for the rich, eh?

URSULA: Oh.

LOERKE: *Travaillez. Lavorato—que lavoro, que lavoro.* You are not an artist. You have never worked as the world works.

GUDRUN: Yes, I have. And I do.

LOERKE: Have you known what it was to lie in bed for three days because you had nothing to eat? In a room with three other families and a toilet in the middle, a big pan with a plank on it? (*He flicks his cigar ash, and it falls into* URSULA's *ice cream.*) And your father making love to a street whore in the corner. Do you understand? How old are you?

[There is nothing in the novel about his father making love to a street whore in the corner, only that Loerke and his two brothers and his sister lived in a wretchedly overcrowded room with three other families and "there might be a woman with my father." I suspect this change sneaked in because of the actor, who constantly chose to make the part repellent, with no pity.]

GUDRUN: Twenty-six.

LOERKE: *Und Ihr Herr Gemahl? Wie alt is er?*

URSULA: Your husband . . .

GUDRUN: Thirty-one.

LOERKE: Come along. I will show you something interesting. (*He stomps his boots again as he jumps down from* URSULA's *table.*)

INT. LOERKE'S BEDROOM. DAY

URSULA *and* GUDRUN *enter, followed by* LOERKE. LEITNER *is sitting up in bed.*

LOERKE: Oh. *Allez, allez.* (*Brings out some drawings.*) I'll show you something. This, this, not this. My factory. *Kolossal!*

(*He lays them out on the bed.* GUDRUN *looks at them.* LEITNER *stares at her, whistling the polka tune they had danced to.* LOERKE *puts another drawing on the bed.*)

LOERKE: Something special. Look.

(*He shows her a drawing of a girl on a horse.* GUDRUN *takes it.*)

GUDRUN: It's beautiful. (*She hands it to* URSULA.)

URSULA: Why did you make the horse so stiff?

LOERKE: Stiff?

URSULA: Yes. Stiff. I mean, look at that stock, stupid, brutal thing. A horse is a very sensitive creature, quite delicate really. But sensitive.

LOERKE: Well, it is not a picture of a friendly horse to which you give a lump of sugar, *gnädige Frau*. It is part of a work of art. It has no relation with anything that's outside the world of art.

URSULA: Yes, but it's still a horse, isn't it?

GUDRUN: Where is she now, the model?

LOERKE: (*Laughs.*) She was a nuisance. Not for a minute would she keep still. Not until I slapped her hard and made her cry. Then she'd sit . . . for five minutes.

GUDRUN: Did you really slap her?

LOERKE: Yes, I did. Harder than I ever beat anything in my life. I had to, for the sake of my art.

URSULA: Well, love has no place in your world of art! (*Leaves the room.*)

LOERKE: *L'amour, l'amour, die Liebe.* I detest it in any language. What does this matter . . . if I wear this hat or another? So love is only for convenience. I would give everything, all your love, for a little companionship in intelligence.

(GUDRUN *listening . . .*)

EXT. SLOPES NEAR MATTERHORN. DAY

BIRKIN *sits on a rock.* URSULA *is pacing around.*

URSULA: Rupert, I want to go away.

BIRKIN: Do you?

URSULA: Mmm, don't you?

BIRKIN: Well, I hadn't thought about it.

URSULA: Mmm?

BIRKIN: But I'm sure I do.

URSULA: Oh, I hate the snow, the unnatural light it throws on everybody. Oh, the ghastly glamour of it all and the unnatural feelings it makes everybody have.

BIRKIN: Well, we can go away. We can go tomorrow. We can go to Verona and find Romeo and Juliet and sit in the amphitheater.

URSULA: Oh, yes. Yes, I'd love to be Romeo and Juliet. (*Flinging her arms out.*)

BIRKIN: (*Laughing.*) A fearful cold wind blows through Verona from out of the Alps.

URSULA: (*Making a snowball.*) Are you glad you're going? (*Responding to his laughing again.*) No, I don't want to be laughed at. Do you love me? (*She crumbles the snow over his face.*)

BIRKIN: (*Crying out.*) Yes, yes. Yes!

URSULA: (*Still pouring snow on his face.*) Do you love me?

BIRKIN: Ugh. Yes.

(*They kiss.*)

BIRKIN: Why is your mouth so hard?

URSULA: Why is yours frozen solid?

(*They kiss again.*)

BIRKIN: Why do you grip your lips?

URSULA: Never you mind. That's my way.

(*They kiss yet again.*)

EXT. MORE SLOPES. DAY

(GUDRUN *is looking into the sun.*)

GERALD: Do you know what it is to suffer when you're with a woman? (*He is walking with* BIRKIN.) It tears you like a silk. And each bit and stroke burns hot. Of course, I wouldn't not have had it. . . . It was a complete experience. And she's a wonderful woman. But how I hate her somewhere. It's curious.

BIRKIN: You have had your experience now. Why work on an old wound?

GERALD: Because there's nothing else.

BIRKIN: I've loved you as well as Gudrun. Don't forget.

(*They stop walking and look at each other in good-bye.* GERALD *clasps* BIRKIN'*s shoulder.*)

GERALD: Have you? Or do you think you have? (*He turns and walks away.*)

EXT. SWISS LODGE. DAY

GUDRUN *and* URSULA *kissing each other.* GERALD *kisses* URSULA.

GERALD: Ursula.

URSULA: Bye, Gerald.

GERALD: Be good.

(BIRKIN *turns and helps* URSULA *into the waiting sleigh.*)

BIRKIN: Good-bye, Gerald.

GERALD: Rupert.

BIRKIN: Bye, Gudrun.

GUDRUN: Rupert.

(*The sleigh starts off.*)

[How is Birkin going to afford living so freely? How has he done so up till now? How will he support Ursula? It is interesting to note how little Lawrence tells us in the novel about Birkin's life, his past, his parents, his financial status. We know a lot about the other characters and their families. At some point Birkin is said to have some £400 a year, but from what? Or whom? Nowhere does the novel indicate that Birkin is a writer, or trying to be one, or going to be one. We assume Birkin is Lawrence. He certainly is in what he says and thinks. But as with all authorial self-portraits, a few major details are left out.]

URSULA: (*Turning to wave.*) See you soon. (*Turns and hugs* BIRKIN.)

(GERALD *looks at* GUDRUN.)

INT. GERALD AND GUDRUN'S BEDROOM. THE LODGE. NIGHT

GUDRUN *is seated on the bed.* GERALD *enters, wiping himself with a towel. He kisses* GUDRUN *on her neck.*

GERALD: Why are you sitting in the dark?

GUDRUN: Look at that lovely star up there. Do you know its name?

GERALD: No. (*Sitting beside her and looking out.*) It's very fine. (*Kissing her hair.*)

GUDRUN: Isn't it beautiful? Do you see how it darts different-colored fires? It's superb.

GERALD: (*Kissing her hand.*) Mmm ... Do you regret their leaving?

GUDRUN: No, not at all. How much do you love me?

GERALD: (*Stops kissing her.*) How much do you think I love you?

GUDRUN: I don't know.

GERALD: But what's your opinion?

GUDRUN: Very little indeed.

GERALD: Why don't I love you?

GUDRUN: I don't know why you don't. I've been good to you. When you first came to me in that fearful state, I had to take pity on you, but ... it was never love.

GERALD: Why do you keep repeating it? That there is no love?

GUDRUN: Well, you don't think you love, do you?

GERALD: I don't know what you mean by the word love.

GUDRUN: Oh yes you do. You know very well that you have never loved me. Well, have you, do you think?

GERALD: No.

GUDRUN: And you never will love me, will you?

GERALD: Why do you torture me?

GUDRUN: (*Putting her arms around him.*) I don't want to torture you. Just say you love me. Say you'll love me forever, won't you? Won't you say it? Won't you say you'll love me always? Say it, even if it isn't true. Say it, Gerald, do.

GERALD: I will love you always.

GUDRUN: (*Giving him a quick kiss.*) Fancy you actually having said it.

(*She gets up and walks away. He stands up as if he has been beaten. Then she falls on her bed.*)

Try to love me a little more and to want me a little less.

GERALD: You mean you don't want me?

GUDRUN: You are so insistent. You have so little grace. So little finesse. You are so crude. You break me and waste me, and it is horrible to me.

GERALD: Horrible to you?

GUDRUN: Oh yes. Don't you think I might have Ursula's room now to myself?

GERALD: (*Slowly getting up.*) You do as you like. You go where you wish.

GUDRUN: Oh I will, but so can you. You can leave me whenever you like, without notice even.

("*The tides of darkness were swinging across his mind, he could hardly stand upright. A terrible weakness overcame him. . . . Dropping off his clothes, he got into bed, and lay like a man suddenly overcome by drunkenness, the darkness lifting and plunging as if he were lying upon a black, giddy sea. He lay still in this strange, horrific reeling. . . . At length she came over to him. He remained rigid, his back to her. He was all but unconscious. She put her arms around his terrifying, insentient body, and laid her cheek against his hard shoulder. . . . There was no change in him. She caught him against her. She pressed her breasts against his shoulders, she kissed his shoulder. . . . She was bewildered, and insistent, only her will was set for him to speak to her. . . . Her warm breath playing, flying rhythmically over his ear, seemed to relax the tension. She could feel his body gradually relaxing a little, losing its terrifying, unnatural rigidity. Her hands clutched his limbs, his muscles, going over him spasmodically. The hot blood began to flow again through his veins, his limbs relaxed. . . . So at last he was given again, warm and flexible. He turned and gathered her in his arms. And feeling her soft against him, so perfectly soft and recipient, his arms tightened on her. She was as if crushed, powerless in him. His brain seemed hard and invincible now like a jewel, there was no resisting him. His passion was awful to her, tense and ghastly, and impersonal like a destruction, ultimate. She felt it would kill her. She was being killed.*")

GUDRUN: (*Screaming.*) Oh my God, Gerald, shall I die?

[This is the other sequence, which I mentioned earlier, over which we had censor trouble. It is a brutal, lunging fuck that Gerald is administering to Gudrun; there is no question about that. And she is, in her own way, reveling in it, enjoying it. As before, we approached Lord Trevelyan, copy of novel in hand, the above passage to cite. As the wrestling scene was for me, this scene was important to Ken, and in his own quiet way he was not going to give in. In the end, the whole film became a package for negotiation: we'll take out two seconds of this if you will allow two seconds more of that. We walked away with a great deal more than we thought we'd be allowed. I have never been certain why Lord Trevelyan, who was not known to be easy to deal with, was, for us, surprisingly easy. I would like to think that he was against censorship to begin with and that he hoped the days of his office would be numbered, and that, with *Women in Love,* a classic novel filmed with relative fidelity, he had the opportunity to move things along in a most defensible fashion. Indeed, the public was not shocked by the film. There was much made of "Full Frontal Nudity" (male), but it was more as fodder for the late night satirical programs. Mind you, the situation was not the same in other countries. Most Spanish-speaking places banned the film entirely or butchered it without our permission; indeed, it is just being released uncut in some of them for the first time. We were fine in America, except for the television networks, to whom we had to deliver a cut version even more brutally butchered than the British censor asked for, which is still the one broadcast to this day.]

EXT. SKI SLOPES. DAY

GERALD *skis alone.*

EXT. LODGE. DAY

LOERKE *is drawing* GUDRUN *as she is sitting with someone else.* LEITNER *is with another young man.* GERALD *returns, carrying his skis, which he throws down and kisses* GUDRUN.

LOERKE: Your form is very good, Herr Crich. Man should have something of massiveness in their stupid form.

GERALD: You don't do sports, Herr Loerke?

LOERKE: Not sport. No, only games.

GERALD: And what sort of games might they be?

LOERKE: Only ones which I enjoy.

GERALD: Yes, but what sort of games?

LOERKE: Secret games . . . Initiation games, full of esoteric understanding and fearful, sensual secrets.

GERALD: Rubbish. Contemptible rubbish.

LOERKE: Why are the English so inept in arguments? You know, there often is another way. (*To* GUDRUN.) *Sehen Sie, gnädige Frau . . .*

GUDRUN: *Bitte, sagen Sie nicht immer gnädige Frau.*

LOERKE: What should I say then?

GUDRUN: *Sagen Sie nur nicht dass.*

LOERKE: *Soll ich Fräulein sagen?*

GUDRUN: Well, I'm not married. (*To Gerald.*) Truth is best.

(GERALD *leaves them.*)

INT. LOERKE'S BEDROOM. DAY

LOERKE *is painting* GUDRUN'*s eyes. She is wearing a silver headdress.*

GUDRUN: Cleopatra must have been an artist. She reaped the essential from a man. She harvested the ultimate sensation. And then she threw away the husk.

LOERKE: I'm not going to play your Anthony.

GUDRUN: Oh. Of course, the very point of a lover is to reach a complete understanding of sensual knowledge.

LOERKE: And today I would be Peter Ilyitch Tchaikovsky.

GUDRUN: Hurray!

LOERKE: The great Russian composer. And you are my bride of six hours.

(*He runs to put a record on a gramophone. She grabs a shawl and starts to dance around.*)

We are on our honeymoon on the Trans-Siberian-Express.

(*The music is playing loudly. He is prancing around in his own dance, contorting his face, hiding behind his hands.* GUDRUN *is kneeling in front of a trunk, looking for more costume, something more suitable for a Russian journey.*)

We're alone in our sleeping compartment. I'm a homosexual.

(GUDRUN, *a veil over her face, reacts to this.*)

A homosexual composer ... who has married to protect his family name from gossip and scandal.

(GUDRUN *is now wrapped in white furs.*)

And you ... you're a scheming, thieving ... nymphomaniac, who's married for fame and fortune.

(*Their dance/charade continues until Loerke falls on the bed, and Gudrun sits beside him.*)

Between two particular people, the range of pure sensational experience is limited. (*He takes a candle that has been burning and places it on his chest.*) One can only extend, draw out, and electrify. One must not repeat. One must find only new ways.

GUDRUN: The train is going into a tunnel. (*She blows out the candle.*)

[This was one of Ken's fantasy scenes: imagining what Loerke was always spouting on about with his mysterious games of sensual experience, and so on. It seemed a good idea at the time, although today it looks more like a trailer for his film *Tchaikovsky*, which he would shortly be filming. It is also a bit reminiscent of the dance scene Hermione performs at Breadalby. It is hardly exemplary of the "secret games, initiation games, full of esoteric understanding and fearful sensual secrets" that Loerke was going on about only a few moments earlier. Martin Rosen really hated it.

INT. GERALD AND GUDRUN'S BEDROOM. THE LODGE. NIGHT

GUDRUN *enters with a suitcase.* GERALD *is sitting on the bed.*

GERALD: Why are you fascinated by that little rat?

(GUDRUN *starts to pack her bag.*)

GUDRUN: I don't choose to be discussed by you. My God, what a mercy I'm not married to you.

GERALD: Well, it doesn't matter whether you choose to discuss it or not. It doesn't alter the fact that you're willing to fall down and kiss that insect's feet. Well, you do it. I'm not going to prevent you. You kiss his feet. But what I want to know is what it is about him that fascinates you? What is it?

GUDRUN: Do you? Do you want to know what it is? It is that he has some understanding. He is not stupid. That's why.

GERALD: And would you like to crawl for the understanding of a rat?

GUDRUN: Well, don't you think the understanding of a rat is more interesting than the understanding of a fool?

GERALD: A fool?

GUDRUN: A fool. A conceited fool. A dummkopf.

GERALD: Wouldn't I rather be a fool than explore those sewers with a rat?

GUDRUN: And what have you to offer as an alternative? An eternity of domesticity at Shortlands? My God, when I think of you and your world and your wretched coal mine, it makes my heart sick! You're so limited. You're a dead end. You cannot love.

GERALD: And you?

GUDRUN: I couldn't love you.

(*She goes through the door and closes it. He runs after her.*)

INT. HALL CONNECTING BEDROOMS. LODGE. NIGHT

As GUDRUN *goes into the connecting bedroom before* GERALD *can reach her. She closes the door.*

GERALD: It may be over between us. But it's not finished.

INT. BIRKIN AND URSULA'S BEDROOM. THE LODGE. NIGHT

GUDRUN *standing there.*

INT. HALL CONNECTING BEDROOMS. LODGE. NIGHT

GERALD *leaning against the door.*

EXT. TOBOGGAN SLOPES. DAY

GUDRUN *and* LOERKE *on a toboggan.* LOERKE *is singing out loud. The toboggan overturns, tumbling them into the snow.* GUDRUN *starts to get up.* LOERKE *takes a flask from his pocket.*

LOERKE: Wait, wait, wait. I've got something for you.

GUDRUN: Oh, Loerke, what an inspiration. What a *comble de joie* indeed. What is it? Schnapps? (*She takes the flask and drinks.*)

LOERKE: *Heidelbier.*

GUDRUN: No.

LOERKE: *Ja.*

GUDRUN: It's made from bilberries.

LOERKE: *Ja.*

GUDRUN: It is distilled from snow. Can you smell the bilberries? It's exactly like bilberries under the snow.

(LOERKE *and* GUDRUN *smell the snow.*)

LOERKE: Listen . . . you're going away tomorrow?

GUDRUN: Yes.

LOERKE: *Wohin?*

GUDRUN: Oh, I don't know.

(*She gets up, as does he.*)

LOERKE: One never does. Where will you take a ticket to?

GUDRUN: Oh, I have to have a ticket?

LOERKE: *Ja.*

GUDRUN: Ah, but one does not have to go where the ticket says.

LOERKE: Then take a ticket to London. One should never go there.

GUDRUN: Right.

LOERKE: You must not go back to teaching! You must not go back to teaching! Leave that to the swine who can do nothing else. You are an extraordinary woman. *Eine, eine, eine seltsame Frau.* Why should you follow the ordinary course? You won't tell me where you will go?

GUDRUN: Really and truly, I don't know. It depends which way the wind blows.

LOERKE: It blows through Germany.

GUDRUN: Perhaps.

LOERKE: Come with me to Dresden. I live alone there. I have a big studio. I can give you work. I believe in you.

GUDRUN: Work?

LOERKE: (*Reacting to seeing something.*) Maria! You came like a ghost. Heidelbier?

(*He offers his flask to* GERALD, *who takes it and drops it to the ground. Then he punches* LOERKE, *knocking him out.* GUDRUN *hits* GERALD.)

GUDRUN: You!

(GERALD *grabs her around the neck and starts to strangle her. She is gasping. Finally he throws her into the snow.*)

GERALD: I didn't want it anyway. I'm tired. I want to sleep.

(*He turns away and walks across the snow. We see him walk farther and farther away, more and more into the distance.*)

EXT. SLOPES NEAR MATTERHORN. DAY

He is a tiny figure, walking across the valley, up the mountain's peaks, trudging, walking and walking . . . He turns back to look below, but all he sees is the bright sun in his eyes and GUDRUN *laughing. He takes off his cap and gloves and throws them away. Slowly he lies down in the snow and closes his eyes.*

INT. BIRKIN AND URSULA'S BEDROOM. THE LODGE. NIGHT

GUDRUN *lying on the bed.*

GUDRUN: Was it vile being dragged back?

URSULA: I didn't even think of it.

GUDRUN: I felt beastly, fetching you here. But I simply couldn't see people. That was too much.

URSULA: Yes.

GUDRUN: I think I'll go to Dresden . . . for a while.

INT. GERALD AND GUDRUN'S BEDROOM. THE LODGE. NIGHT

GERALD *is laid out on the bed.* BIRKIN'*s hand touches his friend's cheek. The room is lit by candles.* BIRKIN *has tears in his eyes.* URSULA *opens the door.*

BIRKIN: I did not want it to be like this. I didn't want it to be like this. He should have loved me. I offered him.

(URSULA *moves toward him.* GUDRUN *enters and looks down on* GERALD. *Then she turns and leaves.*)

INT. BIRKIN'S MILL HOUSE. NIGHT

BIRKIN *sits on one side of the fire, reading.* URSULA *sits opposite him, darning. She sees that his mind is elsewhere.*

URSULA: Did you need Gerald?

BIRKIN: Yes.

URSULA: Aren't I enough for you?

BIRKIN: No. You are enough for me as far as a woman is concerned. You are all women to me. But I wanted a man friend as eternal as you and I are eternal.

URSULA: I don't believe it. It's an obstinacy . . . a theory . . . a perversity. You can't have two kinds of love. Why should you?

BIRKIN: It seems as if I can't. Yet I wanted it.

URSULA: You can't have it because it's impossible.

BIRKIN: I don't believe that.

The End.

Cast of Characters

Rupert Birkin	Alan Bates
Gerald Crich	Oliver Reed
Gudrun Brangwen	Glenda Jackson
Ursula Brangwen	Jennie Linden
Hermione Roddice	Eleanor Bron
Thomas Crich	Alan Webb
Loerke	Vladek Sheybal
Mrs. Crich	Catherine Willmer
Winifred Crich	Sarah Nicholls
Laura Crich	Sharon Gurney
Tibby Lupton	Christopher Gable
Mr. Brangwen	Michael Gough
Mrs. Brangwen	Norma Shebbeare
Contessa	Nike Arrighi
Minister	James Laurenson
Palmer	Michael Graham Cox
Loerke's Friend	Richard Heffer
Maestro	Michael Garratt

Director of Photography	Billy Williams, B.S.C.
Set Designer	Luciana Arrighi
Costume Designer	Shirley Russell
Editor	Michael Bradsell
Production Controller	Harry Benn
Unit Manager	Neville C. Thompson
Camera Operator	David Harcourt
Assistant Director	Jonathan Benson
Continuity	Angela Allen
Choreography	Terry Gilbert
Sound Recordist	Brian Simmons
Dubbing Editor	Terry Rawlings, G.B.F.E.

Dubbing Mixer	Maurice Askew
Assistant Cameraman	Stephen Claydon
Location Manager	Lee Bolon
Assistant to Producers	Tom Erhardt

Color by De Luxe

Approved No. 21973
Motion Picture Association of America

Art Director	Ken Jones
Set Dresser	Harry Cordwell
Wardrobe Supervisor	Shura Cohen
Construction Manager	Jack Carter
Electrical Supervision	George Cole
Property Master	George Ball
Makeup	Charles Parker
Hairdresser	A. G. Scott

Original Music Composed and Conducted By	George Delerue
Associate Producer	Roy Baird
Co-producer	Martin Rosen
From the Novel By	D. H. Lawrence
Written for the Screen and Produced By	Larry Kramer
Directed By	Ken Russell

Made on location in Nottinghamshire, Yorkshire, Derbyshire, Northumberland, County Durham, and London, England, and Zermatt, Switzerland, by Brandywine Productions, Ltd., 52–53 Jermyn Street, London S. W. 1.

Copyright	MCMLXIX
Released through	United Artists

Sissies' Scrapbook

A Play in Two Acts

Sissies' Scrapbook, my first play, began life as a screenplay. I'd just come back to America after ten years in London and was hibernating in the cold winter, in a Bridgehampton house, nervous, for some reason, about making reentry into the big city. I'd made *Women in Love.* It hadn't made me famous or rich (Ken Russell, the director, got all the attention and the three-picture deal from United Artists); even worse, it hadn't satisfied me. I had seen this coming for a while. I simply had not enjoyed making the film, and I found writing screenplays creatively unsatisfying. I thought for a while it was because I was not writing anything that meant anything to me—that is, that I had something invested in, like being gay. But adapting Yukio Mishima's *Forbidden Colors,* a novel very much about homosexuality, had been only a little bit better. And no studio wanted to finance it when I submitted it. No, *Women in Love* had brought me no comfort, no sense of direction, of what to do with my life. And Ken Russell got to make his wretched movie about Tchaikovsky. (When this movie was screened for the UA executives, the lights came up and the chairman said: "Well, I guess Larry Kramer had more to do with *Women in Love* than we thought.")

This realization—that making movies was not the creative outlet I'd hoped it would be—came as a surprise. Throughout the 1960s I had been very much in love with films. New York and London both had exciting film festivals that I attended vigorously. I came to love foreign films particularly. The movie that meant most to me was *Jules et Jim*. Its sheer narrative virtuosity still impresses me. Truffaut uses a Narrator, an unnamed Narrator, to tell the intensely personal story. For whatever reason, this device is rarely used in films and plays. In writing both the screenplay and later the play of *Sissies' Scrapbook,* I wanted to use an unnamed Narrator. Why not? In writing it I also threw in everything that was "meaningful" to me: young men, friends, Yale, homosexuality, fathers, and, of course, love. It certainly was based on the "real."

I finished a draft of the screenplay, only to be confronted by the same problem I'd had with the Mishima: How was I ever going to get it financed? My new American New York agent was not hopeful. A friend read it and said it should be a play. I didn't want to write a play. I was nominated for an Academy Award for my screenplay of *Women in Love,* threw *Sissies* into a box, called a guy I thought I was in love with, and bought a new Mustang for us to drive across country to Los Angeles for the awards. Falling madly in love along the way, of course. I didn't win the Oscar; my coast agent told me I was "hot" and should cash in on it because it wouldn't last long; the guy wasn't in love with me and wanted to go home to Rome, I wanted him beside me even more; I accepted a screenwriting assignment I shouldn't have to somehow keep him with me in our little Loretta Young cottage in Beverly Hills; he left anyway; and I wrote the fucking screenplay—the only thing I have ever written that I am truly ashamed of—and made more money from it than I'd ever made in my life, which I gave to my brother to invest. I returned to New York to turn *Sissies* into a play.

It wasn't all that hard to do. Or so I thought. I had that unnamed Narrator walking around like a master puppeteer, and a set that no designer could ever embody unless we had the budget of *My Fair Lady,* and a cast of characters that, while not as large as *A*

Chorus Line, still required a few more actors than any prospective producer would be happy to pay. My new New York agent didn't like the play any more than my old New York agent had liked the screenplay version of it, but she had heard of a new place called Playwrights Horizons that tried out workshop-type things and got you a director, actors, a couple of weeks of rehearsal, and a two-week run before an audience. It was located in a dance studio in the old YWCA on Eighth Avenue, and you got one big gymlike room that you rehearsed in and built your set in and set up bleachers for your audience in. No critics had ever come because no critics had ever been invited. This was a workshop. You were supposed to learn from it. A young director was found for me by the managing director, Robert Moss, and since I knew plenty of agents and casting directors, a great cast was somehow assembled.

The experience was wonderful. The actors responded to my words; my director, Alfred Gingold, was not the monster Ken Russell had been; and there were no studio executives breathing down my back, pushing and pressuring and questioning every cent and comma. Everybody actually got along with one another. Maria Tucci even made us her special spaghetti. We passed out fliers everywhere we could, and one day the audience came. In fact, they came every performance and filled all those bleachers. They clapped a lot at the end. Most important, though, was that they cried. I had made people cry. I had actually written something that touched people enough to cry. That is a very heady experience for a writer (this writer, anyway), then and now. If this was theater, then I never wanted to make another movie again.

Ever mindful of "what comes next?" I tried to get *The New York Times* to send a critic before we closed. No one answered my calls or hand-delivered letters. In two weeks (all Actors Equity would allow) it was over. Maria made us some more of her special spaghetti and we all said good-bye. Oh, there had been a few people who said they had friends who were looking for plays to produce, but no one actually came forth. One of those who saw the play was the actress Sylvia Miles. One of her friends did call. His name was Michael Harvey. He was rich. He read my play and said he would produce it off Broadway.

He did produce it off Broadway. Everything that had been so right about the workshop production at Playwrights Horizon was awful or went wrong with the off Broadway production at the Theater de Lys on Christopher Street. Most of the original cast was not available, and I was not comfortable with many of their replacements. The set was awful. Alfred decided he was directing Harold Pinter, and we cut out not only the Narrator and a few of the characters, but much of the dialogue as well. Everything I have ever written depends a great deal for its effectiveness on my use (some would say abundant use) of language. But I hadn't learned that yet. I went along with it. It was a very skinny script we opened with. We even had a new title: *Four Friends*. Michael rebelled against producing any play with the word *sissies* in its title. Whatever it was called, it was a disaster. Clive Barnes, the powerful critic for *The New York Times*, arrived thirty minutes late (we waited, of course), and he arrived drunk. (I say it here.) His review the next day began, "With friends like these you don't need enemies." We closed on opening night. Stephen Sondheim, who saw both versions, told me, "You threw the baby out with the bathwater." I am never certain what expressions like this mean, but I have always assumed there was some fundamental problem with the original version that needed fixing, and I could never identify it. Was it the unnamed Narrator? Was it . . . Well, I have never been able to figure it out. Something had gone terribly wrong. And no one had cried except me.

Sissies' Scrapbook was produced by Playwrights Horizons at the West-side YWCA Clark Center for a two-week workshop, December 19–31, 1973. (A much rewritten version, *Four Friends,* was produced at the Theater de Lys on February 17, 1975, by Michael Harvey.)

Sissies' Scrapbook was directed by Alfred Gingold with the following cast:

The Narrator	Mark Suben
Ron	John Colenback
John	Andrew Smith
Dick	Ron Hale
Barry	Curt Dawson

John's Father	Thayer David
Dick's Father	Harrison Endwissel
Barry's Father	Alex Reed
Ron's Father	John O'Leary

Annie	
Susan	Maria Tucci
Nurse One	

Terry	Brad Davis
Other Ron	

Jenifer	Jeanne Hepple
Woman on the Bus	

Laura	
Isabel	Alice Elliott
Barry's Sister	
Nurse Two	

Cast of Characters

The Narrator

Ron
John
Dick
Barry

John's Father
Dick's Father
Barry's Father
Ron's Father

Annie
Susan
Nurse One
} Same actress

Terry
Other Ron
} Same actor

Jenifer
Woman on the Bus
} Same actress

Laura
Isabel
Barry's Sister
Nurse Two
} Same actress

Act One

A word about the setting. It should be naturalistic, without being necessarily totally realistic. Ideally, the stage should be a long one, length being preferable to depth, though depth being helpful as well. The overall feeling should be of one enormous apartment—but on closer scrutiny, and as the play progresses, we will realize that we are seeing, rather, four separate apartments or living areas, each belonging to one of our four young men. Each area, therefore, should reflect this man's personality, income, private life. (RON's is the most expensive, the most "decorated" but also the most impersonal; JOHN's is the neatest and most spartan in terms of excess; DICK's is the least neat, the most studious; and BARRY's is the most bohemian and the cheapest. RON would probably be living on Madison or in the 60s off it; JOHN in the high East 70s about Second Avenue; DICK would live in the Village; and BARRY would be in a railroad apartment on First Avenue in the 90s.) But the areas must flow into one another, be extensions of one another, allowing, particularly at upstage center, where a big table sits, for group activity, a common ground, a meeting place, or just general comings and goings, especially in the downstage area. In each apartment, however, there should be a bed.

At rise, the only light is a central spot, into which the NARRATOR *steps. His identity is solely as the* NARRATOR, *though he will occasionally assume other roles helpful to furthering the action. His appearance is like that of the four men he will be talking about: he is in his middle thirties, clean-cut, pleasant looking. He addresses the audience.*

NARRATOR: Our major event this evening is that someone is going to die. I know we all die a little every day, but this will be the real thing, the grand finale. I hope you'll find it sad and touching. And I hope that some cold, icy chill has already started inside of you.

(*The lights come up on* DICK'*s area as the* NARRATOR *walks off the stage.* DICK *is wiry, intense, probably wears glasses, has dark hair, and wants very much to help people. He is with* ANNIE, *a pleasant-looking, dark-haired girl, sort of elfin. Their scene is light, almost comedic; when it turns sour, we don't remember when things started going wrong.*)

ANNIE: How was your day, Dr. Dick?

DICK: Very pleasant and not particularly unusual, my Annie.

ANNIE: Lots more lovable patients on the couch.

DICK: I love my patients. The sick are not like you and me.

ANNIE: How do you know?

DICK: Well, let me tell you. Let me count the ways. Today I had a day full of misfits. First, a young girl. (*He will mimic each of the people he describes.*) "I hate my mommy. I hate my daddy. I hate myself. And I hate you." Then a little old lady. "I have two very successful sons. They don't love me. There's no place for old people in this world. I want to die." Then a good-looking gay boy. "I've been trying all these years to learn how to be fucked and really enjoy it. At first it hurt. But now it feels terrific."

ANNIE: So that's progress. Congratulations. Don't you wish you had such perseverance?

DICK: To what? I don't want to learn how to be fucked by you.

ANNIE: That's a relief. (*Pause.*) What would you like me to do to you?

DICK: Love me.

ANNIE: Just like that?

DICK: Just like that.

ANNIE: Okay. I love you.

DICK: Terrific. I love you back, Annie.

ANNIE: Now what do we do?

DICK: Immediately? Or in the future tense?

ANNIE: Take your pick. It's your day.

DICK: We walk hand in hand together down life's path.

ANNIE: Ah.

DICK: Isn't that OK?

ANNIE: Suspiciously sentimental. Dick, do you really want to get married?

DICK: Absolutely. Don't you?

ANNIE: It would depend.

DICK: On what? Besides me.

ANNIE: It's the awful *power* of having exactly what you want. I'm sure it's not the freeing, liberating thing you expect it to be. I'm sure it's just another prison. And a far more awful one, because it's one you've chosen.

DICK: My goodness. This sounds like the sudden inability to have a relationship. Wouldn't you at least like the experience of having been married?

ANNIE: But it might be an undesirable experience. Or the end of experience.

DICK: You wouldn't consider a good offer?

ANNIE: I think I've rejected several.

DICK: Really? But nothing worthwhile.

ANNIE: Twenty-five thousand dollars a year and an awfully nice man.

DICK: My goodness, weren't you tempted?

ANNIE: I was only tempted not to.

DICK: I've been hoping for a woman to come along.

ANNIE: Have you?

DICK: Mind you, I wouldn't go out of my way to look for her. But if there did come along a highly attractive individual . . .

ANNIE: So the physical is more important than the intellectual? Men are so disappointing.

DICK: Oh, no. We just want to walk hand in hand together down life's path . . .

ANNIE: My goodness. That sounds suspiciously like the inability to have a relationship.

DICK: . . . with the right and perfect someone.

ANNIE: I had hoped that my psychiatrist would be free from sentimental taint.

DICK: Only for their patients.

ANNIE: Then I must become a patient.

DICK: Not if you're my lover.

ANNIE: Then I will not be your lover anymore.

DICK: And why not?

ANNIE: Because you're next going to say we have to go out to dinner with your father.

DICK: We do.

ANNIE: Your father is a turgid turd.

DICK: I went out with your mother.

ANNIE: She's sweet. My mother is sweet.

DICK: My father is St. Teresa of Avila compared to your mother, who is a head-lopping witch.

ANNIE: My mother is neither sorceress nor saint, but your father casts evil spells on little children. I refuse.

DICK: You have no choice in the matter.

ANNIE: What a fine thing for a psychiatrist to say. Anyway, a single, attractive girl in New York always has a choice.

DICK: Which means . . . ?

ANNIE: Exactly what it says, Mr. . . . what did you say your name was. You think I love you, don't you? Well, your love to me is as the love of the son of the father who casts evil spells on little children. I could not love such a son.

DICK: Why not? I could love the daughter of a witch. He's waiting. We'll be late.

ANNIE: Oh, get the hell out of here. I don't want to go. Can't you see that?

DICK: (*Walking towards a closet.*) Which dress do you want to wear?

ANNIE: Get out, leave my clothes alone!

DICK: They're your clothes, but it's my closet.

ANNIE: They're *my* clothes.

DICK: Annie, we're going.

ANNIE: You're going.

DICK: You're going, too.

ANNIE: No, I'm not, I'm not.

DICK: Why not? Please tell me why not.

ANNIE: No.

DICK: Please!

ANNIE: (*Pause, then very softly.*) I am very ugly.

DICK: Oh, shit.

ANNIE: Yes. I am. I am very ugly. I am too ugly for your father and therefore too ugly for you. The only person I am not too ugly for is my mother, and I am going home to her.

DICK: You are sick in the head. (*He starts to leave.*)

ANNIE: No, I'm not. I am dick in the head.

(*The lights go down on them and come up on the* NARRATOR.)

NARRATOR: That was Dick. And now for Ron. Perhaps I should say here that we have four men to introduce. Now Ron.

(*The lights go down on the Narrator and come up on* RON'*s area.* RON *is tall, quite handsome, slightly going to fat, slightly losing his hair. He gives the appearance of being quite open, but in fact, he hides behind a facade of a good nature, a good sense of humor, and a good sense that his ambition will take him places. He is wearing a bathrobe and goes to open the door, which is buzzing. He admits a blond young man, Terry, very handsome, to whom he will be quite cool and ostensibly pay little attention.*)

RON: (*Turning his back on Terry, thus forcing him to close the door and follow him in.*) Come on in. Make yourself a drink.

TERRY: (*Crosses to the bar and starts to make himself a drink.*) You want one?

RON: (*Off-stage.*) No thanks.

(*Terry looks around, observing. Ron comes back, now clad only in shorts.*)

RON: Let's go, shall we?

(*The lights go down on them and up on the* NARRATOR; *but halfway through his speech, they will come up dimly on* RON *and Terry in bed,* RON *smoking silently and exhaling upward.*)

NARRATOR: Ron had read too much Fitzgerald. He believed in the value of self. Of his own importance, and ability, and eventual pre-eminence over anything he chose to possess. But something got in the way, turning everything ill, like the vestige of an ancient plague, still coming back, still recurring, never ever going away, always, always there. . . .

RON: (*To Terry.*) Look, would you mind going home. I'll give you a ring later in the week.

(*His lights go down and they come up downstage on* JOHN, *sitting alone in a chair, reading* The Wall Street Journal. *He is pleasant faced, not particularly distinctive. He wants everyone to like him and smiles a lot. But in his weakness there is a sadness, which even he does not recognize.* JENIFER *comes in. She is English, quite sure of herself, with no compunction about speaking her mind. She carries a bag full of groceries.*)

JENIFER: I loathe and abhor the American supermarket. John, they are so impersonal. I recognize no one from day to day.

(*The* NARRATOR*'s light comes up softly for a moment.*)

NARRATOR: This is John. And this is Jenifer, whom he loves and whom he will shortly marry.

(*His lights go down.*)

JENIFER: I simply can't get along with her. She stands over me like some harpy, checking my every bit of work, my every move, my every catalogue entry. So much for your New York world of art. In London, with my qualifications, I'd have a much higher position with much higher responsibility. And I'd be trusted. John, whenever is your transfer coming through?

JOHN: Very soon, honey. Then we can go and start everything.

JENIFER: I wish we were getting married over there. There's a little church by the river, by a bend in the river, and you cross over the bridge to the other side, where there's a lovely inn. We could marry on one side and reception on the other. Never mind. I will love a New York wedding.

JOHN: Me too. Do you love me, Jen? I sure love you.

JENIFER: Yes, John. I love you.

(JOHN's *lights go down, and the* NARRATOR's *come up again.*)

NARRATOR: Lastly, we have Barry.

(*The* NARRATOR's *lights go down and* BARRY's *come up. He is tall and blond and handsome, and he knows it. He is also very bright. There is an inability in him to somehow reconcile all of these qualities into a whole. So he sidesteps them in a manner that we shall see. Right now, he lies back on his bed, with his shirt off.* LAURA, *a young woman, very vulnerable, almost asking to be hurt, leans against him, wearing only her underclothes. He responds little to her physically, though she will try to be affectionate toward him, since she is very much in love with him.*)

BARRY: Listen. I'm troubled. I think it's got something to do with you.

LAURA: Good.

BARRY: Why's it good?

LAURA: It's some sort of a reaction. (*Looks at him, waiting; but he doesn't say anything.*) Please tell me. Why am I the cause of your trouble?

BARRY: I didn't say you were the cause of my trouble. I just said I was troubled.

LAURA: No. Not now. Let's not get bogged down in semantics now. Why are you troubled, and what have I got to do with it? (*Again, there is no answer.*) Perhaps we could go for a walk and talk about it. (*She starts to move, but he remains as he is.*)

BARRY: I'd rather stay here.

(*She sighs and lies back against him.*)

BARRY: But you'd rather go for a walk, wouldn't you?

LAURA: That's all right. Let's stay here.

BARRY: Look outside at the moonlight.

LAURA: Why am I in trouble?

BARRY: What? Oh. It's not often someone comes along you like.

(*Her eyes close with relief as she smiles to herself, feeling good.*)

(*Noting her reaction.*) You like me a lot, don't you?

LAURA: Yes.

BARRY: You'd like me to fuck you twenty-four hours a day, wouldn't you?

LAURA: (*Smiling.*) I wouldn't say no.

BARRY: You've been waiting for a long time for me to say something, haven't you?

LAURA: I've been a . . . bowlful of knots, if you can visualize that.

BARRY: I think you're very beautiful.

LAURA: Good.

BARRY: I love the way you make love and look up at me with those soulful eyes. It's very sexy.

LAURA: Good.

BARRY: I'm going to ask you to leave now.

LAURA: What?

BARRY: Good-bye. I'm not going to let our relationship, which you know is a word I despise but which you insist on using, develop any further. Ciao.

(*He moves to get up; she restrains him but is able to for only a moment; he eludes her and gets up and starts putting on his shirt.*)

LAURA: Wait. Wait a minute. People don't just walk out of people's lives like that.

BARRY: I do. I haven't got time for us.

LAURA: Time? You have nothing but time. But what has time got to do with it anyway? It's supposed to be love and affection and need and desire and want!

BARRY: All those things?

LAURA: Yes. All those things.

BARRY: How dumb Americans are, putting it all into words. I shall move to Italy, where the inexpressible is not expressed.

(*He looks down at her, his hands firmly on her shoulders, massaging his grip into her almost painfully, as he sticks the knife in even further.*)

I don't want you, Laura. And I don't need you. I quite possibly might love you, though I'm not certain I know what love feels like. I do feel affection for you, and yes, I do desire you quite a lot. But I don't want you and I don't need you and I really must ask you to go home now because I have an awful lot of things to do tomorrow and I must go to sleep. Good-bye. You're very beautiful, you know.

(*The lights go down and stay down, though after a moment,* LAURA*'s agonizing cry is heard, a cry half stifled, now gently exploding out of her, kept bottled up too long. Then the* NARRATOR*'s light comes up. He is going to now show some slides; this can be accomplished either by his having an actual slide projector or just the button release mechanism in his hand. The back wall of the stage should be filled with the images. A note on the photographs that will punctuate the* NARRATOR*'s speech: We should almost feel the effect of looking through an album, pictures of the four, with or without girls, of the apartment buildings, of their parties, of* DICK*'s first wife, wedding pictures, crazy pictures, even pictures from their college days. . . .*)

NARRATOR: Ron, John, Dick, and Barry were the best of friends. They'd been to Yale together, where they'd been roommates. That was a few years ago. Then they came to New York, to start their climb up the ladder or their walk down the road. Their first apartment was a dump on East 28th Street, with overstuffed furniture, occasional hot water, and bunk-type beds, upper and lower, just like at Yale. They were pretty happy there. It was torn down a few years ago to make way for an insurance building. As life was good to them and they climbed up the ladder, they moved uptown. From 28th Street, to 49th Street, to 90th Street, to 66th Street. John and Dick liked girls, Ron liked boys, though that was his secret, and Barry liked to hurt people. As time went on, Dick got married for the first time, and Ron, John, and Barry carried on alone.

Dick got divorced and moved back in, but then Ron disappeared somewhere, going off without an explanation, returning a few months later, also without an explanation. After a few years, men being men and privacy being privacy, each took his own apartment. These we have just seen. Dick is now going with Annie. Barry has momentarily rid himself of Laura and may or may not take up with Isabel. For John there is only Jenifer. And Ron will date faceless girls while secretly looking for Mr. Right.

(*As the* NARRATOR *finishes, the slides will fade out and the lights will come up on the central area, as the four are playing cards at the table.*)

Ron is on his way to becoming both very rich and very successful in advertising. Dick, a psychiatrist, though poor now, will have a very rough time of it but will eventually come out of it all right. John, a banker, is the one who will soon be dead. And Barry doesn't know what the hell he is going to do. I might add that this doesn't trouble him in the slightest.

(*The* NARRATOR*'s lights go down.*)

DICK: When I was in high school, all I wanted was to learn how to fuck and get into a good college. When I was in college, all I wanted was to perfect my fucking, make good contacts, and get into a good medical school. When I was in medical school, all I wanted was to find a nice wife and become a good doctor. Now I wonder if my fucking is in all that tiptop shape.

JOHN: What was it like, being married?

DICK: Very nice. I hope to do it again someday.

JOHN: Why do you think it didn't work out?

DICK: Some days are better than others. It's the same with wives. And husbands, I might add.

JOHN: Are you and Annie going to get married?

DICK: Changes from day to day.

JOHN: (*To* BARRY.) Are you and Laura going to get married?

BARRY: Laura who?

RON: It's like that, is it?

BARRY: I don't know what you're talking about.

RON: Always the silent, retentive one. Do you move your bowels regularly?

BARRY: Quite regularly, thank you.

RON: I find that very pleasing.

BARRY: Do you? And how is your regularity?

RON: Some days are better than others. It's the same with bowel movements.

DICK: Am I being joshed and sent up? Am I being made fun of?

RON: Doctor, how can you say that?

DICK: I find it very difficult to discern the trend of this conversation.

RON: Fellowship, brotherhood, companionship. I am my brothers' keeper.

DICK: I wonder what will become of all of us?

RON: I shall, of course, succeed.

DICK: But at what cost?

RON: Why, at the cost of my happiness, naturally; I shall be single and miserable unto my grave.

BARRY: John will wind up president of the bank and Dick the head of the hospital.

DICK: And you?

BARRY: I never think about it.

DICK: Isn't it time you did?

BARRY: Nonsense, and never.

DICK: Then what do you believe in?

BARRY: (*Laying his cards on the table and raking in the chips.*) I believe in proper modes of conduct and behavior. I believe in eighteenth-century manners and Henry James rectitude.

DICK: Everyone is entitled to a bad day.

BARRY: Nope. Not in front of me, they're not.

RON: I believe in the tomorrow, in the rich and beautiful tomorrow, with soft skin and golden hair and a penthouse in the sky. (*He takes a swig straight from a liquor bottle.*)

BARRY: It's a good thing you're in advertising.

RON: I also believe in the consuming love. A return by a very special girl of the tremendous amount of love I have to give her.

BARRY: It's especially good you are in advertising.

JOHN: I believe you go from day to day, loving and caring and trying.

RON: (*Toasting by holding up his bottle.*) Here's to us. Everything we always wanted to know about sex, we now know and don't feel any better.

DICK: I believe we're all sick in the head.

JOHN: A hazard of your profession.

(DICK *puts on a record. Music starts from a college glee club record of old Yale songs. The four toast their glasses, then stand up and join arms around one another, swaying to and fro, back and forth, in time with the music. They smile and are very close. The lights dim a bit on them as the* NARRATOR *speaks.*)

NARRATOR: And Gatsby believed in the blue light, and Tonio believed in the blond and the blue-eyed, and Lafcadio believed in neither sentiment nor morality, though his creator believed in the soul's agony metamorphosed into creative force. And Birkin believed in the trust of instinct and the healing power of illness. So many things to believe in. And Barry went home . . . (BARRY *gets up and leaves.*) . . . and John went home . . . (*He leaves.*) . . . and Ron went home . . . (*He leaves.*) . . . leaving Dick to clean up and go to bed.

(*The lights have gone down on the center table and come up on* JOHN's *area, opposite to where the* NARRATOR *is standing. He walks slightly stage center and begins again.*)

NARRATOR: Chapter two. John's Father has a talk with his son on the night before his wedding to Jenifer. John came from the Midwest. His mother, who came from the best of families, had married a middle-aged Englishman, an author who was soon to achieve no little renown. The father and son had never been particularly close.

(JOHN *and his father enter his apartment.* JOHN'S FATHER *is a man of about sixty, of medium height, and quite stout. He dresses somberly, in a dark suit with a vest. He is an intense and staring man, always looking, studying, almost satanically.*)

JOHN: Can I get you a drink, Dad? (*He makes himself a strong one.*)

JOHN'S FATHER: No, thank you. I'll celebrate tomorrow. Liquor only makes me hungry, and when I'm hungry I eat gigantic amounts of sweets, and then I must assuage my guilt by writing, furiously, some horrendously perfect passage for my next book. I'm not quite up to that chain of events.

JOHN: I never knew that about you.

JOHN'S FATHER: I suspect there is a great deal of information each of us is lacking from the other.

JOHN: I've always been honest with you.

JOHN'S FATHER: I'm not speaking of honesty. This is more subliminal and more apt.

JOHN: I don't think I could talk much about whatever that is.

JOHN'S FATHER: Exactly. More's the pity.

JOHN: You mean my sex life or forbidden thoughts, or something?

JOHN'S FATHER: You should just know a great deal about yourself before moving on—to whatever the next step is going to be.

JOHN: Don't you think I'm in control, or whatever?

JOHN'S FATHER: You are obviously in control of the situation which occurs tomorrow.

JOHN: She's just a terrific girl and I know we'll be happy together.

JOHN'S FATHER: That a son of mine is such a romantic!

JOHN: Yep. Seen too many movies, I guess. (*Taking a large swallow from his drink.*) Hey, why didn't you teach me all about—whatever it was you just said I should know about myself?

JOHN'S FATHER: A good question. I was about to . . .

JOHN: Then why didn't you?

JOHN'S FATHER: (*Bluntly.*) You never seemed quite ready.

JOHN: Oh. (*Pause.*) Is it too late?

JOHN'S FATHER: For my teaching you, yes. For your learning, I hope not.

JOHN: Don't make it sound eerie.

JOHN'S FATHER: No.

JOHN: (*Waits for his father to say something more; when he doesn't.*) How is the house?

JOHN'S FATHER: The house?

JOHN: The one you're living in. I love that house. There are seventeen windows in front and twenty-seven in back. Did you know that? Did you know there are twelve oaks and twelve elms and twelve maples, laid out evenly oak one, elm one, maple one, oak two, elm two, maple two? It stretches like that all the way to the river.

JOHN'S FATHER: How interesting. I'll look closer. (*Stands up.*) Here, let me look at you.

(*He motions for* JOHN *to stand up, which he does. He feels his son's body and mid-section.*)

Your midsection feels firm. Stay hard. Don't become a jelly bowl of fat like me. It's hardest to lose around your waist. I was a fine-looking young man, firm, hard. I stood tall, faced the foe, impressed my peers, all that sort of thing.

JOHN: It sounds impressive.

JOHN'S FATHER: It was meant to.

JOHN: Am I some sort of disappointment to you?

JOHN'S FATHER: (*After a pause.*) No.

JOHN: I'm sorry if I am.

JOHN'S FATHER: Never feel sorry for anything, John. I doubt if you'll be able to follow that advice. But pity is a crippling waste of time. Forget it and move on. There is always something better or different or at least a more palatable version of the same thing around the corner. If you can remember that.

JOHN: I'll try. I am a disappointment to you.

JOHN'S FATHER: You came late into my life. I fear more the reverse, that you have been disappointed in me. Was I?

JOHN: (*Softly.*) No . . . of course not.

JOHN'S FATHER: I was. What did you think of me?

(*When* JOHN *doesn't answer, his father suddenly and perversely asks demandingly.*)

Tell me!

JOHN: (*Reacting as if slapped.*) I thought you were . . . weak.

JOHN'S FATHER: (*Smiling.*) Weak. How so?

JOHN: Oh, because you weren't as rich as Momma was, you wouldn't take the long trips she wanted you to take, you hardly ever left your room. It never occured to me you were writing all those books all that time.

JOHN'S FATHER: Yes. I was writing all those books.

JOHN: I guess I misread all the information. (*Trying to be light.*) It's a good thing I didn't read what you'd written. I might know too much about you!

JOHN'S FATHER: (*Sadly.*) Yes.

(*They look at each other for a long moment. Then* JOHN *goes to his father and they clumsily embrace, formally and without completeness. The lights go down on them and up on* DICK, *in his area, where his couch is now prominent. He wears a white doctor's hospital jacket.* JOHN *walks out of his scene and over to* DICK, *where he sits down on the couch to continue the scene.*)

DICK: You used to sneak off senior year, as I recall. It was prom time before you admitted, under intense ribbing, that you were going to see a psychiatrist.

JOHN: Only once a week. A good thing Pop didn't know about that!

DICK: Forget about him. He's a frozen prig.

JOHN: No, he's not.

DICK: What did you and the psychiatrist discuss?

JOHN: Jesus, you're making it sound like some sort of case history. (*Tries to make light of it, flopping back in a reclining position on the couch.*) I said, Doctor, I can't get an erection. When I want to fuck this great-looking girl, it gets all weak and just flops over.

DICK: That's what you told him?

JOHN: (*Softly.*) Yes. And I've never told anyone else.

DICK: You know that I'm safe. I'm your doctor. Is everything all right now?

JOHN: Yes. You bet. Hey, do you know when I was in seventh grade, this guy in class named Warren Munsterberger took his dick out. I knew then I'd never be an ass man. It was unreal! Some guy said, What's that? Are we studying foreign snakes? It came down to his knee. I couldn't make out then, and, if I had to, I couldn't go out and make out now.

DICK: You don't have to fuck for the same reason now. You don't have to fuck the same broads now as you did then. And Warren Munsterberger is probably all worn out.

JOHN: So we talked about it, this doctor and me, for a few months. Once a week. And now I've met Jenifer and I can fuck her good and regular. So I'm going to marry her.

DICK: Is that sufficient reason?

JOHN: I love her. I love her fine. And I'll have grandchildren to make everybody happy, and a nice house, and a terrific job with the bank somewhere overseas like Jenifer wants, and wow.

DICK: Yeah, wow.

JOHN: (*Very softly.*) Dick, I'm afraid.

DICK: (*Looking at* JOHN *for a long moment before answering, carefully considering what he should say at this moment in his friend's life.*) So are we all, buddy. Go home and get some sleep.

JOHN: Won't it be wow?

DICK: Who can tell? If it were only semiwow, would you be able to live with that?

JOHN: Don't I love her?

DICK: You'll find out. Nothing is irrevocable. Go home. Stay out of the sun and hope your head will clear by morning.

(JOHN *pulls himself up; he finishes the remainder of his drink with a big swig, puts a big smile on his face, and does a little drunken dance.*)

JOHN: I'm in love. I love her. Johnny's in love. When Johnny goes marching home again, hurrah, hurrah.

(DICK *looks after him as he goes out into darkness.* DICK *now briefly becomes the narrator for a while.*)

DICK: My father is sitting over there in the corner.

(*The lights come up behind him, on a little fat old man, sitting at the big center table, eating silently.* DICK *comes and stands in front of him.*)

DICK: You want some more cold cuts?

DICK'S FATHER: (*Shaking his head no.*) How is your job?

DICK: Fine.

DICK'S FATHER: Your mother would be proud.

(*And the lights go down on him as* DICK *walks away and returns to narrate.*)

DICK: We never had very much to say to each other. Every time I look at him, I find myself thinking, The bastard's going to die soon, and wondering how that will grab me. Barry's father is a successful farmer. The kind that owns the land and only lives on it.

(*Lights down on* DICK *and up on* BARRY'*s area, where* BARRY *is facing his father, a handsome, older version of his son with a childlike face.*)

BARRY'S FATHER: (*Looking around the apartment with distaste.*) I wish you lived better. What are you going to do now?

BARRY: I don't really know. Maybe write.

BARRY'S FATHER: We don't have any writers in the family. Your great-grandmother Elsa read a lot. Write about what?

BARRY: Some ancient ruins I saw in Turkey. I don't know. I'll sort it out. Yes, I'll do that.

BARRY'S FATHER: How old are you? Somewhere in your late twenties?

BARRY: Jesus, don't you even know?

BARRY'S FATHER: You don't know how old I am. Listen, I'm thinking of stopping your check. You can't be a perpetual do-nothing all your life.

BARRY: Why not? You are.

BARRY'S FATHER: Don't be fresh. Either come home and help me grow the corn or get a job.

BARRY: I'll think about it. If you need me, I'll come home. Daddy, do you remember when I was sixteen and that girl Beverly came down to stay with us?

BARRY'S FATHER: Vaguely.

BARRY: I was in love with her. It hurt me inside. I loved her.

BARRY' S FATHER: That's nice. It happens every day.

BARRY: (*Mimicking him.*) "It happens every day." She didn't want me! She didn't want any of me. I slashed my wrist. (*He offers up the scar.*)

BARRY'S FATHER: Your mother thought you just cut yourself. I thought there was something funny. Why are you telling me this now?

BARRY: I just thought of it. I wanted to.

BARRY'S FATHER: Oh.

BARRY: (*Softly.*) Oh, go to hell.

BARRY'S FATHER: I don't know what to say.

BARRY: I sometimes still want to die. I think I'm going to fly away to death. I want to lie down in the goddamn golden corn and lie in it dead. Next to you.

BARRY'S FATHER: I'll be there soon enough.

BARRY: (*Suddenly feeling sorry for his father and for treating him so, he gives him an impulsive kiss.*) I love you, Dada.

(*Lights down on* BARRY'*s area and up again on* DICK.)

DICK: (*Narrating.*) More about Ron later. His father was evidently nonexistent. No, sir, we don't have many heroes.

(*Lights up on the big table, with the three others sitting around it, the cards in the center. They are looking at* DICK *as if they have been listening to him expounding some point.*)

(*Approaching them and speaking to them.*) Relationships. Based on love. Not need. No albatross. No throat cutting. Independence. Two yet one.

BARRY: Bullshit, Doctor. You're repeating it all by rote. One two three. This is the way we learn today.

DICK: (*Patiently.*) That's right. That's how we learn. One two three. If one doesn't kill us, we go on to two. If two doesn't cripple us, we go on to three. If three doesn't taste nasty and make us sick to our tummy, we go on to four. Why can't you shut up and listen?

JOHN: He has a right to be heard.

BARRY: (*Smiling.*) Yes. It's a free country.

DICK: (*Softly.*) No, it's not. It's a lot of things, but free it isn't.

(*He looks at* BARRY *for a very long moment. Then he quietly picks up one of the liquor bottles from the table and slowly pours it over* BARRY'*s head.*)

BARRY: (*Jumping up.*) What the fuck are you doing, man? Are you all right?

DICK: I'm all right, man, but, man, you have got to be shook up. Where have you been? What are you looking at with your eyes closed? (*Pushes* BARRY.) Huh? Huh? What are you looking at, you unshook-up little twentieth-century product? (*Pushing again and again.*) Free country, eh? Free country? Hit me back! Goddamn it, hit me back!

BARRY: (*He can't and sits down, mumbling.*) You're all fucked up in the head.

(*Lights down on all of them, with* DICK *stepping out and going to run the slide projector. He will now show pictures of* JOHN'*s wedding to* JENIFER, *all kinds of pictures—the roommates, the bridesmaids, the reception, and finally the boat sailing with* JOHN *and* JENIFER *on the deck.*)

DICK: (*Narrating.*) John and Jenifer got married on a Sunday in a church. Jenifer's parents came from England, even though John was just about to be transferred there anyway for his bank. I was the best man—hey, look at me, and I took Annie, she wasn't bitchy that day, and Barry had this new girl called Isabel, who seemed to be very happy and bore a striking resemblance to Laura, and Ron found this old girlfriend named Barbara, and John's parents met Jenifer's parents, and my old man came, and Barry's father sent a telegram saying he couldn't make it but he'd be in later in the month for a corn growers' convention and would be staying at the Yale Club.

(*Lights up on the various areas, with each of the four in bed with a girl.*)

NARRATOR: And that night, John and Jenifer made marvelous love on board their ship. And Dick and Annie made marvelous love. And Barry took Isabel home and let her feel his body exposed. And Ron took Barbara home first and then went home and beat off.

RON: (*Calling out from his area, where he is in bed with a girl.*) I did not! I took Barbara home and said to myself, What the hell, tonight I'll do it with a girl.

DICK: (*Calling out from his area.*) Way to go!

(*Lights down on all of them, as the* NARRATOR *finishes up with some slides of the boat sailing off into the river and a huge picture of a beaming and waving* JOHN *and* JENIFER.)

NARRATOR: We won't see them for a while. But we shall see them. And so now once again there were three.

(*The last photo of* JENIFER *is replaced by a huge picture of a beautiful woman, obviously a model, with the words* Ultima Now *lettered under her.*)

And Ron went back to work, conning the consumer nation.

(*Lights up on Barry, sprawled on the floor, trying to write.*)

And Barry started to write a story which began "I once loved a girl named Beverly . . ."

(*The last slide is of a small bearded midget with the sweetest smile.*)

And Dick went back to the troubles of the world. Soon it would be his turn.

(DICK'*s lights come up. The sofa area is now a consulting room.* DICK *is on the couch in his white jacket, and the* NARRATOR *is sitting in* DICK'*s chair, listening to him.*)

DICK: This is a painful pain in the ass. So was he, that little fat old father you just saw. He lived in his own world and no one was welcomed to it. On a hot day, where we lived, without air-conditioning, he'd sit in his boxer shorts and a T-shirt, with a towel around his stubby neck to mop the sweat. I never realized it before, but I think I found him physically repulsive, not only the fat, but that very white skin, all exposed. Maybe that's why I don't like my own body.

NARRATOR: Maybe. A thought.

DICK: He was a beaten man. So I guess sympathy nudged out distaste and repulsion somewhere along the line.

NARRATOR: A step towards maturity.

DICK: He'd been Phi Beta Kappa and on the *Law Journal,* both at Yale. His mother ran a grocery store and single-handedly put her two sons through Yale. So he'd had the best but nothing went anywhere for him. He worked for his older brother, whom he idolized but who resented him, and then the Depression came along and he just folded his tent and never opened it again.

NARRATOR: All very sad.

DICK: The old lady had had an abortion before I came along, and he once told me that he wanted her to have another to eliminate me, but she wouldn't go through it a second time.

NARRATOR: What do you do for laughs?

DICK: I get married.

(*Lights down on the* NARRATOR *and up on* ANNIE. DICK *takes off his white coat and walks to her.*)

ANNIE: I wouldn't marry you if you had the only penis left alive.

DICK: I wouldn't marry you if your mother became a nun.

ANNIE: You think I'm just one of your freaky patients. All psyched up and no place to go.

DICK: I think you're just Miss Cinderella, afraid to let her Prince Charming take her to the ball. Well, I won't take you to the ball. No, sir.

ANNIE: That's just fine with me. I'm tired of you and I'm tired of life. It's like a soccer game and I'm the only player on my side.

DICK: Good. That's right. Throw in the sponge. You're so obsessed with your own insecurities that you can't see the face for the mirror.

ANNIE: Oh, you act like you're God on high, waving your healing wand at all we poor inadequates in the Valley of the Shadow of Life.

DICK: Not bad.

ANNIE: Thank you. I read it somewhere.

DICK: You'll die if you want to die and live if you want to live.

ANNIE: Oh, platitude, platitude, feh. I don't want to live with you. I don't want to die with you. I don't want to marry with you. I don't even want to eat spaghetti with you.

DICK: That is a turndown if ever I heard one.

ANNIE: You're goddamn right.

DICK: I shall not ask you again.

ANNIE: That's soon enough for me.

DICK: I love you very much.

ANNIE: I love you, too.

DICK: So what are we going to do?

ANNIE: You're the doctor.

(*Their lights go down, and the* NARRATOR *is again front and center with his slide projector, now projecting another set of wedding pictures. First a church, then* DICK *and* RON *and* BARRY, *all dressed in morning clothes. Then a picture of a smiling* DICK.)

NARRATOR: (*Reading from a letter.*) She wrote: "Dear Dick. The doctor gave the wrong prescription. The doctor is a lovely man who falls in love with sick people who want desperately to be loved but can't believe it when it happens. I think you're a liar, Doctor Dick. But maybe so am I. Good-bye forever, Annie.

(*Lights go up on* DICK, *in morning clothes, holding a letter. He turns to another girl,* SUSAN, *cool and composed but looking remarkably like* ANNIE *physically, if not emotionally. She sits on the sofa, doing needlepoint.*)

So, in his loneliness, Dick married Susan.

(*Lights down and the sounds over the loud speaker system of a train, coming to a stop. Then the sound of a conductor's voice announcing:*)

CONDUCTOR'S VOICE: Change at Babylon!

(*Lights up on* RON, *with a suitcase beside him, standing there as if on a train platform. On the other side of the stage stands a handsome blond young man, also called* RON. *They exchange glances. The* OTHER RON *smiles pleasantly and naturally. Our* RON *turns away, then turns back to look. As the* NARRATOR *continues,* RON *continues to size up the* OTHER

RON *to such a degree that the* OTHER RON *loses interest in this fellow who's making such a big deal over coming over to say hello. As the* NARRATOR *finishes,* RON *has approached the* OTHER RON.)

NARRATOR: In another lifetime, Ron Gatz had been a Good Humor man in Pennsylvania. His parents, whom he didn't remember anymore, had been poor, which he did remember. He'd saved up enough money to buy the ice-cream wagon and made enough money from that to put himself penuriously through Yale. He vowed he'd never do anything penuriously again. He came to New York and met a very old man of thirty who had a yacht. This old man of thirty didn't work because he'd inherited his father's fish hook fortune. He sailed all around Long Island Sound with Ron Gatz, and when Ron Gatz left him he became an alcoholic and sailed away, never to be heard from again.

RON: Hi.

OTHER RON: It took you long enough.

RON: What do you mean?

OTHER RON: You made such a big deal out of it all. You see someone you want to say hello to, you say hello.

RON: So hello.

(*Lights down on them as the* NARRATOR *continues.*)

NARRATOR: A few years after the rich old man sailed drunkenly away, Ron was a full partner in his own successful agency. The sky was reached, heaven attained, and there was no one left to meet but Ron himself.

(*Lights up on* RON *and the* OTHER RON, *in bed together.*)

RON: You have an incredible body. Where do you work out?

OTHER RON: Listen, I think It's time I told you something. Since you've never asked. My name is Ron.

RON: Hey, my name's Ron, too. What do you do?

OTHER RON: I'm an actor. A bit of modeling. It's the commercials that pay the rent. What do you do?

RON: Nothing much.

OTHER RON: Okay, I'll let it pass for now.

RON: Let what pass?

OTHER RON: You obviously don't do "nothing much." This is too nice a place.

RON: How do you know I didn't inherit it?

OTHER RON: I just have the feeling you're covering up. That's okay. For a while.

RON: I'm a banker.

OTHER RON: No, you're not.

RON: How do you know?

OTHER RON: The way you said it. Jesus, are you a case.

RON: Then what am I? You seem to know it all. You tell me.

OTHER RON: No, I don't.

RON: Don't what?

OTHER RON: Know it all.

RON: Take a guess.

OTHER RON: You're just another uptight faggot who's hiding. I understand. Do you have any ice cream?

RON: No. I'm on a diet. Don't you really know who I am?

OTHER RON: I hope it doesn't come as a shock to you, but there must be a lot of people like me. How should I know?

RON: Actors do sometimes . From commercials. I run an ad agency. And I'm not going to give you any work.

OTHER RON: And if you see me in the street, you'll pass me right by.

RON: Probably. It depends who I'm with.

OTHER RON: It's your life. You want an apple? (RON *shakes his head no.*) You don't get very hungry for a successful approaching middle-aged man fighting off pudge. That's all right. The chunky look is in.

RON: Where are you from?

OTHER RON: That's the first personal question you've asked me.

RON: No, it's not. I asked what you did.

OTHER RON: That's not a question. That's a categorizer. If I'm a lawyer, I'm safe, respectable, a bit dull. If I'm a writer, hey, that's pretty interesting, but only if I've been published. Hairdressers and decorators aren't your scene. But actors! If I'm an actor, then I'm potentially dangerous because I want something from you.

RON: You must be a pretty experienced whore to be so authoritative about it all.

OTHER RON: That statement rates an automatic "Fuck you." I just don't make dramas where there are no dramas. I see a guy I like, I smile, say hi, talk, fuck, eat, reveal all. It's really not very complicated.

RON: Just like that?

OTHER RON: Just like that.

RON: Where can I find you?

OTHER RON: I'm in the phone book. That is if you'd asked my last name. W-r-i-g-h-t.

(*Lights down on them as the* NARRATOR *continues.*)

NARRATOR: We'll pick up on Ron later. He's really the least interesting of our stories. He'll eventually call Mr. Wright and they'll start off on some sort of relationship. For a while. Until Mr. Wright becomes Mr. Wrong and another Mr. Right comes along. Life will be a series of intended Mr. Rights and imagined Mr. Wrongs. And so it is perhaps for all of us. But it is a boring and uninteresting seesaw. At least Ron will go to his bed a rich man. And to his grave. He will have had his success, but then he never really asked much more of life than this. If he had, Mr. Wright would have been Mr. Right. Barry asked much more.

(*Lights down on the* NARRATOR *and up on* BARRY's *area. To our surprise,* LAURA *is back in bed with him. They are naked and there is a strangeness in the air.*)

BARRY: I want you to come with me, Laura.

LAURA: (*Softly.*) Where?

BARRY: Leave it to me. I'll take you there.

LAURA: Will you hurt me?

BARRY: I love you, Laura. I wouldn't hurt anyone I love.

LAURA: You love me?

BARRY: Yes.

LAURA: That's the first time you've said it.

BARRY: It's the first time I've felt it. I'm glad you came back to me.

LAURA: I've loved you for so long.

BARRY: Why do you love me?

LAURA: Because I do.

BARRY: Tell me that you love my body.

LAURA: I love your body.

BARRY: And my cock.

LAURA: I love your . . .

BARRY: Say it.

LAURA: (*Softly.*) Cock. I've loved you ever since I first saw you.

BARRY: You mustn't talk too much. Talk just gets in the way. I would like to wrap you up with these long white sheets. They'll be like my arms holding you. You'll be all mine—in my protection, and I shall love protecting you. Would you like me to protect you?

LAURA: Yes

BARRY: Good, because there's nothing more I would like to do. Nothing. Laura, dear Laura, my Laura, come with me and let me protect you. (*He has tied her arms gently with the sheets.*) Come with me. Come with me.

LAURA: I'm with you, Bar.

BARRY: I'm going to give you a tap on the back, a little hit slap. I want you to tell me that you like it.

LAURA: Don't hurt me, Bar. Please.

BARRY: I promised you I wouldn't. Didn't I?

LAURA: Yes.

BARRY: Is it all right, then?

LAURA: Yes.

BARRY: (*He slaps her very softly, brushingly.*) Would you like me to do it again?

LAURA: Yes.

BARRY: My Laura. (*Slaps her again, not quite so softly.*) Ask me to do it again.

LAURA: Do it again.

BARRY: Please.

LAURA: Please.

BARRY: Please harder.

LAURA: Please harder.

(BARRY *slaps her quite hard. She shivers, but nothing more.*)

BARRY: Would you like to do it to me?

LAURA: No.

BARRY: Are you sure?

LAURA: No. Would you like me to?

BARRY: Yes.

(*She slaps him feebly.*)

BARRY: That's my girl.

(*He suddenly hauls off and slaps her hard. She lets out a small little groan, and he quickly takes her in his arms.*)

BARRY: Oh, my baby, my little baby. I wouldn't hurt you. I love you. I love you.

(*Lights down on them and up on the* NARRATOR.)

NARRATOR: Laura had come back to Barry. She had gone one night and waited on his doorstep until he came home at three in the morning. He had wordlessly looked at her and taken her inside.

(*A quick, lightning flash of illumination. In the momentary glimpse we get, we see* LAURA *completely bound, hands and feet, to the bed, spread-eagle.* BARRY *is over her. He strikes her with a long thick belt, and she moans. Then the lights go quickly out. After a moment, the lights come up on the* NARRATOR, *sitting in* DICK's *chair, as* DICK, *in his white coat, lies on the couch.*)

NARRATOR: You knew about this aberration?

DICK: I knew.

NARRATOR: What did you do about it?

DICK: (*On the defensive.*) What's an aberration? It happens to turn both of them on. She came back and, in effect, asked for whatever she got. Somewhere inside of her she must have desired exactly whatever she got.

NARRATOR: You don't really accept that, do you? Jews didn't want to die in the ovens. People who stand in front of guns don't really want to be killed.

DICK: (*Very weary suddenly.*) Maybe they do. Well, just look—if we hadn't had centuries of some kind of exterminating—wars, ovens—think how many people we'd have to live with today.

NARRATOR: You don't really believe that.

DICK: I don't really believe that.

NARRATOR: So. You knew about this aberration?

DICK: Yes. I knew. (*Screaming.*) And I felt helpless!

NARRATOR: Did you talk to him?

(*Lights up on* BARRY, *standing dressed.*)

BARRY: (*Yelling at* DICK.) It's none of your damn business!

DICK: (*Who has come to carry on the argument with* BARRY *face-to-face.*) It is too my business. You are my friend.

BARRY: I am your friend, and I am telling you it's none of your goddamn business!

DICK: Then please don't send her out into the world looking so black and blue that any only half-concerned member of humanity would inquire as to her health.

BARRY: I'll be more careful next time.

DICK: You bastard.

BARRY: That, too, is no concern of yours.

DICK: The actions of my friends, indeed of all humanity, are always of concern to me.

BARRY: That is your great mistake.

(DICK *leaves* BARRY, *walks away from him and back to lie down on the couch.* BARRY *walks off.*)

DICK: (*Continuing to the* NARRATOR.) So that was it.

NARRATOR: I see.

DICK: No, you don't. Only I can see. And it's a void. In front of me. I am approaching a void. You think that constant exposure to the—aberrations of my fellow men is a soothing balm to my own sanity? You think my own soul is so elastic?

NARRATOR: For your own sake, I hope it is.

DICK: Barry is the survivor.

(*Lights down on both of them and up on* SUSAN, *who sits, still doing her needlepoint. Eventually* DICK *comes in without his white jacket.*)

SUSAN: Did you have a nice day at the office, dear?

(DICK *looks at her and then just walks away. She looks after him for a moment, then resumes her needlepoint.*)

(*The lights go down on* SUSAN *and come up on* BARRY. *He is clad only in shorts, and he is alone. On his bed, an assortment of ropes and a large, thick, long belt. He is fondling the belt, then suddenly he takes it and whams it powerfully against the mattress. He then throws himself down on the bed, almost in apology—and rubs himself against the ropes, squirming among them, slithering his arms and legs in and out of the coils. He wraps them quickly around himself, trying to tie himself up in some sudden strange submission to the ecstasy it gives him.*

Lights down on BARRY *and up on the* NARRATOR *and* DICK.)

NARRATOR: Barry is the survivor?

DICK: Because he doesn't want to do anything badly enough. And if he fails, it doesn't matter. He's bright, personable, and persuasive enough to always be that necessary extra handsome man the hostess needs for the dinner party. So he'll always eat. Right through middle-age to death. Barry is the survivor. You wait and see. And I hate him for it.

NARRATOR: Are you losing your grip?

DICK: A little.

NARRATOR: Would you like to go into the hospital for a little rest?

DICK: No. Not quite yet. I may still be all right.

NARRATOR: You'll let me know?

DICK: Yes.

(*Lights down on them and up on* SUSAN *and* LAURA, *talking.*)

SUSAN: I'm beginning to worry that he doesn't want to be a doctor anymore.

LAURA: What does he want to be?

SUSAN: Right now, a nothing.

LAURA: So let him be a nothing.

SUSAN: Well, I don't think I can, you see.

LAURA: Why not?

SUSAN: It isn't good enough.

LAURA: For you or for him?

SUSAN: For either of us.

LAURA: Shouldn't he be the judge of him? What would be good enough?

SUSAN: A lot of things. But not doing nothing.

LAURA: If he's not happy, you're not going to be happy either.

SUSAN: Oh, I can be happy. I'm very strong, you know. Women are very strong.

LAURA: I think sometimes that women being strong makes men weak.

SUSAN: I think sometimes that men being weak makes women strong.

LAURA: I suspect we approach our problems in different ways.

SUSAN: I suspect so.

(*Lights down on them and up on the* NARRATOR.)

NARRATOR: Susan was the daughter of a very rich family. She had been to the best of schools and been fed the best of food and been to the best of dentists. Into her slender body a great deal of money had been poured. Now she was married to the best of husbands . . . a doctor. Laura, a poor girl, is potentially the more vulnerable. In fact, the story of her progression from soap opera to stability is the story of survival.

(*Lights come up on* LAURA. *The* NARRATOR *steps back and listens to her.*)

LAURA: (*Caught up in her own emotion and hurt.*) I fell in love with him the first minute I saw him. It's as simple as that. Something passed between us; I saw it happen for him, too, I swear it. We had our first date the following Saturday, and at my place later we made love. It never happened like that for me before. He told me later he went out and fucked another girl the same night. Anyway, I had fallen asleep, after we had made love, only to be awakened by his getting dressed to go home. I was already in love with him, you see, and I had already fantasized the rest of our lives together. Now here he was leaving me already, and I was so overwhelmed with a sense of loss and abandonment that I tried to keep him from going home. That was my first and greatest mistake, and I would do anything in this world to go back to that moment and relive it and play it very coolly, to let him go and see him again the next day and take it slowly. I would have him today, I know, if I'd played it that way then.

(*In the middle of her speech, the* NARRATOR *has stepped into the darkness and been replaced by* DICK, *who now comes forward to* LAURA.)

DICK: (*Vehemently.*) Goddamn it! Why must these things be *played!*

LAURA: Because that's the way it's organized.

DICK: What use to you in any sensible mature long-range scheme of happiness is a man who abandons you on your first closeness, no matter how you had played it?!

LAURA: I don't think you understand.

DICK: Oh, you don't? You don't! It's you, you dumb, dim-witted, helpless, servile, crawling child—begging, needing, waiting to be fed—who doesn't understand. You deserve all the terror and pain you've encountered.

LAURA: Please, I think I'll go now.

DICK: (*Restraining her.*) Oh, no you don't. You came to me and you said, What am I going to do? He wants to tie me up and hit me with a belt, and I don't understand.

LAURA: (*Breaking free of him.*) He can also be kind and loving. There must be disagreeable aspects in each of our natures.

DICK: Wanting to hurt other people, symbolically, actually, unconsciously—or whatever kind of Vaseline you wish to smear over it—is sick.

LAURA: You use that word too much. I think you're too harsh. He loves me. And I've learned to be tolerant.

(DICK *just looks at her, shaking his head sadly. She walks off, and he stands there watching as she walks toward the rear of the stage. Then the lights come up on* BARRY *in bed with* ISABEL. LAURA *watches this for a long moment, not believing her eyes. Then, softly, slowly, she begins to shake, spasmodically, her whole body soon trembling in a fit.* DICK *walks over and tries to comfort her. She runs away from him. The lights go down on* BARRY *and* ISABEL *and come up on* SUSAN, *again doing her needlepoint, as* DICK *comes home to her.*)

SUSAN: Did you have a nice day at the office, dear?

DICK: Don't you ever say anything else?

SUSAN: What did you have for lunch today? Is that better?

DICK: No.

SUSAN: Well then, give me some guidelines.

DICK: I can't do that.

SUSAN: Maybe we should take a nice vacation somewhere.

DICK: Nice? That's your favorite word. I don't know you, Susan.

SUSAN: Of course you do.

DICK: Maybe there's not so much to know. You are so calm and cool and unruffled. Don't you have any pain or agony underneath your shiny surface?

SUSAN: Do you have to make everyone into a patient?

DICK: Everyone is a patient! There's no one sane left.

SUSAN: Perhaps you should change your line of work.

> (*He is so infuriated with her that he hauls off and slugs her. She takes it stoically, almost like a man. He rushes to take her in his arms, trying to comfort her. She stands woodenly as he embraces her as best he can.*)

DICK: We have nothing to talk about anymore. Hold me. Hold me.

SUSAN: Richard, get a hold of yourself.

DICK: No, I want you to get a hold of myself.

SUSAN: You know I don't like it when you act like this.

DICK: We have nothing to talk about anymore.

SUSAN: What are we doing now?

DICK: Passing words. It's a type of farting. (*Picks her up in his arms and carries her to their bed.*)

SUSAN: What are you doing?

DICK: I am going to make love to you.

SUSAN: I don't feel like it.

DICK: Then I'm going to tie you up and rape you.

SUSAN: I don't feel like that, either.

DICK: Then relax and enjoy it.

(*Starts tearing off both her clothes and his as best he can, through the next speeches.*)

SUSAN: It's the middle of the afternoon.

DICK: A perfect moment. Tranquil. Warm sunshine through the curtains.

SUSAN: Could you close the curtains?

DICK: No. I want to see the sunshine.

SUSAN: Everything's got to be your way.

DICK: This time, yes.

SUSAN: Why?

DICK: Because I am sick and miserable and unhappy, and charity begins at home. I am going crazy, Susan.

SUSAN: Nonsense.

DICK: Nonsense. Non-sense. That's exactly what it is.

(*They are both naked now, and he is sitting over her, looking down.*)

DICK: Look between my legs. Look at my friend.

SUSAN: Don't be vulgar.

DICK: My little friend. You will note my penis. That is the specific name for the male sexual organ, Richard's sexual organ, Richard's penis, Dick's dick. (*This causes him to start laughing.*)

SUSAN: (*Hating this and not wanting to listen.*) Richard, please stop.

DICK: Richard's penis belongs to Susan. Susan doesn't want it. Susan doesn't want any of Richard.

SUSAN: Stop it!

DICK: Richard's penis belongs to Susan by rights. It also belongs in Susan.

SUSAN: (*Struggling to get up.*) I won't have you talk this way.

(DICK *starts tying her up in the sheets, propped up against the back of the bed, so that she will look at him.*)

DICK: I want Susan to look at Richard's penis. It wants to go and hide. It doesn't want to get excited and say hello to Susan. It wants to go away and have a long sleep.

SUSAN: Stop what you're doing to me. I'll have to call a doctor.

DICK: I am the doctor.

SUSAN: The doctor is sick.

DICK: I use that word too much.

SUSAN: (*As he fastens the final bonds.*) Do you realize you are tying me up!

DICK: I'm tying you up, I'm tying you up. (*Wrinkles his forehead as some outside thought is getting through to him, which troubles him.*) I want to hurt you. I want to hurt you. Wanting to hurt other people, symbolically, actually, Vaseline . . .

(*He suddenly rushes away from her, out into the darkness of stage center, naked, with only a spot on him, the voices now coming from the loud-speaker, pursuing him as the Furies, while strange pictures of unfamil-iar strangers fill the back wall in huge blowups.*)

PATIENT ONE'S VOICE: Nobody loves me.

PATIENT TWO'S VOICE: I don't love anybody. I don't know how love feels.

PATIENT THREE'S VOICE: I eat too much, get too fat, and hate myself.

PATIENT FOUR'S VOICE: I think I'm having a heart attack and am going to die.

PATIENT FIVE'S VOICE: I think my husband is going to leave me. I can't go on alone.

PATIENT SIX'S VOICE: I have this constant feeling that you're following behind me and licking my ass.

DICK: I can't help you. (*A cry of pain and anguish.*) *I can't help you!*

(*He is now in his office area, pulling down medical books from their shelves, tearing out pages and pages. He walks to a picture of SUSAN and one of ANNIE, and he rips them out of their frames.*)

DICK: Good-bye, Annie, good-bye, Susan, good-bye, Dad, good-bye Dick, adick a dick.

(*The* NARRATOR *in a white coat comes over with a white hospital robe, the kind for patients that ties up the back.* DICK *lets him put it on him.*)

DICK: I can't help them. Help me! Help *me!*

NARRATOR: (*His arms around* DICK.) And so Dick begins his descent into hell. The pieces would have to fall apart before they could be put together again. We call it the Humpty-Dumpty syndrome.

(*The* NARRATOR *leads* DICK *over to the central table, which is now an examining table. A harsh hospital light is lowered. The* NARRATOR *helps* DICK *lie down; he is aided by another man in a white coat, who is seen to be* DICK'S FATHER.)

NARRATOR: A is good.

DICK'S FATHER: B is bad, and C is hopeless.

NARRATOR: D, on the other hand, shows some promise. Not a big promise. Just a little promise.

DICK: (*Mumbling, as if in a drugged state.*) Help me. Help me.

DICK'S FATHER: E and F—forget about. G I personally wouldn't trust, but my colleague from the old country says he has seen worse and that patient lived. H through K. . . . (*Shrugs.*)

DICK: Help me.

NARRATOR: L, M, N, O, P—Okay with a lot of rest and no tobacco, alcohol, starch, sweets, or nighttime hanky-panky.

DICK'S FATHER: Q—well, we all know about Q, don't we?

NARRATOR: R to V, with God on our side and sending a blessing, will possibly give us a few more years. W, X, Y ... perfectly fine, but they're not too important.

DICK'S FATHER: Z I give my personal guarantee would never work in a million years.

(DICK'S FATHER *continues to poke around* DICK*'s body in examination as the* NARRATOR *walks stage center.*)

NARRATOR: While we're exploring the areas of personal hells, personal terrors, and while Dick is, so to speak, under the weather, let's take a look at the inner secret darknesses of Ron and Barry.

(*The lights come up on* RON, *dressed in a flowing caftan bathrobe, facing in the direction of* DICK, *as if he had been watching it or at least sensing it. Suddenly, and quite peculiarly, he begins to dance. The gestures are awkward, like a novice's imitation of how he thinks a ballet dancer dances. It is all rather sad,* RON *trying to do this crude dance. The lights go dim as the* NARRATOR *continues.*)

(*As* RON *continues dancing in the dim light.*) Do you think it's funny, Ron dancing? When he was a little kid, full of freedom and full of happy enthusiasms trying to get out of him, he used to dance around in front of his family. His father called him a sissy for it. That single word sissy was as wounding as calling a Jew a kike. He never forgot it, and he never danced around again so anyone could see him.

(*The dim lights are still on the prone body of* DICK *and on* RON *dancing, and they now come up on* BARRY, *lying in a golden light on the floor with a girl who looks a little like* LAURA *but is in fact his* SISTER.)

Barry's personal inner terror, if you're ready, was that he feared he subconsciously wanted to sleep with his sister. She wasn't well in the head and several times suffered such fear and trembling that she had to be taken away. Once when she came home, they went for a walk in the corn fields, and she did reach over and touch his lips.

(BARRY'S SISTER *on stage does so.*)

He asked her outright if she had wanted to sleep with him and all she did was caress the side of his face and touch his lips again.

(*She does so.*)

BARRY'S SISTER: (*To* BARRY, *who finds this scene exceedingly painful.*) I went to Chicago and I took an apartment and I lived by myself. I'd look out the window and I'd see the lake and . . . I couldn't see the other side, but I knew that far across there was our farm and our house and my room. So I knew there was another side, way over there, somewhere on the other side. But I couldn't see it. And that made me very sad. So then I thought, I won't look anymore, and I pulled the blinds tightly and closed the drapes and turned on the lights, and guess what? I was frightened. And I thought: Barry will come, Barry will come. So I hired myself an ambulance, and I came back home on a moving bed, lying back all the way, back, back, rolling along, all the way home. And I waited and waited and waited, and finally you came home.

BARRY: And now you feel much better?

BARRY'S SISTER: Yes, I do.

BARRY: But what will happen when I go away again?

BARRY'S SISTER: I'll have to start waiting for you all over again.

BARRY: But I'll have to go away again sometime.

(*She reaches out to touch his face, softly. As she does so, he speaks.*)

I'm going away tomorrow.

(*She withdraws her hand quickly.*)

You're sick and I can't help you. Does that make me sick, too? I could fuck you. That's what you want, down deep, and for all I know it's what I want, too. But you'll have to get your help from a man who's not your brother. (*He reaches over and touches her cheek, caresses her lips, perhaps even toying with the idea of going further, certainly feeling the atmosphere of the moment so tangibly that he could perform some subconscious act that he would regret later.*)

(*The dim lights stay up on the three areas for a moment and then go out.*)

NARRATOR: Our continuing saga. Why not tell of heroes? Do we have them? Or only men like these?

(*The* NARRATOR *walks over to* DICK, *who is now sitting in a chair, wearing a hospital bathrobe.*)

DICK: (*To the* NARRATOR.) I always hated Sundays. My folks, they never got dressed on Sundays. Just bathrobes and saggy bodies all day. And no proper meals. Just reach into the icebox and eat for yourself. No one looked after anyone on Sundays. How dare they have made my childhood so ugly?

NARRATOR: Don't you really want to help people anymore? Your records seem to indicate you were a good doctor with some degree of success.

DICK: No. I don't want to help anyone anymore.

NARRATOR: What do you want to do?

DICK: Kill myself or make a lot of money.

NARRATOR: That's it?

DICK: That's it.

> (*The lights go down on them and come up on* DICK*'s apartment area. A big sign, reading "Welcome Home, Dick" is strung up. A record of college glee club songs is playing.* RON *and* BARRY *stand, waiting for* DICK*'s arrival. They are nervous and say nothing but move around,* BARRY *tidying up,* RON *checking himself in the mirror.* RON *has put on some weight, but* BARRY *looks pretty much the same. After a few moments,* LAURA *rushes in with a present. She sees that she's made it on time but senses that no one is in the mood for talking. She and* BARRY *barely exchange looks; he is almost resentful that she has come.* BARRY *continues to straighten things up, and she, nervously, does likewise. Finally, the door opens and* DICK *comes in, followed by* SUSAN *and the* NARRATOR. DICK *looks different, older, more reserved; his hair is now much longer and he wears jeans. Still no one speaks. The* NARRATOR *nods and leaves.* DICK *comes to each of his friends, and after a brief moment, he reaches out to embrace them. It is a touching moment, particularly since no words have been spoken.*)

DICK: (*To* RON.) Don't you look spiffy.

RON: A little nervous. I've got a date.

DICK: What's to be nervous about?

RON: What will I talk about?

DICK: Same things you always talk about—you're getting fatter, you're losing your hair . . .

(*This breaks the ice.* RON *feels his stomach and smooths out his hair.*)

RON: Do I do that?

BARRY: Who is she?

RON: She's . . . someone special.

BARRY: They're all someone special.

DICK: Perhaps he might work out this time.

(*He looks kindly at* RON; RON *is embarrassed by the use of "he."* DICK *pats him paternally on the shoulder.*)

How's advertising? Could I become as rich as you?

RON: You're not leaving the world of the mind? I won't let you.

DICK: No money in it.

BARRY: No money in minds.

RON: Plenty of money in mindlessness. That's me.

(*He pulls out a huge blowup of the* OTHER RON, *posed in an ad layout with lettering, which* RON *now proclaims.*)

Ultima Now for Men!

BARRY: You're kidding.

RON: Our research shows that men now want to stink as much as women.

DICK: Very impressive. Not that I find that particularly surprising. My research has shown that men have long felt that they stink more than women.

RON: True. True. A different kind of stink, perhaps.

DICK: I have found a stink's a stink.

BARRY: True. A stink's a stink.

RON: Ultima Now. A stink for today's stinker.

(*The three laugh softly.* DICK *sees* LAURA *and comes over to her.*)

LAURA: Hello, Dick. How are you?

DICK: I are fine.

LAURA: You looks just fine.

SUSAN: (*Standing apart.*) He is just fine.

DICK: There. You see.

LAURA: Dick . . . I'm sorry about a lot of things.

DICK: Don't be. You seem to be pretty together, and so does he. I guess you didn't need me at all.

LAURA: I've brought you a present.

(*She quickly pulls open her present and, with* SUSAN'*s help, unrolls one of those Yale blue banners, reading "For God, for Country, and for Dick."* DICK *stands back and admires it, nodding his head.* SUSAN, *as throughout, continues to keep a sharp eye on* DICK, *as if he might suddenly either break down or perform some act strange to her.*)

DICK: A most opulent present. My first present in my new life. Chapter two.

SUSAN: Wonderful Chapter two.

RON: Shit, it's still chapter one. I never could understand why you went into that place anyway.

DICK: To see how the other half lives.

BARRY: How does it live?

DICK: Same as everywhere. In confusion.

BARRY: Might be a nice rest. Food any good?

DICK: Fair.

RON: Can't complain, then.

DICK: I loved every minute of it. Ultima Now for Dick. (*Looks at the poster of* OTHER RON.) What are you going to do with him?

RON: He is going to be one famous lad. One hundred thousand dollars a year in modeling fees, his picture all over the world, he'll be an instant celebrity. He'll have the five minutes the world allots us all to be famous in.

DICK: He's got a nice face. (*Pointedly, to* RON.) Perhaps he might work out.

RON: (*Evasively.*) Yeah, that, too. I don't know him too well.

BARRY: (*Gently.*) Get to know your fellow workers.

(SUSAN *wheels out a cake with candles, and they all sing "For he's a jolly good fellow" while the glee club record raises in volume. The lights go down on them. The* NARRATOR *steps forward, holding a book.*)

NARRATOR: A touching, romantic scene, man welcoming home his fellow man, brother to brother. (*Reads from the book.*) "Life is indeed dangerous, but not in the way morality would have us believe. It is indeed unmanageable, but the essence is romantic beauty." That was written in 1910. We've forgotten more than we learned.

(*The lights come up on the big table. Four men sit around it, the four fathers of our four young men.*)

No, this is not our four young men in thirty years' time. At least I don't think it is. Or I hope it's not. Or who can tell? In any event, this scene really took place after much of what we still have yet to tell you. After John's death, for one thing. I just thought it might make more sense to slot it in now. These are the four fathers, of our four young men, who came together when it was too late.

(*The one father we don't know,* RON'S FATHER, *starts off. He is a wiry man, a farmer.*)

RON'S FATHER: My name is Gatz. I'm Ron's Father, but I doubt we'll ever be close.

DICK'S FATHER: What kind of father doesn't see his son for so long?

RON'S FATHER: It was his choice. He left very young.

DICK'S FATHER: And you just let him go?

RON'S FATHER: How do you keep a stray dog home? He never got in touch. There wasn't much I could do.

BARRY'S FATHER: Doesn't seem as if you did too good a job.

RON'S FATHER: Perhaps not.

BARRY'S FATHER: I've at least gone out looking for my boy on occasion. Left the farm and came all the way to New York just to see him.

NARRATOR: (*From the place at the table he's taken.*) Were you aware your son was a very unhappy homosexual?

RON'S FATHER: (*Embarrassed.*) No. (*Coughing.*) No, no, I didn't know that. Well . . . that's . . . too bad.

JOHN'S FATHER: It would appear you weren't too good a father. He had no image to relate to.

DICK'S FATHER: That's a shame.

RON'S FATHER: I don't much understand, but, no, I wasn't a very good father. He was a strange boy to me. I didn't understand him and I didn't love him. He wanted everything romantic, but it somehow come out a battle. We rubbed each other the wrong way. Come to think of it, his mother was pretty romantic. A dreamer. Not that it did much good.

NARRATOR: Perhaps Ron just went out to look for a more romantic life.

RON'S FATHER: Maybe. Sure as hell, it warn't with us.

DICK'S FATHER: Life's no romance. It's dangerous and it's not easy to find the beauty.

BARRY'S FATHER: It's a battle all right.

RON'S FATHER: This country is really too fat. Fat in the bank and fat in the fanny.

DICK'S FATHER: Also too dirty. Dirty sex and dirty spoons.

BARRY'S FATHER: The old days were the good ones.

RON'S FATHER: Now, don't you go tellin' me you want the old days back again.

JOHN'S FATHER: When I was very young, an experience occurred to me which has made it extremely difficult ever since to consider anything either romantic or beautiful. I would repeat it now but for its unpleasantness. I only mention it to illustrate that often early experiences color an entire life. And so it might be with our own sons.

BARRY'S FATHER: What was it? You can tell us.

JOHN'S FATHER: It's quite repulsive.

RON'S FATHER: I've stood up to pretty gamy stuff.

DICK'S FATHER: Perhaps it could help us learn.

JOHN'S FATHER: Do you think that the three of you could still learn?

NARRATOR: The consensus is that we'd like to hear it.

JOHN'S FATHER: My name is Samuel Clayman.

BARRY'S FATHER: I know that name.

DICK'S FATHER: Who's that? Who is he?

JOHN'S FATHER: I'm an author—perhaps not of books that you've read or heard about. But in my own area, I've done quite well. Seventeen novels published—in England they do them in a uniform edition. I have twice been put forward for the Nobel Prize.

RON'S FATHER: What's so gamy about that?

JOHN'S FATHER: Nothing, of course. I state my credentials solely to establish my credibility.

DICK'S FATHER: I believe you.

RON'S FATHER: For Christ's sake, what happened?

JOHN'S FATHER: (*After a nod from the Narrator.*) When I was progressing through puberty, I lived with my parents in a housing project. Next door was a young man going through medical school, or so he said. I had been forbidden the pur-chase of comic books by my parents, and this young medical student offered the exchange of these forbidden fruits in return for allowing him certain physical experimentation.

RON'S FATHER: He buggered you?!

JOHN'S FATHER: No. He used his fingers to explore my rectal area.

(*All the fathers shake their heads.*)

RON'S FATHER: Sounds almost like a buggering to me.

JOHN'S FATHER: I found it both extremely painful and terrifying. I have never forgotten it.

NARRATOR: How do you think it affected your further development?

JOHN'S FATHER: It soured me. I could never conceive of life as anything resembling a romantic beauty. But I've been fortunate. I've been able to create out of this memory and pain, or should I say memory of pain. Others have not been so lucky. Others very close to me, I know. So perhaps *I* have been the bad father.

RON'S FATHER: Well, all your fame and stuff, you gave him that there image you talked of. That you say I didn't give my boy. Hell, my boy would have been tickled pink to have a famous daddy.

JOHN'S FATHER: No, I think I terrified him.

DICK'S FATHER: Because you were so famous?

JOHN'S FATHER: No. I think I terrified him because of something I once did. Or rather said.

BARRY'S FATHER: What was that?

JOHN'S FATHER: I'm not certain I wish to speak of it.

DICK'S FATHER: Not again. Tell us already.

NARRATOR: I think once again we'd like to hear what you have to say—or what you said to him.

(JOHN'S FATHER *looks out into space. The lights go down on the others, and* JOHN'S FATHER *addresses perhaps his son.*)

JOHN'S FATHER: Beware the overbearing pressure of today's sexuality. Beware the innocent slipping into anonymity, the giving of bodies thoughtlessly. It is the most precious thing, the body, that you have to give. And John had said: "I don't think mine is as spiritual a gift to give as all that." And I had said: Whatever it is, it's yours. And therein lies its highest price.

(*The lights go down on him. They go up on, strangely enough,* RON. *In the dim light, he is again performing the strange dancing movements, now half-naked, around his apartment, trying to be a ballet dancer, reaching out to some unseen audience, listening to some unheard music in his ears. The lights come up on the* NARRATOR.)

NARRATOR: So the Fathers talked on. As it turned out, it didn't make much difference that they did. Ron's Father forgot to mention how his boy danced around the living room, full of spirit and happiness, only to be yelled down. Years later, when, in the heat of a violent argument with Dick, who had confronted him, not about his homosexuality specifically, but about his inability to have a satisfactory and open relationship with another man, Ron had said:

(*The lights still on* RON, *who stands there in his seminakedness, speaking as if to* DICK, *as if to no one.*)

RON: Yes, goddamn it, I don't want to see anyone or hear anyone say "Come here" or "Freeze" or "I need you" or "Put your hands up." I'll go to the parks or the places by the beach in the summer. There, in the moonlight, on white sandy beaches, at three o'clock in the morning, I'll join four or five or six other guys. I won't know their names and they won't know mine and someone will pull my pants down and someone else will kiss me. And—can you imagine the feeling of being felt all over by many men—a hand soothing across my chest—someone else's on my back—and then leaning far over, back, back, into someone else's arms, many arms, as a stranger takes my cock and I come.

(*The lights go down on* RON *and up on the* NARRATOR.)

NARRATOR: And how about Barry?

(*The lights come up on* BARRY, *now with* ISABEL *in bed, in identical movements to those of his opening scene with* LAURA.)

BARRY: You're very beautiful. I find you very beautiful.

ISABEL: I think . . . I find you beautiful, too.

BARRY: Do you?

ISABEL: Yes. I didn't know how you felt and . . . I'd been wondering.

BARRY: Were you?

ISABEL: Now I feel much better. Do you think we could take a walk? I suddenly feel like taking a walk.

BARRY: I prefer staying here. But no, let's walk, if you'd like that better.

ISABEL: If you'd rather stay here . . .

BARRY: I have to go away, you know, back to see my sick sister in Indiana. I don't think you and I should get too involved until I make some major decisions about my life. (*As* ISABEL *is obviously very upset.*) What's the matter, Isabel? What's the matter. What's troubling you?

ISABEL: Goddamn it, it's too late to tell me that now.

BARRY: I think you'd better go now, Isabel.

ISABEL: No!

BARRY: I think you're very beautiful.

ISABEL: Would it make you very sad if I walked out of your life right this minute? Because that's what I'm about to do.

BARRY: I don't believe that people just walk out of people's lives, just like that, forever.

ISABEL: You don't? Well, ciao, Barry.

(*And she starts pulling on her clothes and walking off. He shrugs and turns away to ignore her action. The lights go down on him and come up on the* NARRATOR.)

NARRATOR: It was a woman who once said: "I dwell in possibility." Well, what does happen when you've been hungry and wanted food, what happens after you've eaten the ice cream and the apples? The simplest cries of pain seem very silly.

(*The lights come up on* DICK. *He is lying alone in his bed and looking at the ceiling.*)

DICK: I'm still unhappy, and this world shits.

(*Lights down on him and up on* RON. *He, too, lies on his bed, looking up at his ceiling.*)

RON: I am fucking unhappy, and this world shits.

(*Lights down on him and now up on* BARRY, *positioned the same way.*)

BARRY: I'm unhappy, and this world shits.

(*Lights down on him, then up on the* NARRATOR, *then dimly, softly, up on the three men on their beds.*)

NARRATOR: And so, for the moment, we'll leave them. Dick will go off to a rest home in the country to continue his search into how the other half lives. Ron now buys his own yacht and sails away on a long trip. Barry goes back home again to Indiana because he still can't write anything beyond an opening sentence, and without Laura or Isabel he has no toys to bore him. No one had thought about John for a long time. John had written that he and Jenifer were going to North Africa, but no one had received the letter. And so time moves on. New York, with less air breathed by more people, makes growth, even for those already conditioned to surviving as half breathers, more difficult to achieve. But our four, for the moment, are not in New York;

obviously some airs are healthier than others. And with growth, and time—for healing and for health—how useful the future tense. Whether our four thought in terms so cosmic, beyond the casual fear of an unpleasant tomorrow which besets us all, is doubtful. But the situation would soon change. John is coming home.

End of Act One.

Act Two

Time: *Three months later.*

At rise, the lights are quite dim and it takes a few moments for our eyes to become accustomed to this dimness. It looks as if perhaps the stage is empty, but soon we realize that, in JOHN's *area, someone is sitting rigidly in a wheelchair. It is* JOHN *himself. He stares into space; he is completely immobile, motionless, and will stay so. He is catatonic. He sits there in the dim light for many moments. At length,* JENIFER *comes into the apartment, carrying some groceries. She turns on a light, looks at her husband for a brief moment, and goes to unpack the groceries. In a far corner, half-empty suitcases are stacked. She comes back to* JOHN *carrying a container of yogurt and a spoon, from which she proceeds to attempt, as best she can, to feed him. It is a difficult job, and her growing frustration is evident. When she can no longer spoon-feed him, she moves away from him and absentmindedly feeds herself the rest, while gazing at him blankly. The lights go down.*

After a long moment of darkness, the lights again come up on JOHN, *still sitting in the dim apartment. Again, after a moment,* JENIFER *comes in, wearing a different dress, now carrying an assortment of boxes from Saks and Bergdorf's. She puts down her boxes. She looks at her husband, then goes to sit on a chair. She just sits there. She doesn't know what to do. The lights go down again.*

After another moment of darkness, the lights come up a third time on JOHN *sitting in the dimness. After a moment,* DICK *lets himself in and walks into the apartment, carrying a stack of mail. He goes to a hall table, where a huge stack of mail has gathered, and after flipping through the letters he is holding, he adds them to the pile. Then he goes and gets a watering can and goes offstage a moment to fill it with water. When he returns, he is heading toward a row of plants when he finally sees* JOHN *in the dim light. He can't believe his eyes and quickly turns on a light. In the brightness, he drops the can and rushes to* JOHN, *frightened of what he is thinking. He kneels in front of him.*

DICK: (S*oftly.*) John . . . tell me what's wrong. Tell me what's happened.

(JOHN *doesn't answer or even look at* DICK.)

(*Sharply.*) John! Answer me.

(*Still no response. Suddenly, after a long pause,* DICK *hauls off and slaps* JOHN *viciously.* JOHN *doesn't even blink.* DICK *lets out a cry of horror and pain and leans over to take* JOHN *in his arms and cradle and rock him as best he can, softly sobbing and moaning for his friend's anguish. At length,* JENIFER *comes in.* DICK *releases* JOHN *and walks over to the other side of the room to talk with* JENIFER.)

Will you please tell me what's wrong?

JENIFER: I'm afraid.

DICK: So am I. What's wrong?

JENIFER: I'm afraid I've got nothing to say.

DICK: Why does he just sit there?

JENIFER: I'm afraid you'll have to ask him that.

DICK: I tried to. He doesn't seem to want to answer. Perhaps you've noticed that, too. (*When she doesn't answer.*) I said, perhaps you've noticed that, too.

JENIFER: I heard you.

DICK: Hearing me is not enough! I would like a response. A factual response of what the fuck has happened.

JENIFER: I'm not certain it concerns you anymore.

DICK: Oh, you're not? Well, if the janitor came into this apartment to fix a runny toilet and saw your husband sitting like that, it would concern even him. That's how sick your husband looks.

JENIFER: He doesn't have a fever. I . . . I took his temperature.

DICK: That's very considerate. He's not suffering physically.

JENIFER: (*Covering her ears.*) Don't.

DICK: (*Pulling down her hands.*) Don't what? What happened? When did you get back? Why didn't you call? What did you do to him?

JENIFER: (*Defensively.*) What did *I* do to him? Why is it me? Why is it my fault? Why is it?

DICK: Suppose you tell me. If you didn't do anything, there's no need to be so defensive. Tell me.

JENIFER: Don't you understand? I didn't do anything, I didn't do anything. But even if I didn't do anything, I'm afraid I might have done something.

(*She runs off, and* DICK *goes over to* JOHN *again.*)

DICK: John. I'm your old friend and I'm a doctor, too. So I'm a doctor *and* your friend. You look like you don't feel well. Like there's something troubling you. Wouldn't you like to tell me, to try to tell me?

(JOHN *doesn't move. He still is looking into space.* DICK *sees that* JENIFER
is now standing in the corner, watching them.)

DICK: Would you please leave us alone?

(JENIFER *goes off.*)

See? She's left us alone now. Now you can tell me what it's all
about and no one will know but us. You and me. Your old
friend. Your roommate, Dick. We used to share lots of secrets,
didn't we. Tell me what secrets you've got now. (*No response;
sharply.*) John! Tell me what's inside of you, hurting you!

(JENIFER *comes back in.*)

JENIFER: You see.

DICK: (*Walking to her side of the stage.*) I want to take him away and
put him in a hospital.

JENIFER: I won't commit him.

DICK: I didn't say commit him. I said put him in a hospital.

JENIFER: He's crazy. He's lost his mind. He doesn't talk or eat or even
sleep for all I know. I've married a crazy man. I've married a
crazy man. I can't . . . bear . . . stand it.

DICK: We can try to make him better, Jenifer.

JENIFER: I . . . don't want anybody to know. Don't you understand?

DICK: But you can't keep him here like he is.

JENIFER: He's going to be all right. He'll . . . he'll . . . he'll . . . he'll . . .

DICK: No, he won't. Jenifer, I don't give a shit if you let me take him
or not, I'm going to take him. Because if you don't let me, and

anything more happens, it's going to be on your head. Assuming, of course, that it isn't on your head already.

JENIFER: Of all three of his friends, I expected you to be the most understanding. Isn't a doctor supposed to be impartial? Check everything out before he makes his diagnosis? It hasn't been easy on me, you know!

DICK: (*More kindly.*) No, I guess it hasn't. But I only wonder why you haven't done anything.

JENIFER: (*A racking cry.*) I didn't know what to do!

DICK: (*Simply.*) I don't believe you.

(*And he turns to go. The lights go down on* JENIFER *and up on* SUSAN, *who looks up as* DICK *approaches her.*)

SUSAN: I'm your second wife and your third serious involvement. How many mistakes can you afford to make in your lifetime?

DICK: Quite a few.

SUSAN: Well, I can't afford to make too many. Maybe not any.

DICK: And that, my dear, is the difference between us.

SUSAN: You must have known that when you married me.

DICK: Yes.

SUSAN: Then why did you marry me?

DICK: I loved you. I thought I could work it out for both of us. I couldn't. I'm sorry. I take full responsibility, and you may so tell your lawyer.

SUSAN: You did a cruel and heartless thing.

DICK: Until this moment I did not realize it. I accept full responsibility.

(DICK *turns and leaves* SUSAN. *The lights go down on her and up on his father, who sits at the table, eating alone. His father looks repulsive, his white skin sweating on this hot night, sitting in his shorts and T-shirt, with a small towel hanging around his neck to mop away the perspiration.*)

DICK'S FATHER: It's hot.

DICK: Why don't you let me buy you an air conditioner?

DICK'S FATHER: I'm allergic.

DICK: You'll get used to it.

DICK'S FATHER: I'm already used to sweating. Why don't you let me sweat in peace?

DICK: Okay. Perpetuate your agony.

DICK'S FATHER: I'm glad your mother isn't here to see how her son is such a thoughtless young man to his father . . .

DICK: I'm divorcing my wife.

DICK'S FATHER: . . . and such a thoughtless young husband to his wife. Your mother would be very disappointed.

DICK: (*Shrugging and leaving his father.*) Good-bye Poppa. Happy death.

(*And* DICK *walks out on him. He walks over to where* JOHN *is still in his wheelchair and stands for a moment looking down at him, as if trying to look inside of him for some sort of answer.* RON *and* BARRY *quietly come and join him, all three of them now looking down at their good friend.* RON *and* BARRY *have both arrived with suitcases, which they leave at the door to* JOHN's *apartment. After a long moment of bewilderment,* BARRY *turns and walks to the other side of the room, soon followed by* RON *and* DICK. *They stand looking at each other now, these three who have not seen one another for several months. They notice changes.* RON *flips* DICK*'s long hair. Slowly they shake hands and put arms around shoulders.*)

RON: What do you think it is, Doctor?

BARRY: I bet it's her.

DICK: Maybe. Maybe not.

BARRY: You're equivocating.

DICK: Two sides to every story. Anyway, I don't know either side yet.

BARRY: I bet she slammed the door on him, closed up those fat little legs very tightly.

DICK: I suspect it's more than that.

BARRY: It's never really more than that. She walked out on him. Left him high and dry in the middle of the North African desert.

RON: A filthy place, North Africa. We shot some commercials there. If she walked out on him, why is she still with him?

DICK: Guilt. I suspect that if he became a basket case, it has something to do with his trying to keep her with him.

RON: Wow. What incredible need.

BARRY: He became a basket case so she wouldn't leave him. He therefore thinks he loves her.

DICK: A reasonable diagnosis.

RON: What are you going to do?

DICK: It's not going to be up to me. But whatever it's going to be, it's not going to be pleasant.

(*The* NARRATOR *now joins them, dressed as a doctor in white.*)

NARRATOR: Before we go on to the next step, medically, which is a difficult step and an unpleasant step, I wanted to try one last attempt, of a more personal nature, to try to snap him out of it. I thought, comforted by the three of you—trying your damnedest to get through to him—he might respond. I don't know. It's a long shot and probably won't work. But please try your damnedest anyway, will you?

(*He leaves them alone with* JOHN. *The three stand in front of him nervously. Finally* RON *steps forward and makes the first attempt.*)

RON: Hey, fella. Hey, John. Say hello. Will you say hello? Say hello to your old buddies. Ask us what we're doing and how we are.

BARRY: Old Ron's a big deal now. Lots of bread. Prestige. A great apartment. But I'm still a little shit. Why, I'm still such a little shit that the rent man is breaking down my door. And it's not a very firm door to begin with.

RON: I'm still single. Barry's still single.

DICK: And I'm about to become single again, too.

(RON *and* BARRY *react to this with surprise.* DICK *makes a shrugging, helpless gesture.*)

BARRY: So you see, listen, John, if it didn't work out—you can be single again, too.

DICK: Nothing is irrevocable. Free—remember what it was like to be free?

(JOHN *makes absolutely no response.*)

RON: I guess he doesn't remember.

BARRY: Maybe he's free now. Freer than we'll ever be.

RON: No, don't say that! (*He suddenly lunges for* JOHN *and starts shaking him forcefully from the shoulders.*) Goddammit, John, snap out of it. We want you back. We need you back. Don't cave in on us. That makes it harder on us. We need you.

BARRY: (*Pushing* RON *aside and kneeling in front of* JOHN.) Listen. Enough bullshit. You were left? Correct? Well, listen, I was left once upon a time, too. The old lady just went away with the old man, tits, milk, and all. And I crawled around in the dark and cried a lot. Boy, did I cry. And one day you stop crying.

DICK: (*Kneeling beside* BARRY.) Maybe you'd like to cry. Would you like to cry first, John? It's okay to cry. We'll cry with you. Christ, how we want to cry.

RON: (*Kneeling now as well.*) Come on, John boy, let it out. A good healthy cry is like a good healthy shit. And we know how good that makes us feel.

DICK: John, it really is all right to cry.

(*The three of them may be close to tears themselves, but* JOHN *remains as before. The* NARRATOR *comes in and sees that it has been to no avail.*)

NARRATOR: Okay.

(*Two nurses wheel in a hospital table and lift* JOHN, *with the help of the men, onto it. They then push him to stage center, where an elaborate piece of machinery is waiting. A large overhead hospital light comes down over* JOHN *on the table. The nurses begin to attach the wires of the machinery to him.* DICK, RON, *and* BARRY *watch. The* NARRATOR *speaks as* JOHN *is being prepared.*)

NARRATOR: The purpose of electric shock therapy, or EST, also called ECT, electric convulsive therapy, is simply to give the system a jolt. It is an elementary, if crude, attempt to put the marbles back in place. It is a type of therapy, formerly quite prevalent in this country and abroad, that has gone out of fashion, though it is still used quite extensively in Great Britain. Its use is thought permissible when there seems to be no other way. Then the patient is placed in a prone position, given a small amount of muscle-relaxing sedation, and a hard object is placed in his mouth so that he cannot bite his tongue in two. Or an S-tube is pushed down his throat to keep the tongue down and the airways open. Vaseline jelly is spread at the several contact points, and the wires are laid into the jelly. An amount of electricity equal to one and one-half millivolts will be pumped from this machine into John's head. He will hopefully then have a ten-second seizure, like an epileptic seizure. The electroencephalogram, or EEG, waves in the brain must show this convulsion for there to be any benefit. Why it works, nobody knows. (*He starts toward* JOHN, *then remembers some additional information.*) The normal course is six of these, though often you can go up to fifteen or sixteen treatments, given every two days. We're going to stick with six. We won't be seeing it, but in his head, there is successively more minor confusion and amnesia after each treatment, though this goes away after a few hours. (*He again starts toward* JOHN, *but again remembers something he still hasn't relayed.*) It takes two hours after each shock for there to be any reaction.

(*He now goes to* JOHN. *Everyone watches. There is a long moment of tableau and silence. Then the doctor quietly presses the button. The sound of hissing electricity. Everyone looks at* JOHN. *After a second, his body convulses violently for the ten seconds, almost horribly, since we are not used to this, then stops. The lights go out completely into blackness, then come up again after a moment.*)

(*Announcing.*) Shock Number One. No response from the patient.

(*Everyone walks off the stage.* JOHN'*s body remains there, still connected to the machine. Lights go low on him, but he will remain in view throughout the scenes following each treatment. The lights go up on* DICK, *lying on an analyst's couch.*)

(*Without his white coat.*) Dick went back to his first doctor. (*The* NARRATOR *now goes to sit behind* DICK, *in the classic analyst's position. The lights go dim on him so that he is hardly seen.*)

DICK: I wrote you a letter once, saying I was happy.

NARRATOR: I remember receiving it.

DICK: I simply cannot recall why I wrote it—or what feelings prompted it—what were those moments and how could I recapture them. I think I wrote it to please you.

(*There is no response.*)

Is that your only response?

NARRATOR: How would you have me respond?

DICK: So it's still always necessary to answer a question with a question. It's very cold in here.

NARRATOR: Shall I turn on the heat?

DICK: I wrote it to please you! I thought, That man who helped me, whom I visited every day for ten years of my life, is getting old, is going to die shortly, and I am feeling good today, so I'll write and tell him, and he'll think I've done a satisfactory job with that lad. (*Pause; still no response;* DICK *shrugs.*) Still not talking? All these years and cat still got your tongue. What a quiet life you've led. You can help how many people in your lifetime? Fifty? Ten years each; five to eight times a day. Say eight. A working life of at the most forty years. That's not even fifty people. Were we worth it? A lifetime of your devotion?

NARRATOR: I thought so. Think so.

DICK: A-ha! A simple declarative sentence. Listen, there has to be a faster way.

NARRATOR: There is no faster way.

DICK: Only because Siggie said so.

NARRATOR: Only because experience has shown me that there are no shortcuts. Lifelong sores take years to heal.

DICK: All the searching and still no cure for death from cancer. But there's some relief from the pain.

NARRATOR: Children always need instant gratification.

DICK: And adults must learn to suffer. (*Sits up.*) The simple act of returning to you is bondage. I think it's time to tell old Siggie to fuck off.

(DICK *gets up; the* NARRATOR *just sits there.* DICK *looks at him for a long time, then goes out. He walks to the other side of the stage, to his own office, where a patient, a woman, is lying on his couch.*)

DICK: (*Snapping his fingers.*) Get up. Up and out.

PATIENT: Huh?

DICK: Get up. Get up and walk. You will not fall down. You will not die. You will not be struck dead. You will not be punished. You will not die a failure. You can do things you want to do.

PATIENT: You are being simplistic.

DICK: The platitudes of life. They work if you let them. And yes, it will hurt, and yes, there will be periods of pain and anxiety and suffering.

PATIENT: Not only are you talking to me—but you're admitting there may be something worth fighting for.

DICK: Talk about a platitude! (*Vaguely smiling.*) I'm admitting nothing.

PATIENT: (*Smiling.*) Okay.

DICK: There may in fact be nothing. (*Smartly showing the patient out.*) But we'll keep our options open, just in case. (*The patient is gone;* DICK *calls out.*) Miss Young, will you come in please.

(*Linda, a cute young nurse bearing a striking resemblance to both* ANNIE *and* SUSAN, *comes in.*)

You look quite terrific.

LINDA: So do you.

DICK: Would you like to fuck?

LINDA: Perfectly acceptable to me.

(*The lights go down. In the dark.*)

DICK: That was quite terrific.

LINDA: That it was.

DICK: What do we do now?

LINDA: Try it again?

DICK: What's running through your mind right this minute?

LINDA: Right this minute? I'd like something to eat.

DICK: You're kidding.

(*Lights come up on* DICK *and* LINDA, *naked in bed. He is kissing her to punctuate each sentence.*)

She doesn't want to marry me, she doesn't want my money, she doesn't want to tell my wife. She doesn't want to tell my wife's lawyer. All she wants is a good fuck.

LINDA: Yep.

DICK: (*Groaning as he throws himself over her.*) Why can't I relax and enjoy it!

(*The lights suddenly come up very bright and white over* JOHN. *The* NARRATOR, *as doctor, steps forward.* RON, DICK, BARRY, *looking on. The* NARRATOR *now pushes the button.*)

NARRATOR: Shock Number Two.

(*Again, after a few seconds, the huge convulsions of* JOHN's *naked body, accompanied by lighting effects.* JOHN's *body lies pale and wan and unpleasantly. The onlookers are looking rather bad, too. The lights go out completely and then come up, with the* NARRATOR *studying* JOHN *closely.*)

Shock Number Two. No response from the patient.

(*The lights go down on* JOHN. *The* NARRATOR *comes forward.*)

Chapter twenty-eight. Father and son.

(*The lights come up on* JOHN *again, this time with his father sitting beside his son's quiet body. He looks at him, not knowing what to do. He tries to speak, but doesn't know what to say. He somehow senses that the situation is hopeless, that it is too late for words. Finally, he just takes* JOHN'*s hand and holds it in his own. After a moment,* BARRY *comes on.*)

BARRY: I'm John's friend.

JOHN'S FATHER: I recognize you. I met you at your graduation.

BARRY: I remember. I've read all of your novels. All of them. I want to be a writer, too. But I don't have anything to write about.

(JOHN'S FATHER *is silent for a moment. Then, with a cry of pain and anguish, he holds up his son's hand.*)

JOHN'S FATHER: You write about this!

BARRY: (*Very softly.*) That seems rather . . . heartless.

JOHN'S FATHER: (*Softly.*) Do you know how to vomit?

BARRY: I don't understand. . . .

JOHN'S FATHER: Vomiting is a very specific way of dealing with pain. If I couldn't go home and vomit up my pain onto some paper, I would become a cripple.

BARRY: I am a cripple.

JOHN'S FATHER: Why?

BARRY: I . . . I want to love, and I can only hurt. Myself and others.

JOHN'S FATHER: Write about that.

BARRY: It's not so easy.

JOHN'S FATHER: Nothing was meant to be easy.

(*The lights go down softly on them, a dim light still staying on* JOHN. BARRY *walks* JOHN'S FATHER *to his apartment. When they arrive at* BARRY'*s area,* BARRY *pulls out a suitcase from under his bed and shows* JOHN'S FATHER *his ropes and whips and leather accoutrements.* JOHN'S FATHER *looks at them silently.*)

All right. Now you've shown them to me. They are only the paraphernalia of your fantasies. Write about them. Live them and write about them. Use them. Use people. Use experiences. Use your friends, your enemies, your lovers, your dreams, your orgasms. You seem selfish and narcissistic enough. You should be a fine potential writer.

BARRY: What if I'm not any good?

JOHN'S FATHER: Then you'll do something else. No one is any good. It's an irrelevant fear, like all fears. Don't be frightened of failure. It's a waste of time. (*He pushes* BARRY *in front of a mirror and starts taking off his shirt.*) Look at yourself. Look at your blond hair and blue eyes. Look at your smooth hard chest. Look into your brain to find out how it controls this body, how it can control other people's desiring it, how you can control other people. Take the essence of your brain's physical desirings and convert these into art.

BARRY: (*Mesmerized.*) How do I do that?

JOHN'S FATHER: Hate yourself.

BARRY: I do.

JOHN'S FATHER: No, you don't. Not enough. You must hate yourself so much that only by constant work, striving, passionate attempts to prove your worthiness to yourself through your writing, can you survive.

BARRY: (*Almost in terror.*) *That* is terrifying!

JOHN'S FATHER: Of course it is. Why do you say you hate yourself?

BARRY: Because I'm not something else. I couldn't tell you what because I don't know.

JOHN'S FATHER: (*Touching his back.*) Then that's what you write about. What you'd want to be. Trying to find out what you'd want to be. Who you are. It can be very soothing.

BARRY: Would you hold me?

JOHN'S FATHER: (*Removing his hand.*) No.

BARRY: I need holding up.

JOHN'S FATHER: Find it yourself. Tonio Kröger, a dark and talented writer, sailed across the North Sea to the town of his birth. There everyone was blond and blue-eyed, as he had always wanted to be. He felt this longing and pain as he looked at them—looked at them being what he could never be. And he wrote about it. He and I share a marked incapacity to live within our bodies.

BARRY: Why did you touch me?

JOHN'S FATHER: It was a father touching a son's back.

BARRY: Do you *like* women?

JOHN'S FATHER: (*Laughing.*) Do I like them? I have been unsuccessfully married twice, I have had innumerable disastrous affairs, I have an unfailing instinct for choosing the wrong female and the wrong time—that is, if there is such a thing as the right woman and the right time. Do I like women? I like the sexual release. When I've had that, I usually return to my writing.

BARRY: That sounds selfish and unfair.

JOHN'S FATHER: Men aren't fair. Men are weak and submissive and whining. We have made women the aggressors. Do I like women? (*Shrugs.*) But I have helped to make, mold, fashion her into something dislikable.

BARRY: Why do you hate yourself?

(JOHN'S FATHER *slowly takes off his own jacket and shirt and tie and then his undershirt. He is fat and hairy and physically repulsive. He stands there and takes a layer of fat in his hands.*)

JOHN'S FATHER: Self-love. But what is underneath? And underneath the fat thighs and the flesh rolling from the buttocks and the underarms? (*Yanking at his chest hair.*) What infernal use is this? I hate how man can be made.

BARRY: Why do you make it so . . . physical?

JOHN'S FATHER: (*Pushing the suitcase.*) Why do you make it so physical? Despite centuries of protest, despite the fevered attempts of generations of intellectually gifted men, we are still only dogs humping each other in the dead dark of night, one behind the other. These are our basic passions; why deny them or disguise them?

BARRY: Somebody might think you were beautiful.

JOHN'S FATHER: But I do not! And I now care little what others think.

BARRY: Nor do I.

JOHN'S FATHER: Then you have the makings of an artist.

BARRY: How . . . perverse.

JOHN'S FATHER: Exactly.

BARRY: Are you afraid of death?

JOHN'S FATHER: "It's the living ones who die; the writing ones that
survive." I wish I had said that, but it was Henry James, a
solitary, miserable, lonely, unhappy cur who also wrote like
an angel.

(BARRY *reaches over and touches* JOHN'S FATHER'*s chest, runs his
fingers through his hair, then gives the hair a slight pull.*)

You won't get your strength from that. Only from yourself.

BARRY: (*Trying without success to pull at the meager hairs on his own chest
and smiling.*) I thought maybe I could grab a few seeds from
your crop.

JOHN'S FATHER: Look and read and study and suck everything you
can. Try everything you're emotionally and physically able
to try, and then push yourself even further than that limit. And
study your reaction. Study it and dissect it and write it down.
And stoop not into bathos or sentimentality. Keep it lean, pure,
underaccentuated. Make it iron hard, like muscle. Through
it all, insinuate a vein of strength like iron.

(JOHN'S FATHER *has been pounding* BARRY'*s chest as he illustrates,*
making BARRY *feel the muscle and hardness of his own body.*)

Feel it yourself. And vomit it out onto paper.

BARRY: (*Pulling a rope from his suitcase.*) Have you ever had sadomasochistic sex?

JOHN'S FATHER: I have fantasized it.

BARRY: (*Handing him the rope.*) Tie me up.

JOHN'S FATHER: Very well.

(JOHN'S FATHER *proceeds to tie* BARRY *up, first his arms, then his hands*
behind his back. Then he takes other ropes from the suitcase and ties
his legs, then ties his body to the bed. He does a perfect job of it, better
than BARRY *expected and without instructions from* BARRY. BARRY *is*
impressed.)

BARRY: You do a very good job of tying up.

JOHN'S FATHER: Some experiences are universal. We always think
that certain acts, deeds, have existed only in our own lives,
when in fact they are in the provenance of many.

BARRY: What would you do next?

JOHN'S FATHER: Ah, but I am not the writer today. You are.

BARRY: You've tied me up.

JOHN'S FATHER: Only for convenience. You're the writer. How do
you get out of this one?

BARRY: Make love to me. Kiss me.

JOHN'S FATHER: (*Laughing.*) That's too easy.

BARRY: But you said that everything was physical.

JOHN'S FATHER: You have neither set the scene properly nor atmospherically, to bring out whatever latent homosexual or sadomasochistic tendencies might be within me. You will have to try something else.

BARRY: Don't you get tired of spouting such shit?

JOHN'S FATHER: I beg your pardon.

BARRY: Everything you say is a major statement. It's so boring.

JOHN'S FATHER: Is it?

BARRY: It also sounds suspiciously like a big coverup.

JOHN'S FATHER: I don't care what you think.

BARRY: And I don't care what you think. You're too esoteric and out of touch with the realities of today.

JOHN'S FATHER: Which are?

BARRY: Your son, for instance. Do you care what John thinks?

JOHN'S FATHER: Yes.

BARRY: How did it feel, seeing him there today?

JOHN'S FATHER: Very sad.

BARRY: Do you know what's wrong with him?

JOHN'S FATHER: Only that he must be in very deep pain. And yes, it hurts for a father not to be able to get beneath the skin of a son's pain and ease it.

BARRY: But you haven't been a good father. You were never there when he needed you. He was all alone, as you say we all are and must be. But because you weren't there, he is like you saw him today. It's your fault.

JOHN'S FATHER: Stop it!

BARRY: (*Realizing he's hit the vein he's looking for.*) Do you realize the price you've paid for your art? A feeble, crippled son, a son who might die because you denied him yourself.

JOHN'S FATHER: You are too good a pupil. Yes, I realize that.

BARRY Doesn't it make you want to cry?

JOHN'S FATHER: Yes. It makes me want to cry and it makes me want to say to you, I didn't mean it. I would have had it otherwise.

BARRY: Beware of bathos and sentimentality, old man.

JOHN'S FATHER: He was my son.

BARRY: He is your son.

JOHN'S FATHER: What was he like?

BARRY: He is now what he's always been. Very gentle. Afraid of hurting others. Wanting very much to love and be loved.

JOHN'S FATHER: (*Now sitting on the bed beside* BARRY.) And something must have gone very wrong. The love he had to give . . .

BARRY: Jenifer is a bitch. She didn't love him. Not like we loved him, not like Dick and Ron and I loved him.

JOHN'S FATHER: You were his friends and you loved him. Friendship is more important than lovers.

BARRY: There you go with your pompous major meaningless statements again. Who are your friends, Samuel Clayman? Do you have any?

JOHN'S FATHER: Very few.

BARRY: Who can come to you in your time of need?

JOHN'S FATHER: I had hoped my son would. And his children.

BARRY: But you don't have a son anymore. And he won't have any children.

JOHN'S FATHER: How do you know that? How do you know he might not get better?

BARRY: You know it, too.

JOHN'S FATHER: I would like to cry, but I can't.

BARRY: Nor can I.

JOHN'S FATHER: One should be able to cry for a son.

BARRY: Yes, and for a best friend. Will you kiss me now?

(JOHN'S FATHER *bends over to kiss* BARRY, *but* BARRY *bites him on the lip.* JOHN'S FATHER *is momentarily shocked, emits a small cry, then withdraws and stands up. He is now back to himself. He smiles at* BARRY.)

JOHN'S FATHER: Yes. You have been a very good pupil. If you can write about it half as well as you can play with it, then your success is assured.

(*Lights down on them.* JOHN'*s naked body is again wheeled forward by the two nurses, the hospital light is lowered, the nurses make him ready, and the* NARRATOR *as the doctor steps forward.*)

NARRATOR: Shock Number Three.

(*Again the horrible convulsion. This one seems particularly violent.* JOHN *is now pale, yellow, emaciated. The convulsions seem as if they are taking every bit of the remaining life out of him. The lights go out; when they come up, the* NARRATOR *is again examining the body.*)

(*Turning to announce.*) No response from the patient.

(RON *and* BARRY'S FATHER *have been watching.* RON *goes over to the* NARRATOR.)

RON: When is he going to react? (*The* NARRATOR *shrugs.*) What do you mean, you don't know? How long can his system stand all of this? Why isn't he reacting? Shouldn't you be trying anything else? Maybe we should call another doctor in on the case.

NARRATOR: All reasonable questions. I can't answer any of them. Are you related to the patient?

RON: Only as a good friend. His father should be here. He must be late.

NARRATOR: (*Nodding toward* BARRY'S FATHER.) This man isn't his father?

BARRY'S FATHER: No. I'm the father of a friend of his.

NARRATOR: You're his father? (*He nods towards* RON.)

BARRY'S FATHER: No, no. I just thought I might run into my own son here. I was wrong.

NARRATOR: You're a strange group. Everyone here but who should be here.

(*He goes off.* BARRY'S FATHER *and* RON *start walking toward* RON's *area, slowly, talking. The nurses move* JOHN *back upstage. The* NARRATOR *returns without his white jacket.*)

If one wanted to show a foreigner New York, where would one take him? Where could you show him the castles and the moats, the green pastures, the quiet places essential to true creative growth? Where are the vanished churches and the ships? Where are the places where dreams are made?

(*Lights up on* RON'*s area, now used as his office. The big ad blowups of Ultima Now for Men and others. A slide projector is connected, and* RON *is showing, slide by slide, his agency's portfolio of ads to* BARRY'S FATHER. *The ads are of an unbelievable sheen and glossiness, of a nonexistent world.*)

The American dream is pictures and images, fed into the hungry human receiver by the vast machine. The chief fantasy makers now are the ones who, as always, are the best dreamers. Ron was a pretty good dreamer, and, as Barry's Father had been a pretty good dreamer in his own day, they got on just fine.

BARRY'S FATHER: Very impressive. You know, advertising was just coming into fashion as the thing to do when I got back from Paris in the early thirties. A lot of my friends went in to it, did quite well, I believe.

RON: You were in Paris in the twenties? That must have been incredible. I would have given anything to be there then.

BARRY'S FATHER: It was lots of parties. Partying around the world. I was in Paris when it was fun to be in Paris and people did all those crazy things, like discovering the Riviera, and hearing about that guy Picasso, and going to something called a bullfight.

RON: There's no place to go anymore.

BARRY'S FATHER: We were crazy. We drank too much. We never slept. I guess that's when the nervous breakdown came into fashion.

RON: Did you have one?

BARRY'S FATHER: Hell, no. My daughter's had one, but Christ if I know why. She hasn't done a damn thing all her life to break down.

RON: What were your parents like?

BARRY'S FATHER: (*Surprisingly,* BARRY'S FATHER *speaks quite eloquently, as if there suddenly might be more to him than meets the eye;* RON *responds to this.*) My mother filled our house with enormous plants and jungle colors and ornate European furniture. She had considerable imagination, taste, passion, and more than a little eccentricity. She was always running away to read books in some quiet, faraway city, and my father was always having to bring her back. When she died, and he thus lost his consuming interest, he traveled all around the world until, either from boredom or food poisoning, he gave up the ghost somewhere between Hong Kong and Shanghai and had to be brought home himself, in a casket which was placed in the Indiana prairie earth his family had owned for over one hundred years. He left me his name, his goodwill, and a not inconsiderable amount of money. I stood over the twin gravestones of my mother and my father and looked down at them and said out loud, "If the two of you hadn't married and hadn't lived together, why, it wouldn't have mattered at all." That's when I set out to have myself a very good time.

RON: And you have been ever since?

BARRY'S FATHER: You bet. How about you? Do you have a good time?

RON: Only fair. They're more difficult to come by today.

BARRY'S FATHER: I have sired myself one serious son, though. I'm certain that my enjoyments have not been passed on to him.

RON: Did you know Fitzgerald? Was he in Paris when you were there?

BARRY'S FATHER: He was round and about and he could be seen at any of the big parties. But he wasn't a popular fellow, and we were more interested in being popular. I don't think this has changed. (*Nodding toward the slide projector.*) So this is advertising. I don't think my friends are in it anymore.

RON: I guess it is a bit more scientific now.

BARRY'S FATHER: And not nearly so much fun. You know, I don't think you have enough good times. I can tell just by looking at you.

(*At this point, the* OTHER RON *walks in.*)

OTHER RON: Oh, excuse me.

RON: (*Immediately becoming very businesslike; he points to the blowup.*) Mr. Wright here is our Ultima Now for Men spokesman.

BARRY'S FATHER: That so. Is that something pretty special?

RON: We feel that his clean looks, his honest eyes and smile, his good skin, his well-proportioned body—all of these are attributes our potential customers covet. They therefore make the transference from seeing our pictures of him to using our product. It's worked quite well.

BARRY'S FATHER: That so. I guess he is a nice-looking lad. We all looked like him in my day. You couldn't have sold us an ounce of your stuff then—unless you had bottled it in London and called it something like Westminster Balm. Anything English was what was in fashion then.

RON: I guess things are a bit different now.

BARRY'S FATHER: Well, I'm going out to have me a good time. If you see my son, you tell him I'm still at the Yale Club and the convention goes on a few more days or until I get bored. Say, how's about my buying you both dinner?

OTHER RON: I'm afraid I have a date.

RON: And I have to work.

BARRY'S FATHER: Ah, well, some other time.

(BARRY'S FATHER *goes off in one direction, and the* OTHER RON, *after looking at* RON *for a long moment and getting no reaction, goes off in the other direction.* RON *just stands there.*)

NARRATOR: Ron watched them both leave. It was a peculiar experience. One of these men, the older one, represented what he himself would have wanted to be like had he lived several decades earlier. The younger one was today's version of desirability. Yet Ron, who had created this desirability, desired it no longer. And the old man was a big disappointment, too. All that talk about good times. The heroes were gone, he thought to himself. We have no heroes.

(*The* OTHER RON *comes back.*)

OTHER RON: I'm sorry you don't call anymore.

RON: I've been busy.

OTHER RON: Don't you get a kick when we're working together? Crazy little funny thoughts?

RON: How so?

OTHER RON: Oh, in the middle of a session, I sometimes look over at you and think, Hey, I've sucked that guy's cock.

RON: Very unprofessional.

OTHER RON: I think it's sweet. Doesn't it ever happen to you?

RON: No.

OTHER RON: Pity.

RON: Is it?

OTHER RON: Oh, fuck, you're too closed up to talk to. You're a constipated young old man. You never let go. I've never seen you eat too much or care too much or love too much.

RON: Moderation in all things.

OTHER RON: Very boring.

RON: Yes. I'm very boring.

OTHER RON: Doesn't that bug you?

RON: I've also been referred to as uninteresting, and lacking in good times. It doesn't bug me. I'll take my time or wait for my time to take me.

OTHER RON: What the fuck does that mean?

RON: I haven't had my five minutes yet.

OTHER RON: And what the fuck does that mean?

RON: I figure that most people have about five minutes of fame, in the world's scheme of time. Five minutes when they hit the front pages and make it big. I'll have mine one of these days.

OTHER RON: Is that what you're waiting for?! Maybe you've had it, maybe it's passed you by and you didn't even know it. Wouldn't that be a pisser.

RON: No, I haven't had it yet.

OTHER RON: All for five puny minutes. What a boring crock of shit.

RON: What will you have?

OTHER RON: Maybe nothing.

RON: That is boring to me.

OTHER RON: (*As he leaves.*) All I said was that I loved you.

(RON *is now going to walk slowly home.* JOHN'*s body is still dimly evident. When* RON *does get home, he will have a big supermarket bag full of groceries in his arms.*)

NARRATOR: Ron walked slowly home, through the city streets. He did not have the following thoughts: Where are the vanished churches and ships? To whom does it belong, this land: to those fathers who laid those roads leading out to the country—now Greenwich leading to East Hampton to New Haven giving birth to Newtown—those fathers who molded us and made us feared by others? Or to those who followed—adding nothing to this power, adding nothing, only taking, walking towards the next eternity in solitary fear. All is built up now; there are no castles left to build, nor could they be built should we be able to do so. Success is too much cared for, the past not enough. And the music and poetry has gone out of our lives, gone out of our love, our sympathy, our caring, leaving only drama, a stern, unyielding mistress muse.

(RON *is now in his apartment. The doorbell rings. He goes to open it. His father stands there. It is a moment before* RON *recognizes him. He walks back into the room, followed by his father.*)

RON'S FATHER: My name is Gatz.

RON: I know. (*Turning.*) How are you?

RON'S FATHER: You look pretty fit. Your mother's dead, and I thought I'd come to tell you.

(RON *shakes his head, absorbing the information.*)

They told me you was queer.

RON: Who did?

RON'S FATHER: I just heard it. You ain't had no woman.

RON: I've had them. I just prefer men. They're harder.

RON'S FATHER: Harder?

RON: I don't want soft flesh.

RON'S FATHER: Softness used to be much desired. Like a ripe peach.

RON: Well then, it's funny that I'm a fruit who doesn't like fruit.

RON'S FATHER: You needn't be so hard on yourself, lad. It looks to me like you can afford to take it easy, enjoy yourself.

RON: No, I can't. It's all you old ones who speak of enjoying yourself—after the battle is over.

RON'S FATHER: I never fought no battle.

RON: Yes, you did. For survival.

RON'S FATHER: I never looked at it as no battle. I just lived. If I felt swamped under, out there in the middle of the harvest, I just plowed ahead through all the shit. I just lived!

RON: Why didn't you teach me how to live?

RON'S FATHER: I thought I did.

RON: No, you didn't. Because I didn't learn.

RON'S FATHER: Then that's your fault, not mine. I can see you didn't learn. Whyn't you fight me back? Don't you got no outrage or rebellion in you? I fought my father tooth and nail, and you just danced about. You're just a mass of self-pitying blubber. You was a sissy then and you're a sissy now.

RON: Help me.

RON'S FATHER: I don't hardly know what to make of you. All helpless like corn after a drought. I'd like to kiss you and blow the life back into you; maybe my spit would water you back into life. But I can see 'twould be no use. I come all this way lookin' for you. I done found you. And now I'm going to leave you.

(*And he looks at his son with one last look of contempt and leaves him. After a moment,* RON *goes over to put the college glee club record on the phonograph. Then he goes and gets the bag of groceries and sits down with it in the middle of the floor. He is now going to have a compulsive eating jag of astounding proportions, pulling out item after item from his bag, sampling it, setting it on the floor as he attacks another package, then putting this down, occasionally returning to an earlier item, then carrying on, until he is surrounded by the brand names and packages, all of sweets, cakes, cookies, candies, ice creams. He will eventually get vaguely hysterical and wind up in tears. The glee club songs softly punctuate the background.)*

RON: Who wants to go home? Not this kid. Back to what? The old high school grounds where I got my first blow job and gave one? The room I danced around in and got laughed at? The basement next door where some guy stuck his finger up my ass for three *Mutt and Jeffs?* Introducing Pillsbury's Streusel Swirl Cake, topped with nice delicious streusel and crowned with a heavenly glaze. A dessert cake so neat to eat, it's great for snacks and lunch box, too. Betty Crocker Snackin' Cake—the cake you might have mixed before taking your kids to the dentist. Available in six moist, delicious flavors: banana walnut, coconut pecan, chocolate almond, chocolate chip, applesauce raisin, and chocolate fudge. Now a supermoist fudge Betty Crocker Supreme Brownie, and a chewy, chocolate-y Betty Crocker traditional brownie. We make two kinds of brownie because people like two kinds of brownie. First, the supermoist, fudgy kind, made with sour cream and a can of chocolate-flavored syrup in every mix ... Banana Breeze, a luscious, creamy no-cook filling in a crunchy no-bake crust, mealtime magic from Borden-Kellogg-Dole ... Sara Lee cheesier cheesecake ... Hershey's for summer sipping. Sealtest Light and Lively artificial peach ... Royal quivering shivering bittersweet ... This masterpiece deserves every "ooh" and "ah" it gets. ... Entenmann's Royal German Danish Cinammon Twist ... It should have been better. ... Häagen Dazs ice cream so thick it's like a pudding ... should have been goddamn better ... Stouffer's Devil's Food Cupcakes ... We don't belong anywhere ... two dark chocolate, two light chocolate, two coconut white ... lemony lemon, yellow and fine. I am too fat to wear jeans and too scared to take drugs and too balding to grow long hair and too skeptical to believe in pop music. I am caught in the middle of nowhere. Fulfilled Entenmann's Midnight Blackout Cake. Thick heavy inside filling. Mrs. Swanson's home baked in the factory cherry. I couldn't be a writer in Paris or an artist in Greenwich Village. Pillsbury Royal Dutch fudge topping. We were too old for the new generation and too young for the earlier one, the one that went to war and believed in the American flag. Kraft sweet cherry toppings. one of the extra things mothers do. Oh, my goodness, are they good. Working from the outside in, you press your fingers through a thin layer of soft peach fuzz, then into a molten center of concentrated plum raspberry syrup . . . fresh canned pineapple pie . . . fresh concentrated orange muffins for toastier toastings . . . chocolate-flavored chocolate . . .

(*Lights dim down and out on* RON. *The* NARRATOR *as doctor steps forward.*)

NARRATOR: Shock Number Four.

(JOHN *is again wheeled down and prepared. As this is happening,* BARRY *drags a very unwilling* JENIFER *across the stage toward* JOHN'*s body.*)

BARRY: You are going to watch.

(DICK *joins them. The* NARRATOR *presses the button;* BARRY *holds* JENIFER'*s face to make her see. Her face contorts as the electric charge again forces* JOHN'*s body into ridiculous contortions.* JENIFER *is horrified and cries out.* BARRY *and* DICK *drag her away from* JOHN *as his lights go down; the lights come up in a waiting room as* JENIFER *tells her story to* BARRY *and* DICK.)

JENIFER: We went to London and John's transfer came through, so he'd be able to work in the bank there. We found a lovely house in Belgravia, and I started buying furniture. Then the bank asked him to fly to Africa on some sort of business that came up suddenly, so we had to go and live there. He would be gone most of the time, and I was frightened. I stayed in a little house and we had a half dozen black servants. They looked after me, and as long as I stayed home, I felt like a queen. One day I took the road to the river and went walking there, and a white man came along on a donkey. He offered me some water. I was very thirsty, so I drank it. On my way home, I fell into some sort of wild fever. I woke up days later, very pale, very thin, and I couldn't eat for days. I was ugly, horrible. I was angry with John for taking me there in the first place. Then word came from the bank that we would have to be stationed there for at least a year, and I collapsed. John took me off to Tunis for a holiday, and slowly I got better. I told him I wouldn't live with him in Africa, I couldn't. I couldn't face up to it. He said I had to, he couldn't live without me, and he couldn't leave the bank. We had a terrible fight. I went out that night and let some Englishman who was also there on holiday take me to the beach and make love to me. John found us. And he just sat down on the sand, staring at me, looking at me, not speaking. I couldn't even get him to walk at first. But I did. I cried to him over and over that I was sorry, I was sorry, I'd go and live with him in Timbuktu. He seemed to get better. We went back to London. I realized I didn't love him, that it was unfair for both of us to carry on. I told him so. He collapsed again. He just sat there and didn't move, and he hasn't since. I had to mother him, force-feed food into his mouth and help him to the bathroom and tuck him into bed at night. But he still hasn't moved, and I still want to leave him. And it isn't really my fault, is it? I mean, he should have been stronger.

NARRATOR: (*Coming forward to make his announcement.*) No response from the patient.

(*The lights go out. When they come up,* JOHN'S FATHER *is sitting by his son's body and* JENIFER *comes in.*)

JENIFER: I suspect another novel will come out of this.

JOHN'S FATHER: You know my secrets.

JENIFER: I found out the history of your family by reading your books. I didn't have to ask John a thing. It made for a very quiet relationship. My goodness, but you've led an active life.

JOHN'S FATHER: An active life or an active fantasy life?

JENIFER: What's the difference? You've lived them, one way or another.

JOHN'S FATHER: True. Quite perceptive of you.

JENIFER: Don't you want to know what's happened between us?

JOHN'S FATHER: No. I shall imagine it. You can write me later if I'm right.

JENIFER: I've just told his dear friends.

JOHN'S FATHER: They're unimportant.

JENIFER: I can hear them blaming me now.

JOHN'S FATHER: Also unimportant.

JENIFER: Am I unimportant, too.

JOHN'S FATHER: I don't know. I suspect not. Whatever has happened, its provocation appears to have been a major act.

JENIFER: And that makes me important?

JOHN'S FATHER: One does what one does. If it gave you pleasure, remember that. We are free to do what we please, so long as we are prepared for the consequences. You seem to be bearing up under those quite nicely.

JENIFER: You make me sound quite beastly.

JOHN'S FATHER: Yes, we are beasts. No need to feel guilty for truth.

JENIFER: (*Nodding toward* JOHN.) What about him?

JOHN'S FATHER: He wasn't prepared for the consequences.

JENIFER: But they were *my* consequences.

JOHN'S FATHER: No matter. It was his life.

JENIFER: You advocate stepping on the ants of this world? If they get in your way?

JOHN'S FATHER: If they are in my way, it is unavoidable that my bulk shall smother their infinitesimalness.

JENIFER: Yes, I remember that from your books. I wish I had such a fierce outlook. Women are so ephemeral and wispy, when it comes to the ants. Perhaps that's why we're jealous of man's creativity. We create you and then you surpass us. You usurp *our* power. Your testicles take over from our wombs.

JOHN'S FATHER: You are a more interesting woman than I surmised.

JENIFER: You can create with your pen and you can create with your penis. What are we left with?

JOHN'S FATHER: More than you think.

JENIFER: What?

JOHN'S FATHER: Everything. After I have created, with either tool, I am empty. There is only nothingness. Until the vat somehow fills itself again. You, on the other hand, are constantly full, constantly able to be filled. That is the glory of the female organ. It seeks its own constant replenishment. You are always receiving. We can only give. For strength, for everyday peace, I should choose receiving. So much calmer than the constant exertion required of giving.

JENIFER: It's a good thing nations aren't run by your way of thinking.

JOHN'S FATHER: It would be better if they were.

JENIFER: Have you cried for your son?

JOHN'S FATHER: Have you cried for your husband?

JENIFER: Only for certain memories.

JOHN'S FATHER: Such as?

JENIFER: That nonsense you were spouting before. Being filled and replenished.

JOHN'S FATHER: He performed well sexually? Then he wasn't a complete weakling.

JENIFER: Yes. He had a fumbling, childish way of making love. He was very attentive to my needs, to me. And when he knew I was ready, his sort of—plunge and surge up the final mountain was very fulfilling.

JOHN'S FATHER: You see. How more blessed to receive than to give.

JENIFER: Stop it!

JONN'S FATHER: He has.

JENIFER: (*Fiercely.*) You are a constant denial of everything I've been taught.

JOHN'S FATHER: On the contrary. You are a regal affirmation of everything I have stood for. Be proud.

JENIFER: I want to cry for him.

JOHN'S FATHER: Then cry for him.

JENIFER: I want to hold him close to me.

JOHN'S FATHER: He's here, alive. Do so.

JENIFER: (*Tentatively approaching* JOHN.) But he's so pale. My John. Baby John. Your skin is so white. (*Suddenly she rips away the white sheet covering his body and runs her fingertips and then buries her face all over his skin.*) Hold me one last time! (*She looks at him, suddenly hoping that she might be the one to revive him, succeed where all else has failed.*) John, come to me again. Let me hold you. Make love to me. Fulfill me once again.

(JOHN'S FATHER *watches fascinated, entranced.* JENIFER *pulls the hospital robe apart and, her back hiding that part of his body from the audience, tries to revive him with her hands. The moment is a long one.*)

(*While performing the above.*) My John. My baby. Jenifer's John. You belong to me. I want you inside of me. I want John's penis. Please, John! Give it back to me. Please. Please! (*Eventually, her shoulders sag as her hopes and expectations are not fulfilled. She stands there, then finally pulls the robe closed and the sheet back and just remains with her back to* JOHN'S FATHER *and the audience.*) It would appear that I have failed.

JOHN'S FATHER: It's of no importance. The failure.

JENIFER: What is left!?

JOHN'S FATHER: (*Sharply.*) Don't be ridiculous!

JENIFER: (*Again, fiercely.*) Oh, it's not pity I feel, for either you or my late husband, though you are certainly deserving of both. I have only questions to ask—prompted by my own mental deficiencies—my own female inabilities to be as surpassingly bright as our situation urgently requires. You—when your testicles are dry, when your semen sack is empty, you still have your brains. But what can we do, we dim, dumb, brainless ones, kept under the rock too long? We can take your balls away, but how do we remove your brains? Emasculation usually occurs south of the waistline. How can we make it happen . . . north?

(JOHN'S FATHER *goes painfully from his chair to her, limping badly.*)

JOHN'S FATHER: (*With kindness.*) My dear, your very words are your salvation. Your very fierce and honest strength.

JENIFER: I . . . I don't understand.

JOHN'S FATHER: (*Looking at his son.*) He is there and you are here.

(*The lights go down and then up again as* JOHN *is wheeled forward. This time all the preparations are done very quickly. The* NARRATOR *as doctor holds up his button, not even looking back.*)

NARRATOR: Shock Number Five.

(*Again the awful convulsions. No one is present to watch them. The lights stay up and the* NARRATOR *announces, again without even looking back.*)

No response from the patient. Barry, under Laura's prodding, and after John's Father's tutelage, has at last finished a story. He now sets out to discover the secrets of the world.

(*Lights down on* JOHN *and the* NARRATOR *and up on* BARRY's *area, where he lies naked and tied up to his bed.* LAURA, *also naked, stands over him with a belt.*)

BARRY: Hit me!

LAURA: I don't want to.

BARRY: I want you to!

LAURA: That isn't enough. There has to be a certain amount of antagonism on my part. I'm not a vindictive person. I don't have anything against you.

BARRY: Think of it as a favor. I would like to be hit by you. I would like to think, goddamn it, that I am in your protection, that you would always take care of me, that you would bend down to kiss my wounds.

LAURA: All of those things exist without my hitting you.

BARRY: Damn it, I want to see what it's like. I want to experience what you experience.

LAURA: (*Softly.*) I spent so many years getting ready for you, for someone, was it you—smartening up my brain, prettying up my figure, making my virtues as marketable a set of values as I could. (*She is dangling the whip over him as she speaks, softly, touching here and there, doing it toyingly.*) All those years, trying all those roads, all in the wilderness, getting ready. And here we are. Is this it?

BARRY: (*Angry.*) Hit me hard!

(LAURA *hits him not too hard, but she is beginning to feel very sorry for herself.*)

LAURA: Is this it? Are these my marketable commodities? (*She hits him again, a little harder.*)

BARRY: Harder!

LAURA: My mommy would not like to see me or hear me or know the thoughts I am having now.

BARRY: Harder! (*She hits him quite hard.*) That's it!

LAURA: (*Hitting him again harder, now again.*) And is this it? And this? Is this it?

BARRY: Yes. Yes.

LAURA: (*Growing angry, as she begins to really clobber him and get back at him for all the humiliation she has suffered from him.*) But I wanted you to hit me! I wanted to be under you. Under you. I wanted you to be on top of me. Over me and over me. I wanted to be where you are. Under you. I wanted your come on me. I wanted your little white strings that tied me down! (*She is hitting him harder and harder, and his body is now red. He stares up at her in horror. She gives him one last mighty lash.*) I loved you, you prick.

(*And she drops the belt on his stomach, grabs her clothes, and walks out on him. The lights dim on him but stay up. LAURA moves to stage center, drops her clothes on the center table. As she dresses herself, she addresses the audience.*)

No, that was not the last time I saw him. I wasn't all that strong. Not then. He crawled into my bed one night and told me how he'd picked up a little Mexican waitress who he just instinctively felt had wanted to be initiated into the full flowering of his sexual, shall I call them philosophies. He sat there fondling my tit and told me all about it, every physical act he had ordered her to perform on him, and she had evidently been an able and willing pupil. He then read to me; he read the short story he'd finally written. It pleased me a great deal to be able to tell him I thought it was a piece of shit.

(*She is now dressed. She walks to where* JOHN *is laid out.*)

So long, you poor bastard. Or maybe you're lucky. Boy, do I not understand a fucking thing. No answers. Only more questions.

(JOHN'S FATHER *has hobbled on with a cane. He has heard* LAURA.)

JOHN'S FATHER: When I was young and in Europe, I met and listened to a wise old man. At least *I* thought he was wise; most others thought he was a fraud. He told me we wasted too much energy trying to be one person only, when in actuality we are not one individual but many different people. And only in accepting this fact could we ever hope of becoming one. Does this make any sense?

LAURA: Nope. But right now, little does.

JOHN'S FATHER: Men should have it easier than women. Men are freer agents. They can pick up, go elsewhere, keep their looks longer. Women age; they do not have free access to the fuck; they are not so mobile; they are tied to houses and children. Men can have everything. In so doing, they have nothing. Women, in having nothing, have everything.

LAURA: Did anyone ever tell you you were full of shit?

JOHN'S FATHER: Only myself.

LAURA: (*Taken off guard; with a slight smile.*) That's quite endearing of you. (*Looking at* JOHN.) Your son doesn't look like he'll be around too much longer.

JOHN'S FATHER: Unfortunately, he was not strong enough to fend for himself in the jungle.

LAURA: The survival of the fittest?

JOHN'S FATHER: Yes. I can only blame myself for not teaching him how to be stronger. But men are not strong, as I speak of endlessly in my books.

LAURA: So what do you suggest doing about it?

JOHN'S FATHER: (*Smiling.*) No answers. Only more questions.

LAURA: (*Shaking her head and walking off.*) Boy, are you a big load of mouthwash.

(LAURA *goes and sits down next to a woman, who is reading a book; two chairs have been set up facing the audience.*)

NARRATOR: Chapter three. Laura has a strange experience on the Madison Avenue bus.

(LAURA *has pulled out her own book from her bag and starts reading it.*)

THE WOMAN: What are you reading?

LAURA: I guess you'd call it an investigation into the problems of adult life as caused by things that happened in childhood.

THE WOMAN: Ah, mea culpa. I've already read all of those and found myself wanting.

LAURA: Yes. I suppose we all are.

THE WOMAN: I think I'm going to switch to stuff on travel. A little bit more soothing and the end results are more gratifying. I can take a trip to France.

LAURA: I'd love to travel, too.

THE WOMAN: It broadens the mind. Last year, I went to Italy, and before that I went to England, which was lovely. So now I guess it's France. You see, I haven't anything else to do. Do you have any children?

LAURA: No. No, I don't.

THE WOMAN: I had two. Two children and two husbands. The husbands I don't have anymore. Divorce.

LAURA: (*Not certain why the woman is telling her all of this.*) Oh. Yes.

THE WOMAN: My daughter lives down south. She doesn't talk to me anymore. I had a son. He was a teacher at Penn State. He'd just received his doctorate when he committed suicide.

LAURA: (*Stunned.*) How very, very sad.

THE WOMAN: I never knew why he did it.

LAURA: I'm so sorry. I . . . I don't know what to say.

THE WOMAN: Oh, I have a good grip on myself now. I read a lot and I travel a lot. You just can't let things get you down. We're very strong, you know, women. (*Getting up.*) I must get off now. It's my stop. Good-bye.

(LAURA *looks after her as the lights go down and out.*)

(*Lights up on* JOHN. JOHN'S FATHER *is now in a wheelchair. He sits staring at his son.* DICK *comes in, carrying a suitcase, which he puts down. He is stoned on some sort of hard drugs, his hair is very long, and he wears beat-up clothes. He ignores* JOHN'S FATHER *and goes to* JOHN.)

DICK: Good-bye, you old shit. I know I'm never going to see you again. Not in this world.

JOHN'S FATHER: There isn't any other. Where are you going?

DICK: (*Still to* JOHN.) I wish I could have taught you something, some of the things I've learned lately. It wasn't too late for me. I wish to shit you'd have come out of whatever haze you're in. But it's cool, man, whatever you're doing. Don't let anybody tell you otherwise.

JOHN'S FATHER: Which one are you?

DICK: (*Noticing him.*) I'm from column A. No, I guess I'm from column B.

JOHN'S FATHER: I'm his father.

DICK: My condolences. I'm his friend. (*As* JOHN'S FATHER *tries to remember him.*) Yeah, we met. I look a little different now. But don't we all. What's that for? (*Meaning the cane.*)

JOHN'S FATHER: I have trouble walking.

DICK: That must be a hassle.

JOHN'S FATHER: I asked you where you were going.

DICK: Did you? I'm a little zonked. I'm cutting out.

JOHN'S FATHER: Where to?

DICK: (*Does a clumsy little dance step.*) I'm just going off.

JOHN'S FATHER: You were a doctor. A psychiatrist.

DICK: That's it. Doctor Dick. Tracer of lost psyches.

JOHN'S FATHER: Business bad?

DICK: The worst. Hey, you were the writer.

JOHN'S FATHER: I still am.

DICK: No shit. Glad someone is keeping the old continuity going. People still reading?

JOHN'S FATHER: That makes no difference. I'm still writing.

DICK: No shit.

JOHN'S FATHER: No shit.

DICK: No shit.

JOHN'S FATHER: Language as well as reading skills are deteriorating.

DICK: Guess so. Sign of the times. (*Out of his pocket he pulls a knife. He plays with it.*)

JOHN'S FATHER: What do you intend to do with that?

DICK: I thought of killing your son. But now I think I'll have some money off of you first. (*Starts approaching* JOHN'S FATHER, *who stands his ground.*)

JOHN'S FATHER: Why would you kill him? He's practically dead.

DICK: Mercy killing, I think they call it. But first I want some mercy money. How much you got?

JOHN'S FATHER: Yes, it would be a mercy if he were dead. But could you really do it?

DICK: That's what I came here for. You encouraging me to kill your own son? Boy, what a prick.

JOHN'S FATHER: I'd like to see him out of his agony.

DICK: No, you wouldn't. You just want to be out of yours. You're just frightened of me, little old man. (*Close to him now, with the knife under his neck.*) Would be a mercy to be rid of you, too. Fart face. Prick father that made a son to die like this.

JOHN'S FATHER: (*Standing his ground.*) I don't think you're a very convincing killer.

DICK: (*Putting the knife away and turning away.*) 'Course I'm not. I'm not a very convincing anything. Ron, John, Dick, and Barry were the best of friends. They'd been to Yale together, but that was a few years ago. Now look at us. Nothing left. John's the only one left alive.

JOHN'S FATHER: (*Surprised.*) What's happened to the others?

DICK: Death in life, man, death in life. I don't see them. Sad. Real sad.

JOHN'S FATHER: So are you.

DICK: I don't deny it. (*Screaming.*) I do not deny it! (*Grabbing* JOHN'S FATHER.) And there's not a fucking thing we can do about it. We're all cowards, caught in the goddamned quicksand. And we're all sinking right up past our pits. What a joke. It's a bad time of life, man. The worst.

JOHN'S FATHER: I suspect you'll come out of it, along with everyone else.

(*The* NARRATOR *and the two nurses come in and prepare* JOHN *for the next jolt.*)

NARRATOR: Shock Number Six. Sixth and Final Shock.

DICK: (*Waylaying the* NARRATOR.) What happens after this one?

NARRATOR: If this one doesn't work, that's it. His system can't take anymore. Look at him; he's a wreck now.

DICK: So what happens?

NARRATOR: He stays a basket case until he dies.

DICK: Terrific. What a great future to look forward to. Why don't you kill him off.

NARRATOR: Against the law.

DICK: Some law.

(JOHN *is wheeled forward, the hospital light comes down, the nurses have placed the wires to his head, and the* NARRATOR *stands ready with his button.*)

NARRATOR: Shock Number Six.

DICK: Get your scorecard here. Can't tell the players without your scorecard.

(*The* NARRATOR *gives him a look; then, after a moment of silence, he presses the button. This time the convulsions are very slight, almost as if poor* JOHN's *body just doesn't have enough strength left in him to convulse properly.*)

NARRATOR: (*Shaking his head.*) This does not look good. A very poor reaction.

DICK: (*Shouting.*) How can you do this to him! What don't you just kill him off. (*He pulls his knife out.*) I'm coming, John. Peace is coming from your friend Dick. (*He lunges for* JOHN's *body, but the nurses quickly pull the table back and* DICK *falls flat on his face. After a moment,* DICK *pulls himself up.*) Couldn't even do that right. (*He goes and retrieves his suitcase, waves so long to everybody, and heads off.*)

(*The lights go down and then out. They then come up on the* NARRATOR, *without his white jacket.*)

NARRATOR: John did briefly recover. He slowly regained some sort of strength and energy and went back to work at the bank after Jenifer had left him.

(JOHN *begins very slowly, very weakly, to walk across the stage.*)

He was highly sedated throughout each day and unfortunately drank too much throughout each evening. Since the alcohol would not be tolerated by the sedation, and since the evening could not be tolerated without both, John collapsed early one morning . . .

(JOHN *falls down and rolls over and then is still.*)

. . . outside of a Third Avenue bar and died in the gutter before help could come.

(*Lights down on* JOHN. *The music of the college glee club record starts softly. Lights up on another portion of the stage as* JOHN'S FATHER, JENIFER, LAURA, *and* SUSAN *stand around an imaginary grave.*)

His going was noted, but not by his three friends, who were off wandering in their own misery. Before he died, for a dim second's flash, John thought he saw a moment of truth's light—that the inconveniences and anxieties would sort themselves out and even certainly diminish. Everything could be all right. But, as I said, it was only for a second, and then the too thickly woven threads rapidly reasserted themselves and the heavy blanket pulled itself back over the head to suffocate the almost sleeping child. He thought only one thought, over and over again, and it was a thought now shared by his three still living and wandering friends: There must be something better than this, there must be something better than this, there must be. . . .

(*The glee club music has built and is now obtrusively loud.* JOHN'S FATHER *has hobbled on his cane offstage;* LAURA *and* SUSAN *have then walked off in the other direction, leaving* JENIFER *alone by her late husband's grave. She stands there a long moment, then walks away, almost as if she's put it out of her mind completely. The lights dim on the grave simultaneously with their coming up on* SUSAN *and* LAURA *having lunch at the big table at stage center. They are wearing different clothes.*)

LAURA: Do you ever hear from Dick?

SUSAN: No. Briefly, in the beginning. I thought for a moment I was pregnant and we had several discussions, whether I should have it or an abortion. But then it happily proved a false alarm.

LAURA: Where was he?

SUSAN: I really don't know. I couldn't reach him on the phone, so I just wrote him a letter. And he just called me up. Come to think of it, it did sound long-distance. Maybe he has his mail forwarded.

LAURA: How could you not have been more curious?

SUSAN: I guess I didn't care. Do you know where Barry is?

LAURA: Yes. He's in Rome. I even went to visit him.

SUSAN: You didn't! How could you have?

LAURA: I was curious.

SUSAN: What did you find out?

LAURA: I was curious; unfortunately, he wasn't. We had a long talk sitting in the middle of the Piazza Navonna, and the talk turned into a fight, and he just got up and walked off and left me there. That's the last I saw of him—in the middle of the Piazza Navonna. You know, I never know why you stay here. Why don't you take a trip somewhere? With all of your money and all of your freedom . . . why, you could live in London for a while, or Paris.

SUSAN: But I don't know anyone there.

LAURA: You'd meet people.

SUSAN: No. I don't think I would.

LAURA: What do you do all day?

SUSAN: I keep very busy. I've gone back to school. I'm studying for my master's—in sociological evolution. I'm taking courses in statistical evaluation, and in computer analysis.

LAURA: It all sounds incredibly boring.

SUSAN: I find it interesting.

LAURA: I'm glad that you do.

SUSAN: What do you do with your time that's so admirable?

LAURA: I picked a man up in the street the other day.

(SUSAN *obviously finds this vaguely shocking.*)

Do you find that distasteful?

SUSAN: I guess so. I told you I find it difficult to meet people. To make that sort of wholesale gesture.

LAURA: Nothing wholesale about it. Very retail. Do you mind if I tell you about it? I'd like to.

SUSAN: Very well.

LAURA: He was quite handsome, slightly chunky looking, something to hold on to. We went back to his place. He ran an art gallery or something. In the middle of making love, he pulled out a belt and asked me to beat him with it.

SUSAN: Please stop.

LAURA: Oh, none of that is any novelty to me anymore. For what it's worth, I owe that to Barry. Anyway, I for once decided that I was going to beat the shit out of someone. It was the most extraordinary sensation and experience, as if I were getting back at all the wrongs done to me, a true retaliation if ever there was one—"I'll get you because someone else got me." Then very easy to feel the softness, the "I'm sorry I did that to you" tenderness which follows the inflicting. Barry called it having someone in his power, knowing that they trusted him, that he wouldn't go too far, that they were safe with him. How strange to find out so much later.

SUSAN: It all sounds like a very ignorant act.

LAURA: I guess it is. But now I've found out about it. I've experienced both sides. There is a certain enjoyment in acquiring knowledge.

SUSAN: I certainly wouldn't find enjoyment in all of that.

(JENIFER *arrives, rushing in.*)

JENIFER: I'm sorry I'm late. I was up very late last night.

LAURA: Doing what?

JENIFER: Fucking.

SUSAN: I think I may be finished with my lunch.

JENIFER: Did I say something wrong?

LAURA: I think Susan finds us lacking in subtlety.

SUSAN: Yes.

JENIFER: Why? It was quite nice.

SUSAN: What was? The man or the fuck?

LAURA: Why, Susan, good for you.

JENIFER: I don't separate the two. They were both nice together. I'm meeting him later.

SUSAN: You seem to have adjusted quite nicely to our country.

JENIFER: I'm not in mourning or grief, if that's what you mean. Is that what you mean?

SUSAN: Perhaps it is.

JENIFER: I did what I did. There's no reason two lives have to be spoiled just because one person is miserable.

SUSAN: But you did spoil two lives.

JENIFER: I did not. I'm perfectly happy.

SUSAN: (*Getting up and preparing to go.*) I'm sorry. I have to go now.

JENIFER: No. Wait a minute. I must ask you, what do you think I should have done?

SUSAN: I think you should have worked it out.

JENIFER: Just like that?

SUSAN: Yes, just like that.

JENIFER: I notice you didn't do too good a job in that department.

SUSAN: I tried to. I was the one left, if you'll recall.

JENIFER: And you've survived quite nicely.

SUSAN: Yes. Yes, I have, thank you.

JENIFER: So what's your bitch?

SUSAN: My bitch is that we might have worked it out! And the survival of one only would not have been the issue. Rather, two people might have grown together into some harmonious unit of one. My bitch is that two intelligent people ought to have been able to work it out!

JENIFER: (*Incredulous.*) Two intelligent people ought to have been able to work things out!?

SUSAN: Yes.

JENIFER: How ludicrously sentimental and clichéd. You are lying to yourself. Why should intelligent people succeed more than simple folk? Surely we are all still wild animals, breaking out of our cages, our egos at variance with other egos.

SUSAN: (*Interrupting.*) I am talking about love!

JENIFER: Yes, we have the need to love and the need to be loved. But there is also the pendulum swing to the opposite need to hate and be hated. I defy intelligent people to be able to solve this with their minds.

LAURA: (*Quite shaken by this realization.*) Yes . . .

JENIFER: Oh, no, one has to exercise control, artifice, appearance, self-will—and if one loves, then one is capable of sacrifice . . . for a bit! Do you understand me? Do you understand that living is, if necessary, killing other people, if it enables us to go on *living?*

SUSAN: I think you are insane.

JENIFER: But Susan, you have done the same as I have.

SUSAN: *I* have?

JENIFER: You have lost something and survived it.

(SUSAN *sits down slowly, thinking about this.* JENIFER *and* LAURA *draw close to her, almost as if accepting her into their circle as an initiate. The women continue their conversation inaudibly, as the* NARRATOR *begins for the last time.*)

NARRATOR: They will go on. And that is what is wonderful, full of wonder. They will have their lunches and their men. How little they will be affected, now that they have learned, now that we have taught them. Now they have strength. Unfortunately, strength, nobleness, acceptance, virtue, all are quite boring characteristics, dramatically speaking. So we shall leave them. They will go on; they will make do. I say all of this, not with disparagement, but with the greatest envy. They are the strong ones. Never once did they say, I am a self-pitying baboon, swinging on a tree, patting my stomach, licking myself, waiting to be fed, running fast to nowhere. Never once did they say: There must be something better than this.

The End

A Minor Dark Age

A Play in Three Acts

Writing *A Minor Dark Age* was a strange experience.

Brad Davis, or Bobby, which was his real name, had showed up for an audition for *Sissies' Scrapbook*. He'd been sent, not by Stark Heseltine, his agent famous for discovering stars, but by Stark's secretary, Susan Bluestein, who was living with Bobby. He was to be in two of my plays, *Sissies/Four Friends* and *The Normal Heart.* He would have been in three if Lynne Meadow, head of the Manhattan Theatre Club, had not kept us waiting so long for her turndown on *The Destiny of Me,* by which time Bobby had died (as had Colleen Dewhurst, who was to play my mother; oh, the exasperation I still have for Lynne!), and he would have been in four if *A Minor Dark Age* had ever been put on.

Bobby and I had been sitting around talking about his life. He'd told me about it before, but I was asking about it in more detail. *Sissies* had opened and closed, and we were waiting around for something to happen with it or I was looking around for something else to write. We'd become friends. He was a withdrawn and exceptionally shy young man when we first met, and he had not wanted to come to the audition because it was for a gay part and he was afraid I would make a pass at him, as evidently many guys had done over the years, and he wasn't gay. Susan made him come. He was becoming so choosy and difficult about pursuing a career that Stark was losing interest in him. But something about me reassured him, and he took me back to their studio apartment right after a first lunch we had, which almost gave Susan a heart attack; Bobby had never done anything like this. Their apartment in the West Village was a smelly mess, mattresses on the floor, a bunch of cats, a couple of dogs. That's how Bobby lived, and he was boss, at least with Susan. It was a touching relationship, this not particularly attractive over-weight Jewish princess from Long Island trying to become an agent and this gorgeous muscular gentile kid from some hick town in Florida. But whatever it was, it worked; they were together until he died.

I thought I would write a play for Bobby. Yes, Bobby is in it, walking onstage in the very beginning and getting everything going; but so is Penelope Mortimer, an intense English novelist acquaintance who was more nuisance than friend; and so was the central character of *Forbidden Colors,* the Mishima novel I had adapted; but so are other people I don't recognize. When I wrote it I was conscious that I didn't know what the fuck I was writing, or who or what it was about or where it was coming from inside of me. I'd never had that kind of writing experience before. I've read interviews with writers like Pinter and Albee who claim they just sit down and write not knowing what will come out, or some such. I guess this was that kind of experience, only my subconscious was frightening me, something those other guys hadn't talked about. I'd always known what I was doing, more or less. I wasn't used to the unknown.

If *A Minor Dark Age* was a play I never understood, why am I including it here? Until recently I'd never showed it to anyone except Michael Lindsay-Hogg, who directed *The Normal Heart,* who politely told me he wasn't interested. Oh, there was a reading of it once, by something called the American Renaissance Theater, which did it like a comedy. I didn't think it was funny. I still don't.

It seems to be saying something to me now I didn't see then (nor could I have seen it then), about the growth of my interests, the development of my concerns, the arc of my career, if you will. At some point I certainly changed rather radically from one kind of person to another. I became less shy, and I started worrying less about what people thought or said of me. I also became another sort of writer, I now believe: bolder, more in-your-face, with less patience. Hiding less behind another's voice, like Lawrence's or Mishima's. Less concerned with being a "great" writer, like the ones I admired, Fitzgerald, James, Evelyn Waugh. *A Minor Dark Age* (the title comes from something by Walter Lippmann, a leading liberal political columnist of my youth) now seems to me to be the first leap in this new direction. By now I must have realized nobody interesting was writing anything interesting about being gay, which is what I was about, or what I was trying to figure out I was about. By now I must have realized I could not make a living writing about homosexuality and that no one wanted to produce plays or movies about what I was all about. And every gay and lesbian writer I knew, or knew to be gay, knew this sorry state as well. Since, fortunately, the money I had made and given to my brother (and now my nephew) to invest was increasingly sufficient to keep me going until I sorted this out, I think somewhere along about this play I subconsciously decided to make a go for it. I guess you could say I'm still trying to do it.

Homosexuality from my adaptation of *Women in Love* to *Sissies' Scrapbook* to *A Minor Dark Age* to *Faggots* to *The Normal Heart* to *Just Say No* to *The Destiny of Me*—well, there is a path through all of this that I never recognized until now—the very moment I am writing this in my bed at two in the morning waiting for the sleeping pill to kick in. It has been a bad day and a bad evening. I am alone and afraid. I am due to be called for a liver transplant any day now. I have not been frightened. Quite the contrary: I am impatient to get it over with. I have been told I might die from the particular version of the operation I require. David is frightened. I know that. He won't talk about it with me. But I have heard from friends that they sometimes find him crying, which breaks my heart. After all these years I finally have the love of my life. I know he feels the same. Why am I lying in bed thinking of suicide? Swallowing all the sleeping pills that I have in various bottles. I have been terrified of trying to take my life ever since I tried to take my life, which I've already written about in *The Destiny of Me*. For some reason the bottles are screaming at me to get out of bed and gobble them up. How far have I really traveled? A particularly lovely woman in our town blew her head off last week. It was only then that people realized that something must have been bothering her. And today I reread *A Minor Dark Age*. I saw Bobby's face when he told me he had AIDS and heard his voice when he said good-bye to me over the phone and that he could not take what this disease was doing to him and his ability to make a living to support his wife and daughter. I know that the pills I will have to take after my transplant will be twice the number I take now. The rest of my life is going to be one gigantic pill. Why subject David to it?

I have fought so hard to stay alive, to keep others alive, how can I be so callous as to run away from that mission? If I ran away I would indeed be the sissy that my father always claimed I was.

By now I am asleep. Tomorrow I will return to this task of assembling these writings of mine into some sort of order for my editor, before I leave to climb up on that table to be carved up.

No, I don't want to do any revisions on *A Minor Dark Age*. A bunch of people I admire a lot recently read it and were impressed by something or other in it and told me, "You should do something with this." It is what it is, and where I was, and where I still am, where we all still are: a very strange place indeed.

Cast of Characters

Penny   the secretary

Alan   a young man

Alicia Dexterman

Billy   a teenager

Andrew Dexterman

Loren   their son

Scene: A summer house at East Hampton.
Time: Early June 1970.

Act One

The living room of an East Hampton house. Sofas, chairs, a studio couch to stage left, a large dining table stage center, a library and study area to the rear of stage right. Stairs at the rear up to the second floor.

At rise: PENNY *comes in, followed by* ALAN. *She is no more than twenty-three or twenty-four, rather tiny, but beautifully chiseled. He is the same age, dressed in jeans in contrast to her expensive clothes. He is intensely attractive, physical, withdrawn, and also small-scaled.*

PENNY: I'll interview you now. (*She takes a notebook and sharpened pencil from the table.*)

ALAN: (*Handing her a letter of introduction.*) It's all here.

PENNY: (*Taking it without looking at it.*) It would have been nice if you were bigger.

ALAN: What's that got to do with it?

PENNY: You're very compact. Though well proportioned.

ALAN: So are you.

PENNY: What did you do before?

ALAN: (*Thinking it would all be so much easier if she would look at the letter.*) Not very much.

PENNY: Oh, come now.

ALAN: I left school after two months of college and I came to New York to show my poems to anyone. I couldn't handle that trip, so . . .

PENNY: Why not?

ALAN: . . . I went back south and I grew a couple more years and I tried again. This time I stayed. Now I like it fine. But I don't have much of a work record.

PENNY: Why couldn't you handle the first trip?

ALAN: Oh, come on.

PENNY: What do you like fine now?

ALAN: New York.

PENNY: You live with a woman who's older than you are.

ALAN: Yes.

PENNY: Does she keep you?

ALAN: No.

PENNY: How do you live?

ALAN: I get money from home.

PENNY: Do you sleep with her?

ALAN: Of course I do.

PENNY: Do you love her?

ALAN: Yes.

PENNY: Would you leave her?

ALAN: What for?

PENNY: Do you like boys?

ALAN: For sex?

PENNY: Yes.

ALAN: No.

PENNY: Have you ever had sexual relations with a boy?

ALAN: This is a pretty intensive interview.

PENNY: Have you?

ALAN: How do I know the job is worth it?

PENNY: It's worth it. I assume you've already been told that.

ALAN: I hustled a little once, for money. Am I supposed to . . . I thought you just needed a little help around the house.

PENNY: The hustling . . . was that all?

ALAN: I stopped.

PENNY: Why?

ALAN: I liked my "older woman" better.

PENNY: What did you think when you had sex with men?

ALAN: Come on.

PENNY: I have other applicants to interview, should you prove unsatisfactory.

ALAN: Did you advertise in *The New York Times?*

PENNY: No, we did not. There are other ways.

ALAN: You walked up and down Forty-second Street with a butterfly net.

PENNY: Something like that. (*She waits.*)

ALAN: "The Most Unforgettable Experience I Ever Had." (*Clears his throat.*) "When I did it with a man . . ."

PENNY: Keep it simple.

ALAN: I hope you'll write it down. (*She continues to wait and stare.*) There wasn't any love. That's what I thought of. And I used to feel sorry for the guys who were married, sneaking away to the big city to do it. One guy, from New Orleans, he had a wife and four kids and used to come up four times a year, regular as clockwork. That somehow interested me, guys like that, leading double lives.

PENNY: There, that wasn't so difficult now, was it?

ALAN: Can I ask a few questions now?

PENNY: You'll get seventy-five dollars a week, room and very good board, and you'll have a certain amount of time off.

ALAN: Can I ask you a few questions now?

PENNY: I can't tell you exactly when you'll have your time off—but you'll be able to sense when he doesn't want you around and you can take off. The only thing it might take you time to learn is how to sense when he wants you back again. That's hard, particularly if you're off somewhere.

ALAN: ESP.

PENNY: If you've got it, terrific.

ALAN: May I ask you a few questions now?

PENNY: I think we'll give you a try.

ALAN: What has my sex life got to do with it? Am I supposed to go to bed with him?

PENNY: That will be all.

ALAN: That will be all. Hey, listen. The days of serfdom and bondage are over. I'll do the job. And I'll be very polite and conscientious, because this looks like a nice house, and what with the ocean out there, I figure it's not a bad place to be for the summer. But don't treat me like some sort of poor white shit that's come in to clean the windows and forgot to wipe his feet.

PENNY: You forgot to wipe your feet.

ALAN: No, I didn't.

PENNY: You forgot to wipe your feet.

ALAN: No, I didn't.

PENNY: Go back and wipe your feet.

ALAN: I'll wipe my feet off on your tits.

PENNY: I'm sorry you need this job so badly.

ALAN: That's my worry. Not yours.

PENNY: I'll worry, nevertheless.

ALAN: That's very considerate of you. Just what the fuck do I have to do? It's beginning to sound like it's more than general handyman. Or maybe those words take on new meaning out here.

PENNY: Mr. Keller recommended you quite highly.

ALAN: Mr. Keller has been a good friend. I've also been able to trust him.

PENNY: There are some things Mr. Keller doesn't know.

ALAN: So it would seem. Would you like to fuck or something? (*She walks away and puts the pad and pencil away.*) Mr. Keller know you?

PENNY: Seventy-five bucks a week. Christ, I can blow that in three and a half seconds.

ALAN: There must have been a time when you would have done something for seventy-five bucks a week.

PENNY: My father was a chargé d'affaires in Washington. I went to the Madeira School and Wellesley.

(ALICIA *enters. She is a middle-aged woman, more earthy than attractive. She has the look of the suffering intellectual, which she is.*)

This is Alicia Adams. Mrs. Dexterman. This young man, Alan, has joined our staff.

ALICIA: Very attractively. Welcome. I guess. Oh, well, a summer by the ocean never hurt anyone.

ALAN: No one around here has exactly been a rave recommendation for this job.

ALICIA: I'm sorry. I'm really quite pleasant.

ALAN: I meant no offense. It's been the strangest damn interview.

ALICIA: Do you eat a lot?

ALAN: Here we go again.

PENNY: I was coming to that.

ALAN: I eat like a bird. Bread and water will do, and then only once a day. If you don't work me too hard, I can get by on every other day. Jesus.

ALICIA: (*Smiling.*) Do you have any particular favorites?

PENNY: Any particular favorite foods.

ALAN: No, It's never meant much to me.

ALICIA: Pity. We eat quite well. Perhaps we'll reawaken your appetites.

PENNY: Alicia, the staff is my responsibility.

ALICIA: Do you hear that. Alan? You are her responsibility. The sun is out today; I could start on my summer suntan, its first day— and I should let this thought, this anticipation, make me happy. Alan, you are Penny's responsibility. Yes, I must remember that. Yes, I must. It's not that it's *you* who are Penny's responsibility, it's that it's the *staff* which is Penny's responsibility, and I must not tread on younger toes than mine. Yes, I think I can remember all of that.

PENNY: Good.

ALICIA: Good? Oh, I don't think we need give it a qualitative value. Let's just say that it is.

PENNY: It is.

ALICIA: So there will he an extra person to set a place for.

PENNY: Yes. There'll be an extra person eating.

(ALICIA *leaves.* ALAN *looks after her.*)

You wrote poetry?

ALAN: Yes.

PENNY: Past tense?

ALAN: You caught it.

PENNY: Why past tense?

ALAN: Why not? I've fucked. I've eaten. I've slept.

PENNY: Wasn't it any good?

ALAN: I think it was quite good.

PENNY: But there wasn't anything beautiful or meaningful to write about?

ALAN: Something like that. I wish I could do something to shock you.

PENNY: I'm not interested.

ALAN: Oh, but I am. And, yes, you are. (*Slaps her face quite hard.*) Am I hired?

PENNY: That didn't do it.

ALAN: I didn't think it would, but I wanted to try it. It was an essential first. Perhaps I'll just skip to the essential second. (*Starts to unbuckle his jeans.*) Do we actually know two people who behave this way?

PENNY: Yes, you're hired.

ALAN: Would you like to hear how when I was younger I used to think how convenient it would be if I could simply bend over and suck myself off? Self-service. Making other people totally unnecessary.

PENNY: But you couldn't do it.

ALAN: It seems anatomically impossible. For me, anyway.

PENNY: What do you like to eat?

ALAN: We're back to that again, are we?

PENNY: Please choose something. We can then occasionally surprise you. It would give us something to look forward to.

ALAN: (*Starts to circle around her.*) Why don't you choose some sort of food? Why don't you tell me what you like to eat and let me surprise you? Why are you so glacial, Miss Penny? Ice queen. Not bright and shiny. I like ice cream. Any flavor but vanilla. And, when absolutely ripped, I like chocolate things and lemon things. But not together. What do you like, Miss Penny? What the fuck do you like?

PENNY: You are going to be very good at your job.

ALAN: I told you that.

PENNY: What will you do with the money that you need so much? Send it back to Mama and Poppa?

ALAN: Yes. I'll send it to my mother. For her weekly spending money. So she can buy things from the commissary. She's in a mental home. A state mental home. Where people run up and down the corridors shouting, "Come quickly, he's not breathing anymore."

PENNY: What will you do with the money?

ALAN: I'll buy drugs for my father. He has unnaturally large needs for someone his age; the dosages he requires are astronomically large. He must have them to keep going. Or is that my mother? It's quite essential that his work as a dentist must not suffer.

PENNY: What will you do with the money?

ALAN: (*Smiling.*) I've told you. Anyway, it's only seventy-five bucks a week. After you take out whatever you're going to take out, that isn't going to leave very much. Is it?

PENNY: No. It isn't.

(*The lights go down.*)

Scene Two

When the lights come up, they come up as moonlight. The curtains billow slightly over the open windows. After a moment, through the French doors, ALAN *comes in with a young teenager,* BILLY. *Both wear bathing suits.*

ALAN: Come on in.

BILLY: My parents, who are never here, know the owners of this place, who are never here. Let me rub your back dry.

ALAN: I'm dry already.

BILLY: Okay. Then you can rub mine. My name's Billy. What's yours?

ALAN: Alan. You're dry, too.

BILLY: So what?

ALAN: So there's no need to rub you dry.

BILLY: Oh, yes there is. It feels good.

ALAN: You're addicted to the pleasure principle.

BILLY: Why were you out walking on the beach?

ALAN: Why not?

BILLY: This part of the beach is pretty active at night. (*Tries to kiss* ALAN.)

ALAN: Don't do that.

BILLY: Why not?

ALAN: I don't want to kiss you.

BILLY: I'm really sorry about that. I want to kiss you.

ALAN: So I can see. How old are you?

BILLY: I don't want a lecture. (*Tries to hold on to* ALAN, *but* ALAN *pushes him away.*) The rich are not like you and me. No, that's not right. The rich are not like you. (*Starts to giggle.*) I had sex on that beach outside there first when I was twelve. He was a friend of my father's. I seduced him. He had gray hair on his chest, very sexy. For about two weeks I was in love with him. I used to sneak into his bed at night, when he was asleep, and I'd play with him and arouse the hell out of him until he'd fuck me silly.

ALAN: What'd you do when you were thirteen?

BILLY: What'd you do?

ALAN: I fucked a sheep. How old are you now?

BILLY: Fifteen.

ALAN: I guess you should be asleep.

BILLY: No, I should be in bed awake, with you.

ALAN: Okay. Let's go.

BILLY: But you're not gay.

ALAN: No. But I'll sleep with you. I mean sleep sleep.

BILLY: Terrific. What a challenge. I think I'll go home.

ALAN: I have to sleep here in the living room for a while. My room isn't ready yet.

BILLY: (*As* ALAN *pulls the cover off the studio couch.*) You're too boring to stay with. I want to fuck.

ALAN: Then you'd better go home.

BILLY: That's what I said. Nobody there either. What a waste. People waste their lives and my time.

ALAN: You're only fifteen, for Christ's sake. At your age, it's not yet a waste. Just a passing.

BILLY: When does it become a waste?

ALAN: When you're about thirty-eight and have lived exactly one-half of your allotted time. Then it's a waste because you're on the home stretch. There, I did lecture.

BILLY: Do I have to wait till you're thirty-eight?

ALAN: Let's just go to bed. We're not talking about the same thing, and I'm tired.

BILLY: Why are you even bothering to let me stay?

ALAN: I have no idea. Take it at that, will you?

(BILLY *nods; then helps* ALAN *remove the cover and bolsters and fur rug.* ALAN *then flops on the bed and closes his eyes.* BILLY *shrugs and lies down beside him. He attempts to cuddle close to* ALAN.)

Just sleep.

(*Silence as the two settle themselves in and drift off to sleep. Lighting softly modified. At the far end of stage right, a figure becomes dimly visible. He has been there all along, listening, witnessing, but his appearance has not been apparent until now. He slowly rises from his desk or from a big chair.* ANDREW DEXTERMAN *is a large and graceful man, tall, of great bearing and girth. In this darkness, his bulk might seem a bit sinister, but only momentarily. He starts to cross the stage, taking with him a large box of candy, from which he eats pieces, one after the other, quickly, noiselessly. He looks down at the two sleeping youths, standing there for what seems to be some time, as the light again modifies, as if dawn were coming closer, and he is still there looking down at them. At one moment,* BILLY *awakens to see* ANDREW *towering above him.* BILLY *smiles sleepily, as if in a dream, and holds out his arms to* ANDREW. *The lights go down.*)

Scene Three

The bed remains unmade, but its inhabitants are no longer in it. ALICIA *enters with the morning coffee and newspaper, followed by* ANDREW. *They sit stage center, and she pours coffee.*

ALICIA: Did you sleep well?

ANDREW: Yes.

ALICIA: Where did you sleep?

ANDREW: In my room, in my bed.

ALICIA: I'm sorry the summer is starting off with so little promise.

ANDREW: Is your writing going well?

ALICIA: Quite well. I've settled a major structural problem.

ANDREW: Good.

ALICIA: My heroine will have a mastectomy. Just the metaphor I've been looking for. I quite like this house, don't you?

ANDREW: So far.

ALICIA: I hope we don't have any neighbors who talk to us.

ANDREW: Mostly weekend types, I suspect. Until August.

ALICIA: We must do something about August.

ANDREW: What would you suggest?

ALICIA: A higher fence or a cruise.

ANDREW: (*Smiling.*) By August, we shall have transmitted so many unfriendly vibrations that I don't think we'll have to worry.

ALICIA: Would you mind if I went back to England for a visit?

ANDREW: Yes, I think I should mind. I thought we agreed you'd stick the summer out.

ALICIA: All you need is a cook.

ANDREW: Which you do better than anyone else. Why do you want to go back?

ALICIA: It seems time. It's been three years. I'll completely loose my accent. They won't know me. I could buy new underwear.

ANDREW: All substantial reasons.

ALICIA: I want to see Hotspur.

ANDREW: I see. I thought you were finished. Discharged.

ALICIA: I'm both of those. One is never "finished." I want to see him.

ANDREW: Can I help?

ALICIA: However could you help?

ANDREW: Well, I guess I can't with that attitude. (*Starts methodically eating from a plateful of biscuits and toast, until the plate is empty.*)

ALICIA: No.

ANDREW: Are you having difficulty writing?

ALICIA: No. Now that dear Penelope is about to lose her tit, it will all flow quite nicely. Metaphors are so helpful. Everything's unblocked. The fury unleashed. Perhaps dams should be built with metaphors. Or nuclear power stations. Do you think you ought to tip off the president?

ANDREW: If your writing's going so well, why do you want to interrupt it with a visit to England?

ALICIA: Perhaps I'd fall in love again.

ANDREW: Do that here.

ALICIA: The master suggests I do that here. I don't feel like doing it here. It requires atmosphere and place. I've read in the gossip columns that lesbianism is in. "What famous English movie star parenthesis female close parenthesis is living a secret bohemian Greenwich Village life with what famous American fashion model parenthesis also female close parenthesis question mark end quote. I didn't know the word bohemian" was still in usage. Do you think life in Bohemia, when there actually was a Bohemia, was really all that raffish?

ANDREW: I have no idea. But it's an interesting question.

ALICIA: I'm glad.

ANDREW: You have a way with interesting questions. You've always had an interesting mind.

ALICIA: Thank you.

ANDREW: You're quite welcome. Please don't follow it up with "But are interesting minds enough?"

ALICIA: They're not.

ANDREW: No. They're not.

ALICIA: We both have incredibly interesting minds.

ANDREW: To the point of satiety.

ALICIA: Andrew, why ever have you brought me here this summer?

ANDREW: You said you wanted to come. You hadn't been to East Hampton since you were a girl.

ALICIA: But those were different days. Those were days when the pound was worth five dollars and England had the Suez Canal and books cost five shillings to buy and own forever and didn't turn yellow quite so quickly. Do you know that my teeth are yellow? (*Takes his hand and his arm and holds them like some relic.*) One ancient arm, yellowed within, how holy? Mother Church, how holy?

(ANDREW *grabs back his arm in annoyance.*)

No, of course, your bones are white, quite white. But why? I don't think you drink milk anymore, or not nearly enough to whiten bones—but perhaps you overdosed on it sufficiently when you were young. How is your writing going, my dear?

ANDREW: Sufficiently.

ALICIA: Sufficiently overdosed. Can you use that? It's yours.

ANDREW: A gift?

ALICIA: Ah. but I shouldn't use it. For I shall have used it first, and when those youthful scholars dissect us—they'll find I'd waged undue influence on you. We mustn't have that. Particularly not when it's the reverse which is true.

ANDREW: I hope you don't mean that.

ALICIA: Of course I mean it!

ANDREW: I've left you alone to do whatever you please. I've been particularly conscious of attempting not to influence you.

ALICIA: How could you not have influenced me, you monstrous talent? What you deny me in my waking life, you taint within my dreams.

ANDREW: Nicely put. Alicia, I'd like something more to eat.

ALICIA: (*Getting up.*) Andrew, do you remember?

ANDREW: What?

ALICIA: Anything. Everything. How we met, or why we met, or why we're still together. Loving and unloved.

ANDREW: I love you.

ALICIA: I remember that.

ANDREW: Good.

ALICIA: No, it's not good. I remember that from long ago. What would you like to eat?

ANDREW: Toast and peanut butter. (*Smiles.*)

(ALICIA *goes out.* ANDREW, *alone, runs his hand round his midsection. This is a characteristic gesture of his, repeated, often unconsciously, throughout, particularly during or after or before eating. He goes to look out toward the sunshine and the ocean. He walks out on to the terrace and returns with a bathing suit. He walks to stand in front of a large wall mirror, where he proceeds to undress. Naked, in front of the mirror, he studies his body with great seriousness. He does not like what he sees.* ALAN *comes in from the beach, wearing a bathing suit. He looks at* ANDREW *as* ANDREW *studies him, then bends to put on his suit.*)

It's quite ugly. The body is quite ugly. The body can be quite ugly. Sit down.

(ALAN *does so.*)

You're the new boy.

ALAN: Yes.

ANDREW: Your name is Alan.

ALAN: Yes.

ANDREW: You wrote poetry.

ALAN: Yes.

ANDREW: Everyone does that when young.

ALAN: Do they?

ANDREW: I watched you sleeping last night.

ALAN: Did you enjoy it?

ANDREW: Did you? No, let's not start off playing games. There were two of you in that bed last night and you were both beautiful and I hope you enjoyed each other as I did and . . . And I want you to feel free to do whatever you wish in my house. Freedom.

ALAN: Thank you.

ANDREW: Make use of it.

ALAN: I'll remember that.

ANDREW: How is Mr. Keller?

ALAN: Mr. Keller sends you his regards. No, his love.

ANDREW: Did the two of you make love last night?

ALAN: No.

ANDREW: Why not?

ALAN: I didn't want to. Freedom.

ANDREW: I hope you didn't for any reason feel constrained. I thought you young ones of today were meant to be spirits of freedom.

ALAN: Are we? Is that what you're trying to be?

ANDREW: Do you know that this morning I went early into the village and consumed the following: one-half of a chocolate cream pie, one apricot tart, one cherry turnover, one half-pound of assorted bakery cookies, one concoction of mocha cream and devil's food, one half-pound slice of a cake triple layered of cheesecake, chocolate, and strawberry jam . . .

ALAN: Are you proud of that? That's quite a bit.

ANDREW: I am mortally ashamed. But I'll shortly go inside and write. What will you do?

ALAN: What do you want? I'm on the payroll, remember?

ANDREW: Go and write me some poems.

ALAN: I won't do them anymore.

ANDREW: Why not?

ALAN: It's a waste of time.

ANDREW: That sounds suspiciously as if you're no longer able to.

ALAN: How do you do it, year after year, hell, day after day?

ANDREW: One finds ways. (*Turns suddenly and goes.*)

ALICIA: (*Returning with a plate full of toast and peanut butter.*) Good. He'll be working soon. He won't need this, then. (*She offers it to* ALAN, *who shakes his head no.*)

ALAN: He wanted more food?

ALICIA: Has he had an eating jag? No wonder he's writing so regularly.

ALAN: I've read several of your novels. And I liked the movie they made of *Sweet Pumpkin.*

ALICIA: Did you? I'm not so certain that I did. There's something about seeing all those famous faces, playing basically inconsequential people, which falsifies the entire experience. I wish

one of those Frenchmen who get those marvelous performances from amateurs had done it.

ALAN: I liked it.

ALICIA: Do you want toast and peanut butter?

ALAN: (*Again shaking his head no.*) Why aren't you writing yourself?

ALICIA: I'll work myself up to it. The house will settle down and
there won't be anything else left to do. Everyone will be busy
doing something.

ALAN: What will I be doing?

ALICIA: Penny will find something. Hasn't anything been . . . spelled
out to you about your duties?

ALAN: Spelled out? No.

ALICIA: Well, you are extraordinarily decorative for a start. Perhaps
that's all you're meant for.

ALAN: I hope not.

ALICIA: I mean in life.

ALAN: I know you mean that as a joke.

ALICIA: No. Do I? Well, maybe I did, through it is quite logical. Why
shouldn't people be paid for the attractiveness they exhibit?

ALAN: They are. It's called prostitution.

ALICIA: Perhaps it's wrong to consider it pejoratively.

ALAN: No, it isn't.

ALICIA: (*Starting to go off.*) The young, who know so much . . . You're
very young to have such firm ideas.

ALAN: But that's the only time when ideas are firm. It's later on that everyone seems to crack up.

ALICIA: Have you never . . . cracked up?

ALAN: I guess so. I didn't think of it much at the time.

ALICIA: Tell me about it.

ALAN: I took too many pills once and got committed. They gave me shock treatments to bring me down.

ALICIA: How awful. Your brain might have been damaged. How could they do such a thing to you? Why, I'm incensed!

ALAN: My father gave them permission.

ALICIA: How dare he?

ALAN: He's a dentist. I guess the hospital figured that was all the medical permission required. Anyway, it calmed me down.

ALICIA: Are you friendly with your parents?

ALAN: They're fine.

ALICIA: Do you love them?

ALAN: Yes.

ALICIA: It doesn't sound to me as if they're worthy of your love.

ALAN: Is that something one decides for oneself?

ALICIA: How extraordinary you are. Tell me about them.

ALAN: My father drank too much. He had to keep moving his office, from one town to another, just to save his practice. My mother was a drug addict.

ALICIA: Why aren't you writing? The inner turmoil those two must have caused can only be the marvelous foundations for a creative spirit.

ALAN: Tell me about your parents.

ALICIA: I beg your pardon?

ALAN: You asked about mine.

ALICIA: Mine were not very interesting.

ALAN: Oh, no one thinks their own story is interesting.

ALICIA: Nonsense. Too many people think their own story is interesting. Witness the market glutted with their attestations to same.

ALAN: Without all this hoopla, couldn't you just tell me?

ALICIA: I was a minister's daughter. I grew up outside of London, amidst much guilt, fear, and other ailments long since thought only the provenance of American Jewry. I was totally mystified when I married Andrew to find that he was actually angry that I was encroaching on his private preserve.

ALAN: What was your father like?

ALICIA: I find your continued interest remarkable.

ALAN: Don't.

ALICIA: He had white skin—torpid, I would call it—except that that summons up hot days and we lived in an only marginally heated curate's house, filled mainly with hand-me-down sticks of unupholstered parishioners' furniture. There were eight children; I believe I was somewhere in the middle. If I think of torpid, perhaps the heavy underwear and the thought of his sweating skin beneath it comes to mind. I could not bear to think of touching him, or allowing him me; after all, he was a man of God and not a father. You can imagine what difficulties my sexual life presented to me when at last I received the tardy but nevertheless natural call to the fuck.

ALAN: Tell me.

ALICIA: You are very beautiful sitting there. You are perfectly proportioned and you have a skin which seems to have a healthy life of its own and you have curious eyes which do indeed seem to be interested.

(ALAN *comes over to her chair and sits on its arm and bends to kiss her. At first she just allows this without response, but she then takes him into her arms, almost her lap, and rocks him as she and he continue their embrace. When they finish, he looks for a long time into her eyes.*)

ALAN: Tell me.

ALICIA: Now I don't think I want to.

ALAN: Nothing is changed. Tell me.

ALICIA: I have been institutionalized four, maybe five times. It wasn't that I tried constantly to kill myself, I don't even remember if that was the issue or not; it's just that I didn't seem to have the will to move from minute to minute. London is very gray for a very long time, from approximately October through May, and long hours spent traipsing to and from an analyst's couch on Harley Street are particularly eternal in the sense that one never sees the end in view.

ALAN: Were you married to Andrew?

ALICIA: Oh, yes. I married him very young. We were both something of early twenty prodigies; we came to the world's attention, or what we thought of as the world, at that age, and we thought we were wonderful. He was already lecturing on his varied and sundry ways to save the world, creatively, artistically. Everyone was listening, but no one was paying attention. I'd had two novels published, pure flights of fancy on my part, on the tangled webs of infidelity, a subject I was totally unfamiliar with but one on which I was soon to become an expert.

ALAN: You're talking like a book. Like you're writing all of this down. Come over here. (*Gets up and tries to lead her to his studio bed.*)

ALICIA: I will not.

ALAN: Please come with me. I want to lie down with you.

ALICIA: It's broad daylight.

ALAN: So what? Don't you like to be seen?

ALICIA: Of course not.

ALAN: (*He begins closing the full drapery that lines the window wall, and the room becomes dimmer.*) Come and lie down with me.

ALICIA: Alan, please don't.

ALAN: Come and lie down.

(*She does so. He unbuttons her blouse and lays his head against her breasts. She puts her hand up to his head and rests her own head on top of his.*)

ALICIA: You weren't brought here for this.

ALAN: I know that.

ALICIA: What are we going to do?

ALAN: Right now? Fuck. We'll worry about the later later.

(*The lights go down.*)

Scene Four

The lights come up on the large round dinner table, lit by candles. It is late evening. The remains of dinner on the table. Around it are ANDREW, ALICIA, PENNY, *and* ALAN. ANDREW, *who has eaten and drunk mightily, continues to drink throughout the scene and to reach out and eat anything that might be left on the table or another's plate. A tape recorder is playing.*

ANDREW'S VOICE: The strategic movement recommended by Mr. X in his carefully considered argument will only lead to one discovery—one that he has not foreseen. We will discover that the world cannot be divided, that allies are entangling, puppet regimes treacherous, and most of the third world politically irrelevant. But we shall discover it too late, after unnecessary expenditures of costly amounts of lives, manpower, and money. At that point, we will be able to start anew to address ourselves to seeking an objective end that all men can understand and one which faithfully expresses the best and oldest but long forgotten traditions which brought us here in the first place—to be the friend and champion of those seeking to be free—and only this . . .

ANNOUNCER'S VOICE: (*After a pause.*) You have been listening to novelist Andrew Dexterman in Washington. *An American's Opinion.* July 19, 1945. Tune in next week.

(PENNY *turns machine off. There is a long moment of silence.* ANDREW *drinks more.*)

ALICIA: You were the only one who was right.

ANDREW: I was.

ALICIA: You were the only one who was right.

PENNY: After all these years, for the truth to finally come out.

ANDREW: Oh, it has nothing to do with truth. I saw things in one way and they saw them in another and their way prevailed. It's always easy to condemn in hindsight.

PENNY: But weren't you certain then?

ANDREW: Yes, I was certain then. And I am now. But there's nothing more a pain in the ass than a fellow who's certain. Isn't that right, Alan?

ALAN: I'd say so, but only when the certain fellow wants everyone else to believe him. There's nothing wrong with being certain and just knowing it within yourself.

PENNY: But sometimes the world must be told things it doesn't want to hear. For its own good.

ALAN: Ah, but then I don't know much about that. I suspect it's in very good hands, being in Andrew's hands, I mean.

ANDREW: Thank you, young fellow who knows so much.

ALAN: I don't know anything. That's what I'm trying to tell you.

ANDREW: Do you know enough to caress my wife's body, to feel her skin, warts and all, to feel her wrinkles and her dried-up tubes with your fingers? Do you know enough to stick your thing up her and give her your pleasure?

ALAN: I don't think any of that requires knowledge. More instinct and affection.

PENNY: Andrew, have some more coffee.

ALICIA: (*Who has been staring at* ANDREW.) You did have to do this, did you?

ANDREW: Yes, I did. And I do. Why not? Do we have some tacit understanding that I must keep my eyes open and my mouth closed?

ALICIA: Why yes. I've lived by that understanding for years.

ANDREW: (*To* ALAN.) Was she good?

ALAN: (*To* PENNY.) May I have some more coffee, please?

ANDREW: You are staff! You are the hired help! You are a worthless child with only an unwrinkled cock to prove your purity. You are an emaciated remnant of some future unborn self. You are a pain in my ass which I have elected to house under my roof.

ALICIA: That's enough, Andrew.

ALAN: Would you like me to go?

ANDREW: No. You're not leaving me yet. You're not leaving me until I have milked you dry, until I have sucked out of you whatever you can give me that I can take and what I can take that you won't give me.

ALAN: You sound very . . . satanic.

ANDREW: Oh, goodness me, no. I wish I were. I am only fat and forceful and incredibly stubborn.

ALAN: What do you want?

ANDREW: Didn't Mr. Keller tell you?

ALAN: Mr. Keller told me that you liked to have pretty young things about. I take it that Penny and I constitute pretty young things.

ANDREW: Mr. Keller told you more than that.

ALAN: Mr. Keller told me to read the end of chapter fifteen of your wife's third novel. I have committed it to memory: "Beware the overbearing pressure of today's sexuality. Beware the innocent slipping into anonymity, the giving of bodies thoughtlessly."

ANDREW: (*Begins to roar with laughter.*) Good old Keller. He's turned to literature at last. Beware, beware, beware ... That's what he's told you. I'm not dangerous, boy. I just like a little beauty now and then, to remind me of just how ugly I am. It keeps me in my place. Look at you! Small and perfect you. Isn't it amazing how such a little tidbit can keep me in my place. My brains have been picked by the greatest scavengers in the world, and a little pretty ninny is the only effective antidote to my poisonous presence. Do you understand that, boy? Do you comprehend that?

ALAN: Yes. Yes. I understand it.

ANDREW: Good.

ALAN: All of my life, scratchers and pickers, dirt farmers like you, have come and looked at me and poked and touched and wanted, and I've looked them sadly in their eyes as I look at you and I say, "Fuck off." I came this way, I came packaged this way, and it's mine, not yours or anybody else's unless I choose it to be. I have no price on my head. Or rather, if I choose to have one, I'll do the setting.

ANDREW: You came here.

ALAN: I came here. I came to see. If I want to give myself to you or to anyone else, I'll do the giving. You won't do the taking unless I do the giving.

ANDREW: You set your own rules?

ALAN: You bet I do. What's more, you know it, which is why you like me here. You weak bastard, you like to be told off. Go to bed, fat old man, and sleep it off. Go to bed and feel fat and ugly and sorry for yourself and have yourself a cherry pie before you go to sleep, and maybe, just maybe, have a hope and a dream that pretty little Alan will come and kiss you goodnight.

ANDREW: Would you come and kiss me good night?

ALAN: Maybe Penny will help you up and tuck you in and touch your flesh and tell you you're beautiful.

ANDREW: I don't want Penny. I've had Penny.

PENNY: Come along, Andrew. Let Penny take you to bed.

ANDREW: (*Laughs.*) Pretty little Alan. A hope and a dream!

PENNY: Come, Andrew. Come with Penny.

ANDREW: Come. Come. (*He starts up on* PENNY's *arm, first grabbing the remnants of the cake plate and whatever pieces of food he can carry. They stumble up the stairs and out.*)

(ALAN *comes to* ALICIA *and stands with his arms around her shoulders and neck.*)

ALICIA: (*At first touching his hands, then getting up and walking away from him.*) I solicit no sympathy.

ALAN: You're talking like a book again.

ALICIA: I am a book. My books are my only reason for living.

ALAN: That's stupid.

ALICIA: Is it?

ALAN: Let another human being be your reason for living.

ALICIA: But you'll be a waste of time. Don't you understand that?

ALAN: I hope not.

(ALICIA *comes to him and kisses him. He responds. She breaks away from him.*)

ALICIA: The youth clutched at her like a mouse begging for a cat.

ALAN: I'm only something to write about.

ALICIA: What higher compliment!

ALAN: You love him very much.

ALICIA: Of course.

ALAN: He treats you very badly.

ALICIA: But that's why I love him.

ALAN: Do you want me to kick you somehow? Would that help?

ALICIA: It might.

ALAN: That's very stupid, too.

ALICIA: Yes. It is. I wasn't aware that intelligence had anything to do with love.

ALAN: No. I guess not.

ALICIA: Tell me about your . . . girlfriend.

ALAN: No.

ALICIA: Does she mother you?

ALAN: Tell me about your other affairs. Were they sons for you?

ALICIA: I have a son.

ALAN: Tell me about him? Do I look like him?

ALICIA: Hardly.

ALAN: Would you like me to? Or him to look like me?

ALICIA: My mind doesn't work that way. It's cold out now, isn't it? One forgets how country nights are so much colder.

ALAN: Where is he? Where has he been?

ALICIA: A mother learns not to ask questions. That's the really tormenting thing, the not knowing. I wonder about him often. What does he think and do? What does he do for sex? What creativity have we been able to pass on to him? What will he amount to?

ALAN: Don't you talk with him?

ALICIA: Would you answer those questions if your mother asked them?

ALAN: No.

ALICIA: Goddamn it! Must you be so . . . cool? Must you be so patient? Show me your guts and your . . . passion! Even your love-making is . . . beatific. Those big blue eyes looking so lovingly on the vanquished. I hate tenderness.

(ALAN *starts walking out of the house.*)

Good-bye, tenderness. Good-bye, weak little boy. Good-bye, milk pudding. Wait!

(*He stops and looks at her.*)

Oh, you poor baby. You poor lamb in a den of literary lions. What aren't we going to do to you. . . .

ALAN: Listen, I don't know how many times I have to tell you, all of you. I can take care of myself. I can protect myself. I can open myself up and let things hurt me.

ALICIA: Oh, but you can't. Only we know how to do that. Only we know the secret.. And we've had so much practice.

ALAN: You don't know. You only know how to hurt back.

ALICIA: I'm going to bed now. Good night.

ALAN: Good night. I'd still like to sleep with you.

ALICIA: Good night.

ALAN: I want to make love to you.

ALICIA: Good night.

ALAN: Good night.

(*She leaves him standing there and starts across the room and up the stairs as he watches her.* PENNY *starts down the stairs, and she and* ALICIA *meet midway and talk to each other as* ALAN *looks up at them.*)

PENNY: He's asleep. You need some rest, too.

ALICIA: That I do. How are you?

PENNY: I'm fine.

ALICIA: It seems to be taking us longer than usual to settle in, don't you think?

PENNY: I suppose so. It seems like a long time every time. We'll be settled soon. Get some sleep.

ALICIA: You, too.

(*They kiss each other good night, as friends.* ALICIA *goes upstairs and out.* PENNY *comes downstairs toward* ALAN. *She begins to clear the table.* ALAN *has been vaguely perplexed by the ally nature of their meeting on the stairs.*)

PENNY: Help me clear the table.

ALAN: Please.

PENNY: Oh, don't start anything now. Please help me clear the table. (*She suddenly sits down, quite tired. She just looks into space, probably for the moment not even aware of his presence. Unconsciously, she moves items on the table around in meaningless movements.*) Yes, she's right. It's cold.

(*Touched by this,* ALAN *comes over to her and stands behind her, putting his arms around her in much the same way as he did shortly before with* ALICIA.)

PENNY: I'm so very cold. (*She begins to cry, softly. She turns and buries her head in his stomach, as he continues to comfort her.*) So very cold. (*Pulling away from him.*) I don't want to be made love to. Fucking is not the answer to everything. You just think you can make love to anyone and put everything to rights. Not with me. Not with me.

ALAN: (*Touching her face.*) Poor Penny.

PENNY: Stop it! You really are infuriating. Go home, go away, leave this house!

ALAN: Have you ever been to Morocco? I went to Morocco once. I couldn't handle it. A complete stranger saw I was all wound up and he gave me a couple of pills and sat with me while I calmed down and finally went to sleep. I only slept for a couple of hours, and I was still shot to hell when I woke up, but it was a kindness on his part. I couldn't look him in the eye, that next day. Or whenever I saw him again. (*He tries to turn her face to look at him.*) I guess I felt that, in my fear, I'd told him things, I'd blurted things out, that I'd never told anyone before. I've always wanted to find him again and say, Hey, look, it all came out all right. And thanks.

PENNY: What did you blurt out to him?

ALAN: Do you really want to know?

PENNY: Yes.

ALAN: Well, I'll tell you, but first, you tell me what you would tell that man, that stranger, if he were here right now, trying to comfort you. And I'll bet that what you tell me is just what I told him, or near enough.

PENNY: What should I tell you?

ALAN: Whatever it is that's frightening you so.

PENNY: Nothing is frightening me.

ALAN: Okay. I see. I was a long way from home, in Morocco there, and I felt very cut off, not at all like me, because I usually like strangers and don't mind being cut off. Cut off from what? I always think to myself, there's nothing to be cut off from. But something about the desert not far from my window, and something about the beggar cripples that used to haunt the hotel, and I guess something about airplanes that never came in when they were expected, I guess all of that clutched me up. I got scared, and what with no one to talk it out with properly, to let the poison out of my system, yes, I was pretty overcome with fear. I wasn't there alone, mind you. I went with a very pretty blond man, Angelino, though he was English. I'd met him in London and he was hung up on me. We'd never made love, no, I wouldn't let him, those were my rules, and that was cool with him, he didn't force me to do anything, and made me more than feel that he was merely pleased, pleasured, to have my company along. But there were all these pressures closing in on me, what was I doing there and should I or should I not be doing this or that or something other, and I was getting fully blocked off from being able to think things through properly. (*He has his arms on her shoulders, her neck, calming her, massaging her brow, warming her, helping her.*)

PENNY: Why didn't you make love to him?

ALAN: Now there you go asking me. And you've just a moment ago criticized me for trying to do the very same thing.

PENNY: He loved you.

ALAN: You know that? Yes, he did. You sound like quite a romantic thing.

PENNY: When I was sixteen, I thought I lived in prison. I used to dream it all the time, night after night, so that eventually I lived in it in the daytime, too. I lived in a prison, within four walls closing in on me. I could see the bricks and feel how cold they were, and how hard my bed was and how much everything smelled. I could feel inside my stomach the frustration of my sex not being properly released. I wanted men, strange men, strange towering, gigantic men, from the next cells, to break through to me and grab me and, and, and drown me somehow and wash me all over in, in, in . . . their . . . I made up fantasy stories about men on the street, selling themselves over and over to different people, selling their bodies to live with, their hugenesses commanding exorbitant prices from the hungry, the hungry, I was hungry, many hungry men and women who walk the streets, looking to be fed. I dreamed it over and over again. I imagined it, coming, coming over me over and over again.

ALAN: There's nothing wrong in any of that.

PENNY: It's not right and it's not wrong. I know that. It's just one particular story that's forced itself on me to live with it when I want to live with another story, whatever it might be. I want to live some other story.

ALAN: Full of pink and drooping green trees and streams and warm sunshine.

PENNY: Men in white suits. Men with smooth, small bodies. Men without animals inside of them. Gentle, floating men.

ALAN: Like me?

PENNY: I . . . I don't know. I don't know you.

ALAN: I'm just not very good at interviews.

PENNY: I am. I'm very good. I always give the right answers.

ALAN: But don't you see, I'm trying to tell you that there aren't any right answers. It's just the story for now. It can be a very nice story, if you can let it just be the story for now. Not an old story. Just a now story. Can you let that happen? Can you live a story just for now?

PENNY: I don't know. I don't think so.

ALAN: Well, sooner or later, you're going to have to try. You wrote the old stories down already. You've read them, and I've read them, and, well, it's just time to write some new ones.

PENNY: I haven't been able to do that. Andrew, he lives in such torment, lately it's been worse, much worse. . . .

ALAN: Shhh. I don't want to hear about Andrew.

PENNY: (*Holding on to him.*) Love me, love me, love me.

ALAN: I love you.

PENNY: You don't. You don't know me.

ALAN: At this moment, I feel love for you.

PENNY: You just say the words. You say the words to please me. Why do you want to please me? I can't do anything for you. Not a thing.

ALAN: Why do you have to do anything for me?

PENNY: Why do you say the words?

ALAN: I say the words because I feel the words. I feel love for you.

PENNY: And what about tomorrow, and the day after that?

ALAN: We haven't come to that part of the story yet.

PENNY: I don't want to come to that part of the story. Little boy body, perfect, beatific ... (*They kiss tenderly.*)

(*The lights go down softly.*)

Scene Five

ANDREW's *library-study area, stage right, his writing area, his domain, his refuge.* ALAN *sits in a chair beside* ANDREW *at his desk. The next day.*

ANDREW: How old are you?

ALAN: I'm twenty-four.

ANDREW: When I was twenty-four, I had finished four years of college and spent two years abroad. We seem to be slowing down our progress, not hastening it.

ALAN: What's the hurry?

ANDREW: Ah, but that's just it. We always were in quite a hurry. It gave us a sense of urgency, that marvelous feeling that there just wasn't enough time to do everything. It felt . . . good. That's nothing that interests you. (ALAN *shrugs.*) Perhaps I should try another tack.

ALAN: Where do you want to go?

ANDREW: Mr. Keller told me that he picked you up on Forty-second Street, hustling for money, and that when he took you back to his apartment, you were very impressed by the large number of books he had in his study. Is that correct?

ALAN: That is correct. (*Pause.*) If you're waiting for me to say that I'm impressed by the large number of books in this house, I am.

ANDREW: Would you care to tell me why?

ALAN: Have you read them all?

ANDREW: Most of them. The rest will be useful sometime or other.

ALAN: Well, then, I'm impressed by that, too. Now, do you want to suck me off or anything specific? Am I supposed to pretend that we met on 42nd Street, or what?

ANDREW: Why have you stayed?

ALAN: Why not? Every minute a new adventure.

ANDREW: What do you think about?

ALAN: In what way?

ANDREW: What do you think about all of us?

ALAN: There are three of you, and I guess I think different things about each of you.

ANDREW: Mr. Keller sent me some of your poetry. It's rather good.

ALAN: But not good enough.

ANDREW: No, not quite. Not yet. Is that why you stopped?

ALAN: There's no point in doing it unless it is good. Very good.

ANDREW: Those things take time. And you seem to indicate that you have a great deal of time.

ALAN: For certain things.

ANDREW: But not for hard work.

ALAN: I don't know about that. I consider this hard work.

ANDREW: But you said you liked being here.

ALAN: I do, in a certain way. In another way, I don't want to be here. This is a very curious place and I find myself constantly surprised.

ANDREW: You seem to be creating most of the surprises yourself.

ALAN: For you, perhaps. I do what I feel like doing.

ANDREW: I find that fascinating.

ALAN: Oh, come on. So do you.

ANDREW: I've just wanted to observe you in action. Feel free to do whatever it is you want to do, you feel like doing.

ALAN: Mr. Keller told me all of that. I have felt free. It's all of you who seem to have dampers put on your actions by my being here.

ANDREW: Put a pretty young thing, or in your case a handsome young thing, in the middle of a pack of crones, and it has a way of upsetting balances or metabolisms or whatever quo is status. Now Penny is an interesting case in point. Young though she may be, she's very old.

ALAN: No, she's not.

ANDREW: Are you interested in Penny?

ALAN: I'd rather hear about her from her.

ANDREW: Well, I'd like to tell you about her. She has led an extraordinary life. Shortly after her birth, she almost died from rheumatic fever. Her mother had been abandoned by her father, and she, together with three other siblings, all lived in a shack by a railroad crossing. There weren't enough sheets for all of their beds. I don't know if you are familiar with the symptoms of rheumatic fever, but a great deal of bleeding ensues. Consequently, she bled constantly onto the same sheet. She told me it was heavily caked with layers of blood. A very unfortunate childhood.

ALAN: Yes.

ANDREW: Ah, but then her adolescence was no better. She was taken away from home by someone who called himself her "uncle," someone who in actuality had been a lover of her mother's, someone who had made a financial arrangement with the mother to buy Penny's body. They went away to live in a small house in Baltimore. She was thirteen and he was thirty-five and she bore him several children.

ALAN: I find that hard to believe.

ANDREW: She bore him a number of children. They were all put up for adoption, and Penny, at my instigation, has had herself rendered incapable of bearing children again.

ALAN: Otherwise, she might have borne some of yours as well.

ANDREW: Perhaps. Or yours. I'm more in the habit of taking precautions, or seeing that precautions are taken, than her "uncle" was or any of the men who followed. I think you must be the only male relatively near to her own age that she's allowed near her.

ALAN: She told you about it?

ANDREW: Of course. She told me she rather enjoyed it. She said there was a softness to you that was a new experience for her.

ALAN: A softness?

ANDREW: I'd consider that a compliment. You must think of yourself in comparison with all of the other men who forced themselves upon her, all of the brutal instigations, impositions, insistences. You do see that, don't you?

ALAN: Why are you harping on this? Do you think I forced myself on her, even "softly?"

ANDREW: Do you think she was willing with you, or perhaps, shall I say, just responding like Pavlov's dog?

ALAN: Whatever you're talking about, I don't think it's in my line.

ANDREW: No, perhaps not. Perhaps we should talk, not about Penny, but about something or someone else. Now Alicia is an interesting woman, don't you think?

ALAN: The master certainly knows what's going on in his own house.

ANDREW: Yes, he does.

ALAN: More like some god knowing what's going on in his world.

ANDREW: Thank you.

ALAN: God with a small "g."

ANDREW: Even so. Shall I tell you about Alicia?

ALAN: You will anyway.

ANDREW: But don't you want to know about her? About her poor background?

ALAN: Her minister father, the sexual guilts . . .

ANDREW: Ah, I see she's beat me to it. That's a writer for you. One must be constantly on the alert. Quite right. Well, then, she's saved us a little time.

ALAN: Do you have a thing for poor people? Penny and Alicia both.

ANDREW: Humble origins, do you mean? My goodness, no. I mean, it doesn't arouse me in any way, if that's what you're asking. I come from just that sort of a beginning myself.

ALAN: Which would explain it.

ANDREW: Now, don't you want to hear about me? I had so looked forward to telling you about myself.

ALAN: Now look here, tell me what the fuck this is all about.

ANDREW: A little spiky show of temper. Good. Pacifists are such a boring group.

ALAN: What am I supposed to think listening to you go on and on, what am I meant to feel, how am I to react . . . ?

ANDREW: Now, does any of that make any difference to you?

ALAN: Not one bit.

ANDREW: Then why ask it? Just relax and converse.

ALAN: Relax and converse. Just like that. Well, I had a dream last night, doctor, that you came to sleep with me. I was about to be embraced by a beautiful young boy named Sandy, but you came and took me instead.

ANDREW: And naturally this disappointed you?

ALAN: Yes.

ANDREW: I see.

ALAN: Do you? I was disappointed only that the beautiful young boy wasn't a beautiful young girl.

ANDREW: Had you considered how disappointed I might have been to see you in his arms rather than mine? Or to see him in your arms rather than in mine?

ALAN: *You* were disappointed?

ANDREW: Perhaps we dream the same dream.

ALAN: There was more. Sandy had to move his wife out of the way first, before he could take me in his arms. This seemed to take a certain amount of exertion; even though she was a light woman, she seemed very heavy—or he just simply was awkward in removing her.

ANDREW: It makes sense, doesn't it?

ALAN: Yes.

ANDREW: Have you ever walked the empty streets of a city, late at night, after the rain, with few people about except panhandlers, other derelicts, ugly bodies looking for comfort? It's all ugliness, late at night. You know that? That's what it's all based on—the entire system of values which runs our lives, this world. And what is so incredibly sad and useless, or so it seems to me, is how little use you make of you. You have been given the world's most valuable currency and you don't know how to spend it.

ALAN: That's true only for you. It's not valuable to me.

ANDREW: Then you are a fool.

ALAN: No! Only to you. I think you're a fool. I think, I think you squander even more valuable things—your brain and your body, maybe even your talent, though you think you create out of your pains and your agonies. Why do you hate yourself so?

ANDREW: Why don't you like yourself more?

ALAN: How . . . how should I spend . . . me? Why do you quibble over me, why do you disapprove so? . . . Let me . . . let me tell you about my father. . . .

ANDREW: The alcoholic dentist?

ALAN: No. He was the father who brought me up. My actual father died before I was born. I only heard that he was a singer—like a troubadour—if they have them nowadays—and he went from town to town—he was Dutch, and he came to this country with a beautiful girl he'd met traveling through the country towns of France. My head is splitting wide open. What use are all these words, they can't express what either of us feels—how I want that song, that man, that . . . two strong arms, warmth, pointing me in the right direction, which way, letting me go there myself, not telling me I must be beautiful, letting me go there myself but having confidence I'll get there, do you understand that, what I want . . . ?

ANDREW: Yes. We need a place to stay.

ALAN: My head is splitting open in two.

ANDREW: (*Holds* ALAN'*s head.*) Sit up and behave.

ALAN: Hold my head, goddamn it! Please. Take it, take your hands and hold on to my head, and please keep on talking, you were saying, we need a place to stay, we need a place to stay . . .

ANDREW: (*Holding the boy.*) You want to wander forever, oh, I think we all would like to think we could do that. But we can't, we can't, complete freedom isn't given to anyone, and if it is, it's only a prison in disguise, because nothing happens.

ALAN: A prison—yes, a prison. I don't understand, I don't understand anything, you're taking away everything. Can you explain it to me?

ANDREW: Tell me.

ALAN: Whatever. What am I doing here? Where am I going? And why there, rather than somewhere else? Why do I answer the phone one day and not the next? Why do I fear tomorrow and long for it today? What have you learned in your years that I will need to learn in mine? And will I learn it?! And . . . and more important, much more important, will it be worth learning? Don't ask me to go. Don't send me away. If I'm not doing what you want me to do, don't send me away. I'll learn anything, I'll learn. I'm stopped up, I'm plugged up. Help me get it loose, get it out. I want to be clean. I want to be empty and cool, like the space of a church which is empty. Oh, Jesus, how would that feel?

ANDREW: Fine. Cool and empty.

ALAN: Rub harder, press harder. Make your fingers like sticks and stick them through my brain, skewer my head and put little messages into it, big messages, ram them through and hope I'll learn.

ANDREW: You'll learn.

ALAN: How do you know?

ANDREW: I'd say you were on the border of collapsing. That's when we're usually ready to learn. When all of the pieces have fallen apart, that's when we're ready to start putting them together again.

ALAN: Yes. Yes. *Yes! (He grabs* ANDREW's *arms and wraps them around him.* ANDREW *buries his face in the boy's shoulder.)*

End of Act One.

Act Two

ALAN *bustles in efficiently carrying a sheaf of papers, an armful of books, a list of items that must be taken care of. It is now several weeks later.* PENNY *and* ALICIA, *both wearing robes, are having their morning coffee.*

ALAN: I'm embarrassed to say that I'm enjoying all of this.

ALICIA: That too will pass.

PENNY: Enjoy it. Be my guest.

ALAN: I'm sorry if I've taken over from you. He seems to give me all these things to do.

PENNY: He trusts you. That's important.

ALICIA: Trust?

PENNY: Alan is such a good worker, don't you think?

ALICIA: Oh, yes, such a good worker.

ALAN: Okay. Forget it.

PENNY: And so efficient. A born secretary.

ALAN: Assistant.

PENNY: The terms are interchangeable.

ALICIA: Like so many things in life. Now what were you going to ask us? How can we be helpful to you, little man?

ALAN: Do you have any idea where I might find this quote? "From the beginning he was a *necessary* writer, a chosen writer. And it is this experience of observing a man proving himself equal to the greatest of tasks—explaining the world to America and explaining America to itself—which provides the constant excitement in his work."

ALICIA: Yes, I remember that. I remember when we first read it. How touching it was, that evening. The article arrived from England, for it was in England that it first appeared . . .

PENNY: You'll find it in the supplement file, somewhere around volume sixty-two.

ALAN: Thank you.

ALICIA: . . . and we sat around the fire in the country. We were living in upstate Massachusetts then, or downstate Vermont. What was the difference. He read it through once, quietly to himself, and then he handed it to me and I read it. And then, quite spontaneously, I started reading it aloud, there was no one else there, softly at first, then more . . . robustly, as if *I* were announcing it to the world. He just sat there, and tears came to his eyes, and then they came to mine, too. (*There is a silence.*)

ALAN: I'll check that file. (*He goes.*)

PENNY: (*Looking at* ALICIA *for a long moment.*) What would it take to bring tears to your eyes now? I guess that sounds soppy. I'd cry. Goddamn it, I'd cry.

ALICIA: Whatever for?

PENNY: Whatever for! For what wasn't! That's what for.

ALICIA: But nothing ever was, not from the very beginning, not from when I was a child, not from when I married him, not from when you came. Now it's just someone else who's taken your place. You're the one who should be crying.

PENNY: Actually, I think it's all very funny, which should give you some idea about my capacity for love or feeling.

ALICIA: Yes. That's what he did to me, too. We should cry together, in black Greek dresses, nodding and bobbing our bodies in unison, wailing for our son lost in the war, our husbands never returning. Nothing changes. We just eat better now.

PENNY: (*Getting up to go.*) You're too much of a defeatist for me. I thought that all along. I never said it before, because I've been fond of you, but I've always thought you were a fool. I still think so, only now I think I am, too.

ALICIA: Why? What could you have done?

PENNY: Obviously nothing. I didn't even know anything was happening, and it happened. I think it might even be time for me to move along. Hit the road. Whatever.

ALICIA: Ah, that I couldn't do. I may have the worms inside, but goddamn it if I know how to get rid of them. One gives cats a pill once a month and no worms. (*Shrugs.*) Where would you go? I'd miss you. Don't go. No, don't go.

PENNY: There must be another aging and infirm writer around who can't file. He'd call me back soon enough. When he couldn't remember how the final chapter was now meant to come out. Oh, he needs us more than he'll ever admit.

ALICIA: Or less than we'll ever admit.

(*She pours herself some more coffee; she looks at* PENNY *to see if she too wants more.* PENNY *nods and* ALICIA *fills her cup. They sit.*)

(*At length.*) What he doesn't know, what he doesn't know now, is that he'll only hate himself even more. So strange. That's the only reason women are good for men: there's nothing from a woman that a man must have. They don't envy us our bodies. Or our minds. So we're safe. We are always horribly, unsatisfyingly safe. (*Gets up.*) Whatever you make up your mind to do, come and tell me. (*Starts walking up the stairway.*) I would give anything not to be safe.

PENNY: No, you wouldn't. Or you wouldn't be here.

ALICIA: You're wrong. My heroine has had her mastectomy. She isn't safe. I live all of her anxiety and fear. I dream for her. I have her nightmares, her hysteria. I cry out for her rejections. I live with her danger and it frightens me. And that's what I need, to be alive. You don't understand that; perhaps it's best to wish that you never do. (*She is gone.*)

PENNY: I still say you're the fool! (ANDREW *comes in.*) She's the fool and you've made her one and you've made me one and may you someday know it. Good-bye, you bastard. Good-bye, good luck, good fucking. What does a small boy's ass feel like? Tight and white and smooth and hairless. Do you pretend it's a cunt? Or do you pretend it's you a thousand years ago in some former life? Or some life to come? What do you pretend?—because it can only be pretending.

ANDREW: You always had an original and quite accurate insight into what made me function, which is why I like you around. There's no need for you to leave. I hope you won't leave. What do I pretend? Do you have a pad?

(She immediately takes up a steno pad and starts taking down his words.)

When he was young, he dreamed of removing his body hair, of waking up one morning and finding it mysteriously and miraculously gone, revealing his body gentile pure, white and stylish, smooth and desirable. When each morning found the wish not granted, he found he must resort to other, more positive actions. In the distant town, in their local store, to which he journeyed out of embarrassment lest his mad desires be made known locally, he purchased his first depilatory, a strange cream which, when applied, gave off a pungent odor, quite like cat shit. With it came the hair, guillotined off, smoothly, sharply, quickly. Ah, to appear tomorrow on the beach, naked, pure, desirable, wanted, freshly minted . . .

PENNY: And then the miracle, like all miracles, was over. The grayness of the third morning, the stubble from the still working furnace, belching up ashes of reminder . . .

ANDREW: You've been with me too long. Perhaps you should go.

PENNY: How long will it take you to train him to fill in your blanks?

ANDREW: He already fills in my blanks. Or rather, I his.

PENNY: Don't be smug.

ANDREW: You no longer know your place.

PENNY: Can you blame me?

ANDREW: I thought I'd trained you better.

PENNY: I don't think we ever came across this contingency. I don't think I did.

ANDREW: Of course we did. When we delved in Japanese myth, and researched the catamites, when we tried our *Death in Venice* bit. The story was quite well received.

PENNY: ". . . a crucially important story. The men to compare him with are literary artists driven by historical imagination. . . ."

ANDREW: I never understood that. I don't know very much about history. I consider that one of my biggest lacks.

PENNY: Oh, I can tell you about a few others. Would you like some coffee?

ANDREW: Please.

PENNY: Would you like me to tell you what I think they are?

ANDREW: No.

PENNY: Drink your coffee before it gets cold. Are you hungry?

ANDREW: What is there to eat?

PENNY: What sort of mood are we in today? Midday meal, midnight snack, or last supper?

ANDREW: The condemned ate a hearty meal.

PENNY: One hearty meal. (*Gets up to go and get it.*)

ANDREW: No, don't go. I'm not hungry. I feel very fond of you, very affectionate towards you, very warm, protective.

PENNY: Give me a trust fund before you jerk off. I'm not like that. People don't feel warm towards me. I'm not a warmth-inspiring person. I provoke respect because I am efficient. Efficiency does not give birth to trust funds.

ANDREW: You're older now.

PENNY: Than when I came here? Or when you found me?

ANDREW: Than yesterday.

PENNY: How sentimental of you.

ANDREW: You begin to sound just like Alicia.

PENNY: You never counted on our being such good friends, did you?

ANDREW: I never thought about it.

PENNY: Of course you did. You thought it would make her jealous as all hell, and that amused you.

ANDREW: Is that what you thought? It was much more subliminal than that. No—much more basic. Jealousy had nothing to do with it. More hunger. Speaking of which . . .

PENNY: I'm going. (*She heads towards the kitchen.*)

ALAN: (*Coming in in his bathing suit.*) Do you mind if I go for a swim? The references you wanted are prepared. Wait, first, before I go for a swim, come here with me.

(*Takes* ANDREW *by the hand and leads him over to the door to the terrace.*)

ANDREW: Here, what are you doing?

ALAN: See what a beautiful day.

ANDREW: Go for your swim.

ALAN: Come with me.

ANDREW: I never appear naked, or partially naked, in public before dusk.

ALAN: No one will see us. We can go to the cove.

ANDREW: We seem to be upsetting my apple cart.

ALAN: The ladies.

ANDREW: They prefer to be called women now. Yes, the women. Yes, the women are upset. Does that amuse you?

ALAN: No, of course not. I feel very self-conscious about them.

ANDREW: How do you feel about yourself?

ALAN: I want to tell you something. I don't want you to feel that this sudden conversion of mind came quite so unexpectedly. That one day I was black and the next day I was white, like some sort of magical transformation.

ANDREW: But that is what happened.

ALAN: Yes, and I try to deny it. I wrote my first poem yesterday, my first poem in maybe fifteen months.

ANDREW: I'd like to see it.

ALAN: Seeing it is unimportant. I wrote it. I don't want to know why I wrote it, what might have brought it about. The main thing is I wrote it, when I thought I might never.

ANDREW: So you attribute it to me, my influence, and you're grateful.

ALAN: (*Angry.*) I told you I don't want to go into it. Don't get so smug that it's you. Don't. Don't do that.

ANDREW: I . . . I'm sorry. Yes, I mustn't be smug.

ALAN: And, don't back down either.

ANDREW: No, I mustn't back down. No, I mustn't do that either. (*As* ALAN *turns away.*) What's the matter?

ALAN: I've got you buffaloed. In a corner. Say what you want to say, feel it any way you like. I shouldn't tell you what or what not to think.

ANDREW: Why am I buffaloed?

ALAN: Forget it.

ANDREW: Why!

ALAN: Because you're afraid you'll lose me.

ANDREW: Yes. You're right. Go for your swim.

ALAN: I told you once they put me away in a hospital. When I woke up, when the pills had worn off, there was a young doctor there, smug as can be, looking at me, sitting by my bedside, just waiting to be superior. "I'm not going to leave here," he says to me, "until you tell me why you did it." I looked at him for a very long time and finally said that he could sit there forever. I wasn't going to tell him a thing. And I didn't. I didn't know anyway, which is something he didn't know. A few months later, I was out of the hospital, of course, and back in school, only the school wouldn't let me stay unless I went to speak with their doctor a few times a week. I didn't mind because he was a lovely old man, very old-fashioned, but kind, kindly. One day, out of a clear blue sky, I started writing poems, something I'd wanted to do for years, but never done, never been able to do for some reason. I asked him, Why now? Why have I started now? And he just said, Why not? You did it, and the important thing is only that you did it.

ANDREW: Yes. Go for your swim. I'll watch you from the shore.

(ALAN *touches* ANDREW, *then goes out.* ANDREW *watches after him, then starts pacing the room.* PENNY *comes in with some food, recognizes the mood, and leaves it.* ANDREW *starts eating as he takes a microphone from a tape recorder, presses proper buttons, and begins talking into it.*)

How long before boredom? The luxury of summer is being withdrawn from me; I am outlawed from the district from which I came and of which I wrote. I shiver with the portent of the approaching icecap. My curiosity, my zest of mind, are getting the better of me. My confidence ebbs away. My books have not been much use. Whatever good I have accomplished seems an illusion. My private life is running out of time. And the only one I can talk to is you. The questions become more awful and the possible answers more frightening.

ALICIA: (*Comes to stand at the top of the stairs.*) Andrew.

ANDREW: (*Startled.*) How long have you been up there?

ALICIA: Oh, Andrew, had I just walked in on you this minute, I could write your words and movements for the last ten. I've finished.

ANDREW: What have you finished? With me?

ALICIA: Didn't that happen a long time ago? I have finished with my novel. Penelope has had her mastectomy and she has won.

ANDREW: Won what?

ALICIA: She's alive. She's survived. What do you mean, "won what?" She's fucked her way to the end of the tunnel and she's come out alive.

ANDREW: Minus a tit.

ALICIA: She's stronger than she was when she had two.

ANDREW: How did you arrange that? It sounds like a contrivance.

ALICIA: Why? She met a man, a film director, that's very contemporary, don't you think, not a very good film director, but one with a good head on his shoulders who cares for her as she is. And that's the important thing, don't you think?

ANDREW: A film director?

ALICIA: He is not particularly well endowed, in genitalia as well as talent, and he has a penchant for premature ejaculation, which often leaves her unsatisfied, but how long are the simply sexual standards meant to be important? She decides not very long, and takes him for his other qualities.

ANDREW: Whatever they may be.

ALICIA: Exactly.

ANDREW: My God, Alicia, have you left something out? He has no talent, he has no cock, he seems to have nothing but an ability to be her companion, like some sort of lapdog.

ALICIA: He is amusing, he enjoys extroverted social life, he has many friends who are interested in the current happenings of their world.

ANDREW: How extraordinary.

ALICIA: Additionally, he is a moderate eater.

ANDREW: A paragon. Wherever could one find him in real life?

ALICIA: I have no idea. I write fiction. Is that what you're going to say? Andrew, why do we pick at each other so? The weather is so lovely here. You've not even been to walk by the ocean. We came here so we could walk by the ocean, so we could work happily side by side—did we ever really do that, we were going to try. I have two breasts. You never ejaculated prematurely. You satisfied me. Years ago. We had friends. We went places.

ANDREW: And I ate moderately.

ALICIA: I don't care about that.

ANDREW: Leave me alone, Alicia. I resent it when you assume your saintlike countenance, when you walk down stairways like a Mother Superior in a home for palsied victims.

ALICIA: We are palsied.

ANDREW: We are not.

ALICIA: I don't want to fight. Don't raise your voice.

ANDREW: I want to fight! Yes, let's have an exchange of loud and banal tortuous insulting words. If I had to choose your main drawback, the one thing about you which drives me crazy, which is driving me crazy day by day as we work and live and eat and you look at me with those saintly critical eyes, always looking, if I had to choose only one thing, it is that *you don't fight back*! I don't want looks. I want words and actions, hard fists against my chest, spiteful words which let the venom out, get it out, get it all out! (*Shakes her.*) Fight me back, goddamn it! Hit me! Tell me you hate me! Tell me anything directly! Tell it to *me*! Not in the form of relaying me the plot of your new novel. Not in reminding me of some past you say we lived together, but which I just don't recall—not that we weren't there together, I just don't think we were there in the way your memory seems to dredge it up. Alicia, hit me hard. Open yourself up to whatever is bottled up inside of you.

(*She tries to turn away from him.*)

ALICIA: All I wanted, Andrew, was help. (*Runs out of the house.*)

ANDREW: And help is the one thing no human being should ask from another. We do, but we should be strong enough not to.

PENNY: (*Entering to clear the tray.*) Do you really believe that?

ANDREW: Leave me alone. I thought you were going. I thought you were hitting the road.

PENNY: Ah, yes. So I am.

(*She picks up the tray and takes it into the kitchen.* ANDREW, *in frustration, puts the microphone down and slowly goes upstairs. There is a long moment of silence and emptiness. Then a man enters, just as* ANDREW *is leaving. He is about thirty, and he has the look of someone who has been running a long time. He puts his suitcase down and looks around, smiling at familiar things, like the study, some words of* ANDREW'*s he reads, the bits of food about.* PENNY *comes in from the kitchen.*)

Loren!

LOREN: Hello. So you're still here. You must have the longevity record.

PENNY: I'm leaving. This is my last official act. Cleaning up after Daddy.

LOREN: Why are you leaving?

PENNY: What's happened to you? Where have you been? You look pretty good.

LOREN: You look exactly the same. And this place—just like all the others. Instant at home in a place that isn't. Do you think they ever bought any furniture, that it's all stored away somewhere and has been for years, from before I was born? I wonder what it looks like. Maybe a lot of it would be beautiful, like art nouveau.

PENNY: There isn't any furniture stored away.

LOREN: Maybe they never told you. Maybe they've forgotten about it themselves.

PENNY: There'd be storage rental to pay. I'd know about that.

LOREN: No, but maybe it's in someone's barn, up in New Hampshire.

PENNY: Loren, there isn't any furniture.

LOREN: Did they worry about me? Did they wonder where I was?

PENNY: If you were wandering about the face of the earth only as a gesture to pique their curiosity, you should know that you failed. Oh, once in a while, there'd be an "I wonder what's become of Loren" from your mother and a grunt from him. How did you find us here?

LOREN: I rang up Mr. Keller. I asked him not to let you know, in case I decided not to come.

PENNY: That's very considerate of you. And Mr. Keller. Mr. Keller has been working very hard lately in your father's behalf, it would seem. Oh, listen to me. I sound like an old lady headed for Palm Beach and, my God, that's just how I feel. How have you been, Loren? You look well. Your skin is clear, something my mother always figured was worth ten extra points. You look trim and fit. You were a little pudgy when you went away last time. Stay thin. It may come in handy.

LOREN: For what?

PENNY: If you haven't learned for what on your worldly travels, maybe you'd better go out again until you find out.

LOREN: "I traveled with the sea breeze. It whispered to me and I went with it. I closed my eyes. The world, still unborn and formless, must be shaped. Do not mock this journey, dearest one. It was a noble calling, good and fruitful, with no little innocent bliss."

PENNY: This is the new text. (*She picks up and reads a piece of manuscript.*) "We may be heroic after our fashion, disciplined warriors of our craft, yet we are all like women, for we exult in passion, and love is still our desire—our craving and our shame. And from this you will perceive that we poets can be neither wise nor worthy citizens. We must needs be wanton, must needs rove at large in the realm of feeling."

LOREN: That's not bad.

PENNY: That I leave for you to find out. Good-bye, Loren, and welcome home. Welcome, welcome, welcome.

(*He grabs her in his arms.*)

Go away, goddamn it, as I could never do. Go away and find your answers somewhere else. You won't be a son here. You'll be an appendage. And some shitty reminder that they loved each other once, enough to come together and bring you out of it. And they don't want to see that anymore.

LOREN: Poor Penny. What's happened?

PENNY: (*Touching his face.*) Have you been hurt on your journeys with the sea breeze?

LOREN: (*Breaking away.*) Where's my mother? How is she?

PENNY: Your mother is . . . I don't know. Removed. She doesn't strike out anymore. She talks only about the past or her new book. She . . . exists. We're friendly, I don't know how or why, but we need each other. She used to use me as a conduit, for information; she'd ask me questions about him, and I'd answer as best I could. But she doesn't do that anymore. Why did you come home?

LOREN: It seemed time. I was tired and unhappy, and the old life seemed good for a moment.

PENNY: Why did you go away?

LOREN: Thou shalt not covet thy father's mistress.

PENNY: That wasn't the reason. You could have had me.

LOREN: There might have been just a tiny bit of guilt attached to that. To go along with the rather larger amount that went along with having you in the first place. It was easier to go.

PENNY: Yes, it's always easier to go. So I shall go. I guess you can have my room. It's quite nice, with an ocean view. I'm going to take a last walk by the beach. I'll see you before I go. (*Kisses his cheek and leaves.*)

LOREN: (*Reads from another piece of paper.*) "We are a long way from the mood of my first work, the hope of the early settlers who had grown sick of narrowness and were all for pushing on into the realm of the unknown world of unlimited opportunity—"

ANDREW: (*From the upstairs landing.*) Stop reading that! How are you?

LOREN: I like what you're writing.

ANDREW: (*Starting down.*) Do you? If you were only one of my critics.

LOREN: I never understood a lot of it.

ANDREW: You never tried.

LOREN: No, I never tried. Same old Andrew.

(*They embrace awkwardly.*)

How are you, Dad?

ANDREW: I hate this place.

LOREN: You've put on a little weight.

ANDREW: A lot of weight. I get hungrier as I get older.

LOREN: It's a problem. Have you tried jogging? Or working out at a gym? You might like a gym. You meet some pretty interesting characters.

ANDREW: What are we babbling on about? Why are you home?

LOREN: Same old dad. Right to the point.

ANDREW: What's wrong with that? It's . . . it's good to see you.

LOREN: Maybe we could beat around the bush for a while.

ANDREW: Whom have you seen? Your mother, Penny?

LOREN: A rather different Penny.

ANDREW: I don't know what to do with her. One just can't throw out a faithful retainer after years of loyal service, but that's just what I want to do.

LOREN: What did she do to rate that?

ANDREW: Grew up, I guess. Ah, well, perhaps it's for the best.

LOREN: That's what you said when I left.

ANDREW: Well, wasn't it? You seem older, more mature, more in control of yourself.

LOREN: Do I? Was I going around peeing in public?

ANDREW: More or less.

LOREN: I was frightened of you.

ANDREW: I know. Are you still?

LOREN: I've just come home. I'll have to see.

ANDREW: Penny has been replaced with a twenty-three-year-old young man named Alan.

LOREN: Replaced? In all ways?

ANDREW: Yes. He's a poet.

LOREN: I . . . see.

ANDREW: Do you? I don't. Tell me where you have been these past few years. I have a new and morbid curiosity about the young, young things. Have you loved?

LOREN: Did we have that kind of relationship—that we exchanged these kinds of confidences? I never told you a thing. But then you never asked. Is it now tit for tat? Is that it?

ANDREW: You and your mother. Two against one. Loren, why are you home?

LOREN: I got terribly frightened and I came home.

ANDREW: I get frightened now, too.

LOREN: Like father, like son?

ANDREW: I rather doubt that. For your sake, anyway.

LOREN: Maybe I would have liked to be like you.

ANDREW: I hope that the frustration and agonizing that goes on daily in the body has not been passed on from father to son.

LOREN: But it has.

ANDREW: I'm sorry then.

LOREN: I don't want the sympathy. I just want to know how to cope with it.

ANDREW: I can't tell you that.

LOREN: Do you love him?

ANDREW: I don't think I let myself think of that.

LOREN: What have you thought about then?

ANDREW: I've thought about myself, about my reactions to his reactions to my actions. About his actions caused by my actions. About what makes him tick. About what I might do to make him function otherwise. He's an object of study. Does that sound awful?

LOREN: Yes.

ANDREW: So be it. There you have it.

LOREN: You're writing about him. In other words.

ANDREW: I'm writing about me.

LOREN: It's the same thing.

ANDREW: I suppose so. It isn't so awful. Perhaps, when you're older. How did you find us? Through Keller?

(LOREN *nods.*)

How is Keller?

LOREN: I gather he's been working a little harder than usual for you.

ANDREW: He sent me Alan, if that's what you mean.

LOREN: I thought he was a lawyer, not a pimp.

ANDREW: He sent him to me as a poet who was talented, but who was not writing, who was frightened of his talent.

LOREN: Since when have you turned into a Red Cross for frightened writers?

ANDREW: A lot has happened since you left. I started lecturing at several schools. I found I enjoyed my contact with the young. I was interested in what they did and said, their reactions to my work, my problems. And I found that this contact kept me younger, kept me alive, more in touch. . . .

LOREN: I could have done that for you, as I was growing up. I think I'll go and take a swim. (*Goes to take his suitcase upstairs.*)

ANDREW: I don't think there's a spare room. You'll have to sleep down here.

LOREN: Penny is giving me her room. Maybe I'll ask her not to leave just yet. We can stay together, two orphans in the storm.

ANDREW: Loren.

LOREN: Yes.

ANDREW: Welcome home.

LOREN: Thank you, Father.

ANDREW: Can't I say that it's good to have you home again?

LOREN: I can't imagine why. Will you write about me now?

ANDREW: I hadn't thought about it. Never mind.

LOREN: (*Going up.*) Thanks, Dad. It's great to be back. Never knowing what the next moment will bring. Just like growing up all over again.

ANDREW: Loren?

LOREN: Yes?

ANDREW: Don't go. Come back. Come down here. Let me talk.

(LOREN *comes back down, leaving his suitcase on the stairs, and together they sit in* ANDREW'*s study area.*)

Thank you.

LOREN: What's wrong, Andrew?

ANDREW: I don't know. I've been going through a very strange patch. I don't know why I'm here. Pieces are falling away from me, instead of coming together, sticking together.

LOREN: I . . . I'm sorry to hear that.

ANDREW: Why am I sleeping with a boy?

LOREN: Do you consider me the expert?

ANDREW: I must have done something to bend you in that direction.

LOREN: I'm not queer. I'm nothing. Neuter. For every blond boy, there's been a dark-haired girl. It's really quite meaningless. I blamed you for it, which suddenly now seems not to be true anymore, as if you, too, now are meaningless, and I've outgrown you. If you want to sleep with him, sleep with him. If relating to him gives you pleasure, have it. If sticking yourself into his ass gives you a feeling of power or returned youthfulness or simply an experience you've never had and want to try, take it, do so, whatever. You're a writer. You know all of this. Why are you asking me? Why is he having this affair with you? Have you asked him that?

ANDREW: He says he doesn't know. That it's just happening. That it isn't necessary to question it, it's just happening. Let it go at that.

LOREN: Just what I say to you.

ANDREW: Your generation seems completely uninterested in cause and effect. Why is unimportant.

LOREN: Things just happen. May I go now?

ANDREW: Yes, go now. Has this been so embarrassing for you?

LOREN: You're much softer now, Andrew. I actually find you quite touching.

ANDREW: Am I?

LOREN: I . . . I can't tell you why your pieces aren't sticking together. Mine aren't either. I don't think that Alan is really what's troubling you. And I think you know that.

ANDREW: It's the writing. The writing isn't going very well.

LOREN: From what I've read, it seems to be going very well.

ANDREW: Bits and pieces. Isolated patches. Nothing fits together very well. I don't know what I'm writing about.

LOREN: Why, you're writing about you, and this boy, and presumably about your wife and young mistress, and now me—all of us readily around you, placed here by your will.

ANDREW: Why do I get frightened?

LOREN: Oh, Andrew, do you really think I know? Or anyone does?

ANDREW: I hate it here.

LOREN: You had all your life to make a home for yourself. For us. Why didn't you?

ANDREW: I needed flexibility.

LOREN: I don't know what that is. Along with freedom, security, love, it's a foreign country. We don't speak their language very well. We never have. I gather my mother is not in such terrific shape.

ANDREW: Isn't she? She's annoying me as much as usual. I'd get rid of her if I could. Does that sound awful?

LOREN: Yes.

ANDREW: But it's honest. You youngsters forever talk of honesty.

LOREN: Wouldn't you miss her?

ANDREW: Yes, I would miss her. So what. One misses a place one has visited long ago but will never see again. One becomes nostalgic. I would gladly trade her for the resultant bout of nostalgia.

LOREN: Poor Daddy. I find it very refreshing. It may in fact be the reason I came home, to find you like this.

ANDREW: I'm going into town . . . to shop. So, you're home. The little image of myself, grown into manhood.

(*A very frustrated* LOREN *watches him leave. After a moment,* ALAN *and the young boy,* BILLY, *come in from the beach, wearing bathing suits.*)

ALAN: Who are you?

LOREN: And who are you? (*To* BILLY.) And you? I'm Andrew's son.

ALAN: He hasn't talked about you. But your mother has.

LOREN: You're Alan.

ALAN: Yes.

LOREN: My name is Loren.

ALAN: This is Billy.

BILLY: I'm your neighbor.

LOREN: How old are you?

BILLY: Here we go again. I'm a stunted midget of twenty-five. I don't shave and don't have hair under my arms or around my thing because I've plucked it all out with my mommy's tweezers. I prefer to stay young looking at any cost. Jesus, why can't a fifteen-year-old fuck and suck like everyone else?

LOREN: They just usually don't. I'm happy to meet the exception which disproves the rule. How do you do?

BILLY: Okay.

LOREN: You seem incredibly sexually oriented for one so young.

BILLY: Nothing else to do around here all summer.

LOREN: I wish I had been so open at your age.

BILLY: Want to fuck?

LOREN: Not now. Maybe later.

BILLY: Okay. Don't worry. I'll get you.

LOREN: Maybe you will.

ALAN: Billy, go home, will you.

    (BILLY *shrugs, leaves, a bit sulkily.*)

LOREN: What do we say to each other?

ALAN: I'm happy to meet you.

LOREN: Ah, but am I happy to meet you?

ALAN: Does any of this make any difference? Your mother will be happy, now that you're back.

LOREN: I'm nervous about seeing her, now.

ALAN: Now that you know all about me.

LOREN: Yes.

ALAN: Well, try this on for size. When I first came here, I was attracted to your mother. We went to bed together.

LOREN: Why did you leave her?

ALAN: She gave me something that was important for that moment, and then he came along and gave me more. I still get from him something that's making me work and grow, that I need right now.

LOREN: People seem disposable items to you.

ALAN: Aren't they for everyone? I'm just not hypocritical about it.

LOREN: Aren't you? Give me hypocrisy, then. It's beginning to seem even necessary. Have you been through Penny, too?

ALAN: We've made love, if that's what you mean.

LOREN: You've been a little cyclone, haven't you?

ALAN: At each moment, I felt love for them. I needed them and they needed me. It just didn't sustain with Penny. She fights herself too much. So does your mother.

LOREN: And my father is a saint, giving openly without dispute.

ALAN: He seems to need more than they do, and hence has more to give.

LOREN: You make it all sound very simple. Like an equation.

ALAN: I don't think about it.

LOREN: And if someone else came along who had more to give, and who needed even more, then off you'd go, into the night.

ALAN: Perhaps. It would depend on just how I was feeling at that moment—nourished or in need of different nourishment.

LOREN: Perhaps you're in the midst of founding a new school of philosophy. You could call it the selfish school.

ALAN: Or the honest school. Look, this is a debate that must have gone on for centuries. We're not going to solve it. My name is Alan. I'm your father's secretary. I'm happy to meet you.

(*He holds out his hand.* LOREN, *after a pause, takes it, shaking his head in wonderment.*)

Good. I'm glad you're home.

LOREN: You're knocked me off balance, you fucker.

ALAN: I'm sure you'll pull yourself back up and together.

LOREN: Are you? No, I'm not together at all, and you're not helping matters much.

ALAN: Maybe you should go then.

LOREN: Oh, no! It's much too interesting to go.

ALAN: Then welcome.

LOREN: What's my father like in bed?

ALAN: Suppose you tell me about your sex life?

LOREN: What would you like to know?

ALAN: Nothing really.

LOREN: I'm sorry you're not genuinely more curious. I'd like to tell you about it.

ALAN: Then please tell me.

LOREN: You're very vulnerable.

ALAN: No, I'm not. I try not to be vulnerable at all. If you want to know, that's my secret.

LOREN: I say your secret is a load of shit. You are wide open to being hurt, and to being desperately needed by someone who can give you what you need. That's why you're here. Penny obviously has little to give you, except a body and a pleasant efficiency which must get wearing after a while. My mother—

my mother needs and wants my father and only my father. You could only get so much from her before she would withdraw into her unreal memories of a haunted past. If it was really haunted, or if she just prefers to think of it that way. Artists, you know. Leaving my father . . .

ALAN: Perhaps . . . perhaps you're right. I don't think about it. It just happens . . . in a certain way.

LOREN: Then perhaps one of these moments you will start to see things clearly and for yourself—and not through someone else's eyes.

ALAN: Do you?

LOREN: See things clearly? Heavens, no. But I try and I want to, which is two steps ahead of you.

ALAN: You make everything so . . . intellectual, so . . . you analyze too much. I just . . . just feel. I'm sorry you don't understand that, what it means to feel things, inside of you, without putting words to them.

LOREN: How do you know I'm not capable of that, too?

ALAN: (*Touching* LOREN'*s face.*) Do you experience the chemical property of skin? I knew a woman who said that any relationship was really founded on how two people's skins felt to each other. (*Removing his hand.*)

LOREN: I'll stay the one person in this household unseduced.

ALAN: You're reacting intellectually, not emotionally. How does my hand feel?

LOREN: Like a hand. I know what skin feels like. I know what it's like to have in my arms someone who feels lovely to me. Your arguments are kindergarten arguments, or will be if the present rate of advancing juvenile precociousness is maintained. No, I don't want to be a rung on your ladder.

ALAN: (*Starting up the stairs.*) Welcome home. Yes, I think it will be interesting for you. (*Goes out.*)

(*After a moment, Alicia comes in from the terrace. She stands there for a long moment, looking at her son. He turns, and they smile.*)

LOREN: Hello.

(*Then they embrace.*)

How are you, mother?

ALICIA: Oh, Loren, I don't know. How are you? Where have you been? What have you been doing? How long will you stay? Oh, we have so much to catch up on. (*She breaks away from him and goes to nervously light a cigarette.*) My goodness, I'm shaking. Is it so hard for mothers to face their sons after long absences? Why did you go away for so long? Why did you go away at all? Stupid me, forgive such silly questions.

LOREN: Don't be nervous. I've had marvelous years, years I want to tell you about—the places and people and experiences, and the things I've thought. I'll stay a while, if you want me to.

ALICIA: Yes, I want you to. Very much. We'll have all sorts of time to talk. What will we talk about first?

LOREN: Mother, I know things aren't well for you.

ALICIA: Of course they are!

LOREN: Penny's told me what's happening. I've met Alan. Please relax. There's nothing you have to shield me from. We can talk and work things out.

ALICIA: Can we? Oh, Loren, I don't think talk will do anything anymore. Not a single thing. Except complicate matters. And they're so complicated, so crystal clearly complicated. I no longer want to sort them out. I no longer wish to know why things are the way they are. I just want each day to quickly blend into the next one and the next one after that. I want the sun to keep on shining. I want people to come and go. I want to sleep great amounts and wake up to read a book, perhaps a good mystery novel, or something without sex and questions. I want to be like a cat, just sleep when I have to and wake up, and actually be amused by running round in circles chasing my own tail. That sounds like heaven. My own circumscribed circular world, with only me inside of it. Does all of this sound silly? It sounds like I'm getting old. I should move to Florida, no, the south of France, overlooking the ocean but far enough away not to hear the babbling people. The beachifying people. That's what I'll write my next novel about, beachifying people. I must stop rambling and gobbling so, like a turkey. . .

LOREN: Mother, stop please, you're killing yourself . . .

ALICIA: Am I? How am I doing that? I'm sorry. Yes, I must calm down. Perhaps a trip into town. We could buy some pencils, or yesterday's newspaper, or some fancy cakes for your father. There's so much to do.

LOREN: We'll make things to do.

ALICIA: Make things to do! I don't want to have to do that. I want things to happen spontaneously because we're happy. Oh, Loren, I'm a middle-aged mother who still wants her world full of sugar candy and lace things. Why can't I grow up!

LOREN: Perhaps he won't let you.

ALICIA: On the contrary. His actions constantly remind me that the real world is one I do not wish to enter. Imagine him sleeping with a boy. A little, lovely, boy, so smooth and tender and soft. I slept with him, too, you know. Yes, I did. I'm quite proud of that. Penny has slept with him, but he came to me first. Why do you think he left me, Loren? Why do you think he came and went so quickly? Will you sleep with him, too? My goodness, I never thought of that. We may have to constantly find him new sleeping companions, like some rare animal in the zoo who requires a special diet. Are you ready to be eaten by the soft and lovely Alan? Can we feed you to the Alan? Loren, come here, please, come here and let me hold you.

LOREN: (*Holding his mother.*) It's all right, mother. It's all right. We'll go out and find other things.

ALICIA: I don't want to go out. This is my home. I must stay at home.

LOREN: Get some rest, mother. Take a nap. Then we'll go for a long walk by the ocean in the moonlight, after dinner, when you're rested and calm and we can talk. Would you like that? Doesn't that sound nice.

ALICIA: Yes, that sounds fine. I'll take a nap, that's what I'll do, and rest up for our walk in the moonlight.

End of Act Two.

Act Three

It is after dinner, a late dinner. The lights are low, perhaps only candles burning down. There is moonlight from outside. The study is dimly illuminated. The dining table contains the remains of what must have been a fine and lavish meal. At rise, ALICIA *is bringing in a large cake, with candles on it. The others—*PENNY, ANDREW, ALAN, *and* LOREN—*react with surprise.*

ALICIA: This is my farewell to Penny cake. I have made it myself, from entirely natural ingredients. I must make it clear that this is not a cake to celebrate your leaving, but to celebrate the sweetness of your many years here, and the happy hours we spent together. What it all boils down to is—I wanted to get you a present, but I didn't know what to get you. In the end, everything in this house is always reduced to nutritional components anyway, so why not for you.

(Handing her a big knife to cut the cake.)

I hope you understand.

PENNY: Thank you. Yes, I do. Now who am I asked to kill with this weapon?

ANDREW: Another bottle of wine, this fine wine! Alicia, you have outdone yourself.

ALICIA: Yes, I've thought so.

PENNY: (*Cutting cake and handing it around, first to* LOREN.) I consider this not so much a farewell to Penny cake as a welcome home to Loren cake.

LOREN: That's too much.

PENNY: They're entirely natural ingredients.

LOREN: Perhaps I can split it in half and give half to Alan.

PENNY: Alan will have his very own piece. And so shall Andrew. And Alicia, will you have a piece?

ALICIA: Absolutely. Do you know, I even put in some carrots.

ANDREW: (*Who has uncorked a wine bottle and poured himself a huge glass of wine.*) May I propose a toast? Does anyone mind if I propose a toast?

ALICIA: Don't be boring, Andrew.

LOREN: Let him propose a toast.

ANDREW: Shall we call a council and vote on Andrew's proposing a toast?

ALICIA: Get on with it.

ANDREW: Shall we get on with it, Penny?

PENNY: It's got nothing to do with me anymore, thank God.

ANDREW: Alan, do you enjoy toasts?

ALAN: Let's hear it, Andrew, and I'll tell you.

ANDREW: It is a memorized toast, that is . . .

ALICIA: That means it's a long one.

ANDREW: . . . it is an important passage I have committed to memory. A passage by a writer other than myself. Should anyone be able to guess who it is . . . (*Downs the wine.*) "The mystery of the Word is great . . . ."

ALICIA: Oh, this is a long one.

PENNY: Yes, it is. (*Takes* ALICIA'*s hand in commiseration.*)

LOREN: I've never heard it.

ALAN: Neither have I.

ANDREW: ". . . the responsibility for it and its purity is of a symbolic spiritual kind; it has not only an artistic but also a general ethical significance; it is responsibility itself, human responsibility quite simply, also the responsibility for one's own people . . ."

ALICIA: (*To* LOREN.) You've heard it. You probably just closed up your ears.

PENNY: Or you didn't understand it. I never understood it.

ANDREW: ". . . the duty of keeping pure its image in the sight of humanity. In the Word—that's a capital W, mind you—in the Word is involved the unity of humanity, the wholeness of the human problem, which permits nobody, today less than ever, to separate the intellectual and artistic from the political and social . . ."

PENNY: You do go on, you know. You go on and on and on. I'm glad I'm leaving you, you fat fart of a windbag.

ALAN: Shut up.

LOREN: "In the Word is involved the wholeness of the human problem." I like that.

ALICIA: I liked it too, once. 1 just can't find the word I want anymore.

PENNY: Yes, you are a fat fart of a windbag.

LOREN: We heard you the first time.

PENNY: (*Standing up.*) A fat fart of a windbag. *Whooooosh.* (*Blows out a candle on the cake intentionally.*) Those are my words for today. And yesterday. And tomorrow. In the Word is the unity of the fart of a windbag. Will anyone quote me twenty years from today?

ANDREW: Little girl, have you packed? Are you leaving my house in order?

PENNY: I am leaving your house. It will have to seek its own order.

ANDREW: And not a minute too soon.

PENNY: A very clever arrangement of words. "And ... not ... a ... minute ... too ... soon." The unity of the Words. So clever, one following the other.

ANDREW: Good-bye, little girl.

PENNY: (*Standing up unsteadily.*) Now listen to me. I am leaving. And not a minute too soon. I am sorry to be leaving. Because I don't know where I want you to forward my mail. I find that very sad. You have made me sad. I think you're all a load of ... tripe. If you be greatness, give me the bums. I thought I had the bums. But I don't think I did. I had the great ones. Boy, have I had the great ones.

ALAN: Penny, how about calling it quits and going to bed.

PENNY: I have called it quits. Good-night, all. I made my farewell speech: I have loved you, each and every one of you. In my own way. I have tried to be of help. Because I believed in what you were doing. I leave now. Good-bye. I . . . I don't love you anymore.

(*She gets up and walks, as best she can, toward the stairs.* LOREN *goes to help her, but she refuses his help. She slowly goes up and out.* ALICIA *turns from looking at* PENNY *to looking at* ANDREW. ANDREW, *annoyed, picks up the bottle of wine and his glass and goes to his study, where he will sit and drink and stare into space.*)

LOREN: Good-bye, Penny.

ALICIA: Yes, good-bye to Penny. I used to want this day. As always, when it happens it either happens too late or it doesn't make any difference anymore.

ALAN: Now you'll wish me to go away—so you still have something to wish for.

ALICIA: I have wished you away, ever since you came into my arms. My god, Loren, I don't want you to hear any of this. I . . . I'm sorry.

LOREN: Don't be sorry, Mother.

ALICIA: Oh, but I am. I don't want you to hear or see anymore. (*She goes to* ALAN *and caresses his head and his face.*) I don't want you to see anymore or hear anymore to know about me. (*To* ALAN.) Yes, you are beautiful. For one single moment you made me feel beautiful. I feel sick to my stomach. My wonderful meal has come back to haunt me. Would you take me to my room?

(ALAN *gets up, starting to help her.*)

Will you forgive us, Loren? Will you excuse us? (*She sits down again.*) No, I must stay with my son on his first night home. Will you leave us alone, please?

ALAN: Of course. (*Starts to go upstairs.*)

ALICIA: No, you must go to Andrew. He's sulking in the study. No one is paying any attention to him. Go and ask him if he wants anything more to drink.

ALAN: I think I'll go to bed.

ANDREW: (*Calling from the study.*) Alan! Come here. We have work to do.

(ALAN *goes to the study.* ANDREW *throws open his arms. After a long moment,* ALAN *goes to him and allows himself to be embraced.*)

Have something to drink. (*He pours some of his wine into* ALAN'*s mouth.*) Drink, child, drink. Your father's in the clink. Your mother's dancing in another's arms, so drink, child, don't think.

ALICIA: (*She and* LOREN *have sat and listened to the above.*) So there you have it. (LOREN *doesn't know what to say.*) No, of course, there's nothing to say. Nothing to say. Please, I beg of you, tell me about yourself. Tell me anything!

LOREN: I came home . . . because I was frightened. (*Wants to cry.*)

ALICIA: Oh, my poor, dear son. And you came home to find us frightened, too. We should know better at our age, don't you think? But why? Why should we?

LOREN: I just hoped you would.

ALICIA: Now you know our secret.

LOREN: I met a woman who looked like you. We drove through the country, across the country. We made love in so many motel rooms across the country. We wandered around the French Quarter one night and she took me back to our room and she beat me. She laughingly tied me up with sheets and then proceeded to pound the shit out of me with my belt. Then she left me. And she looked like you.

ALICIA: I apologize for her!

LOREN: Oh, don't be silly. I don't blame you for that.

ALICIA: Tell me more. I've been so selfish, only telling you about my problems. Tell me about yours.

ANDREW: (*Yelling from the study;* ALAN *sits at his feet, staring into space.*) Yes, Loren, tell her more!

LOREN: (*Standing in the middle, between the two of them.*) Tell her more! Tell me more! You're pulling me in two! Nothing's changed. Nothing's changed. What is there to tell you that can change anything? I came home needing *help.*

(*He falls into a heap on the floor.* ALICIA *runs to him.*)

I can't walk. My feet don't walk. They don't move. They won't carry me, go one in front of the other. . . .

ALICIA: Andrew . . . Andrew, help us. . . .

ANDREW: (*Not getting up.*) Get up, Loren. Get up and walk.

LOREN: I can't.

ANDREW: Get up on your two feet and walk.

ALAN: He's frightened, Andrew. You should go to him.

ANDREW: Go to your room! This isn't your concern.

ALAN: Isn't it? Good night. (*Gets up; passing by* LOREN, *he touches his head.*) Good night, Loren. I understand. I'll see you tomorrow. (*He goes up the stairs and out.*)

ALICIA: What's wrong, Loren? Can you really not walk?

LOREN: I can walk. I don't want to. I told you I was frightened. No one listens to me, though. I only see your fears. I want to get rid of mine.

ANDREW: (*Coming to him.*) Let me help you up, son. (*He does so, and* LOREN *allows this.*) There. Come. Let's sit down and all talk this out.

(*They all sit at the table.*)

Now, where have you been?

LOREN: It just seems that I'm always waiting.

ANDREW: Try and tell us for what.

LOREN: Just for something nice to happen. For someone to love. For some nice person to be there and be interested and to answer my interest. So we can hold each other and love each other and feel each other's bodies and enjoy that. Is that so much to ask from life—to wait for?

ALICIA: No, no.

ANDREW: Yes. It is. Because it doesn't happen.

LOREN: How can you say that?

ANDREW: Why can't I?

LOREN: Because you're ... you're gobbling up people like it's going out of style, like you're at some last supper.

ANDREW: I *am* at a last supper. Why shouldn't I taste some new flavors? Why not?

ALICIA: Why?

ANDREW: I'll tell you! Each day, each day brings something new to be frightened of. Did I ever think I would be frightened of ... of the Asian masses, or hordes of unemployed blacks, or food shortages, or taxes taking most of what I earn, or Arab retribution which has destroyed the entire free world's economy ... highway holdups. I never thought I would be frightened of any of that. Why shouldn't I eat and eat and eat as if there's no tomorrow? Why deprive myself?

ALICIA: And what of us?

ANDREW: Eat yourself. Love where you can. I no longer possess rights over you. I renounce them.

ALICIA: You are a crude and careless man.

ANDREW: Am I? Why must I be forever bound to you? To your needs? You drive me crazy with your complaints and needs. Can't you take care of yourself?

ALICIA: Not when you've taken care of me all these years. I don't know anything else.

ANDREW: Then you must learn. I haven't taken care of you all these years. I've tolerated you all of these years. And you've been fool enough to accept it, to tolerate me back, to let it go on and on and on like an arid desert, never allowing yourself to see the truth, that we were and are empty.

LOREN: Stop it!

ANDREW: (*Pleading to his son.*) But we *are*! Can't you see that? Why must you be blind, too? You've been wandering the world. I don't know what the hell happened to you, but you come home sobbing that you can't find love. Well, goddammit, there's nothing that says it's there waiting for you and that it's your due right. Nothing is there; nothing is easy; nothing is guaranteed. You've got to go out with your bare hands and wrench out what you can. Get up off the floor!

LOREN: I think I would rather not, that I would rather be the coward, than to be like you.

ANDREW: That's fair enough. I told you to be your own man. Find out who that is.

LOREN: How does one find out? You tell me! You who have just discovered how to suck cock. You tell me.

ANDREW: It's a hell of a lot more tasteful than you slobbering there on the floor.

LOREN: Everything boils down to sex in your world, and it scares me shitless.

ANDREW: There's nothing scary about sex.

LOREN: There is when it destroys families. And yes, there is because it's all bodies and rejections. Don't you know that? Go out and get it with my bare hands? You just take. From weak people who give from fear or need. You don't know what it's like to be loved. You're too quick on the grab to wait and find out if they really want you—because you know that if you waited to find out, you'd probably be rejected. Out of hand.

ANDREW: (*Sadly.*) There's truth in what you say. That's why I act as I do.

ALICIA: Oh, Andrew, what a horrible admission. I've loved you.

LOREN: And you shit all over her!

ALICIA: Loren!

ANDREW: (*Placing his hands on hers.*) Yes, Alicia. I've known that. Only there was nothing I could do with it. Nothing. Because I haven't loved you for a very long time. Is this such an awful thing to say? I don't think so. I should have said it years ago. My love, I don't know, it just disappeared many years ago. It went little by little, until one day I woke up and found myself in bed with a stranger.

(*She walks away, across the room.*)

I'm sorry. No, I'm not sorry, because it's the truth.

(*She starts climbing the stairs.*)

I'm as guilty as you for letting it go on and on, all these years. But, by my actions, I thought I was showing you that . . . I wanted out.

(*She goes out.*)

LOREN: Go up to her.

ANDREW: I can't.

LOREN: I'll go to her.

ANDREW: (*Grabbing him back.*) No, you don't. She's got to face this herself. If she kills herself, that's her decision. You can't give her any more love than you do, which is already too much, and she knows it's there—but it's not what she needs, not a son's love. She's got to face this herself. And she'll only hug you and kiss you, and that's not what you should have from her either.

LOREN: Andrew, what am I going to do?

ANDREW: You're going to leave us in our hell and get the hell on with your life. Get out! Go tonight! Go and fuck yourself silly until you find your answers.

LOREN: Is Alan your answer?

ANDREW: Don't be silly. He's just another piece of meat. Same as Penny was, only not as efficient. People are all objects to me, Loren, and that's the particular cross I must bear. They satisfy me for a while, calm me down, divert my attention, but in the end, I have only my ugly self to contend with. And that's when I write.

LOREN: But you write like an angel.

ANDREW: So they tell me. Now you know the price for angelhood. Will it help you? Do you want to write?

LOREN: No, I don't think so.

ANDREW: Then something else will come along.

LOREN: Right now, I'm going to follow your fuck myself silly advice. There was a young boy here this afternoon. I'll look for him on the beach.

ANDREW: Come back a minute. I'm sorry I wasn't a better figure for you to look up to. That somehow my being such an object of terror has extruded you towards your own kind. But, by my own words, I can only say that even had you a loving father, as I had, it can still turn out the same. (*Embraces* LOREN, *and* LOREN *finally returns the embrace.*) I wish we had done this many years ago. Now go out there and do what you will. And I hope the kid's got a strong ass.

(LOREN *goes out and* ANDREW *fetches and opens another bottle of wine. He drinks from it and then:*)

"Who are these coming to the Sacrifice?
    To what green altar, O mysterious priest,
Leadst thou that heifer lowing at the skies,
    And all his silken flanks with garlands drest?
What little town by river or sea shore,
    Is . . . is . . . is emptied of this folk, this pious morn?
And, little town, thy streets for evermore
    Will silent be; and not a soul to tell
        Why thou art desolate, can e'er return . . ."

(*He shivers involuntarily.* ALAN *appears at the top of the stairs and starts down.*)

ALAN: Penny and Alicia are together.

ANDREW: Planning their strategy, no doubt.

ALAN: I don't think so. Comforting each other.

ANDREW: Yes, perhaps that.

ALAN: Where's Loren?

ANDREW: Gone looking for comfort, too.

ALAN: Which leaves only us. Do we need comfort as well?

ANDREW: Yes, I think so.

ALAN: Will it bring you much satisfaction? Or peace? Or whatever it is you seem to need so much of?

ANDREW: Perhaps you're better than Penny. You do have a rather crude but effective understanding of me.

ALAN: Why do you have to say it so harshly?

ANDREW: I'm accustomed to using words properly. Camouflage, disguise—sentimentalization are not for me.

ALAN: Could we talk about you and not your work?

ANDREW: I don't separate the two.

ALAN: I do. I'm going to make you do so, too.

ANDREW: Ah, the child begins to grow.

ALAN: Shut up. The child was fairly well grown when he got here. If anything, he's beginning to age.

ANDREW: Have we done that to you? Made you conscious of your mortality?

ALAN: There you go with your words again. Tell me how you *feel* about me. Put it into nice simple words, basic simple emotions, like love or hate or nice or not so nice.

ANDREW: You're very . . . nice. Something like that?

ALAN: Dig a little deeper.

ANDREW: A little deeper . . . let's see. I think you're a very fine fellow. How's that?

ALAN: Shitty. I'm in love with you, Andrew. I don't know why, it has nothing to do with sex, it has to do with some feeling in the pit of my stomach which makes me need you and want to cling to your big bulk. That makes me feel bigger, more necessary, in a way that I've not felt before. Do you think, now, that you could answer me in a more effective way?

ANDREW: No.

ALAN: Why not?

ANDREW: It's not my habit to explain these things.

ALAN: Is that because no one has ever asked you to before? Or are you just running away?

ANDREW: I'll explain it on paper and then you can read all about it.

ALAN: I don't want to read about it. I want to hear you tell me.

ANDREW: Go to bed. Go away.

ALAN: Is it so awfully hard to say what you feel?

ANDREW: When I'm prepared to say what I want to say, I'll call you in and we can discuss it at length.

ALAN: You're a very unfortunate man. Good night.

ANDREW: Come here! (ALAN *walks on; forcing* ANDREW *to go and grab him back.*) I said come here! You imbecile! What right have you to come and exercise your wiles. You stupid representative of beauty, come into my house to taunt me with your body and your eyes and your graceful movements and your skin . . .

ALAN: Stop composing.

ANDREW: Stop composing! (*He hauls off and is about to hit* ALAN *when instead he clutches at him clumsily and pulls him into his arms.*) I'm not used to the kind of words you want to hear, and you shan't hear them from me. If it isn't enough that I allow you here, that in my own way this is my indication of my need for you, than leave me, get out. I won't suffer your impertinences.

ALAN: Such funny words for love.

ANDREW: I said nothing about love. Why do you love me? I am a very unlovable creature. What can you possibly get from me that's desirable?

ALAN: I told you. You fool. You seem to make all love physical. An acceptance of your body.

ANDREW: I believe most men do. And I hate how I am made.

ALAN: Only, I think, ones who think they are ugly.

ANDREW: I am ugly.

ALAN: Only to yourself. If you could only realize that there are other things in you which I respond to, which I enjoy holding. You have an inside as well as an outside.

ANDREW: How repulsively put. Anyway, my inside is mine alone.

ALAN: No, it isn't. Not when I feel some of it, too, and want to feel more. Oh, I know you think that the insides are only for your books. But I want to try to teach you that they are for others as well.

ANDREW: This is pathetic. Please go to bed.

ALAN: Only if you'll come with me.

ANDREW: I'll be up shortly.

ALAN: No, come now. Otherwise, there's no reason to come at all. If you can understand that.

ANDREW: Yes, yes. I'll come. I'll come.

ALAN: Don't make it sound like such a defeat.

ANDREW: Damn it, now don't you start with *your* words. Must you have complete and total victories?

ALAN: Of course.

ANDREW: Damn you.

ALAN: You try in every way to do so. Is it only my physical body that you love?

ANDREW: I can't separate that from the rest of you. Don't ask me to.

ALAN: I think I will. Would you love me if I were not quite so nice on the outside? No, probably not. I'll accept that. It's nothing new. Do you realize how insulting that is for me?

ANDREW: Insulting? You ingrate.

ALAN: In some ways, you're a very dumb man.

ANDREW: In these matters yes. It's all so ... like some sort of biological laboratory experiment. You want my insides; I don't want to give them, I don't know how to give them. I want your outsides, and you want to give me your insides. We're frogs on the cutting room table.

ALAN: Come to bed, Andrew. (*Leads him by the hand up the stairs and out.*)

(*The lights go down to denote the passage of time. When they come up, the stage is dark and empty, lit only by a few remaining candles. Then* LOREN *comes in, carrying the limp body of* BILLY. *He places him down on the studio bed and kneels beside him sadly. Then he goes out again. When he returns, he is carrying the body of* PENNY, *and* ALICIA *is following behind him. He places* PENNY *on the bed next to* BILLY. *Then he goes and makes a stiff drink, which he gives to his mother.*)

ALICIA: Thank you.

LOREN: Sit down, Mother. (*Makes her do so.*) Could we try and piece together what has happened?

ALICIA: They went swimming together.

LOREN: But there's blood.

ALICIA: Blood? Yes, yes ... of course. She tried to cut her wrists. Upstairs. I ... I found a knife in her room. I went ... rushing out the back deck and down the stairs to the ocean.

LOREN: I went walking. I heard Billy calling. I thought it was for me.

ALICIA: (*Crying out.*) Andrew! Help us!

LOREN: Tell me what happened.

ALICIA: What is there to tell? It's in the past, already in the past, completely in the past.

LOREN: Mother, Mother, speak sense. We'll have to call soon, and they'll ask questions. Tell me now.

ALICIA: When I left your father, when he told me he no longer loved me, I went up to my room to weep. I found I couldn't. I went to Penny's room. She sat there, on the corner of her bed, not knowing what to do. Should she pack, should she stay, where would she go—so many possibilities for choice often make for no choice at all. I know that. She looked at me and she cried, Hold me, make me feel warm.

(ALAN, *pulling on a robe, comes running from upstairs.* ANDREW *stands, also in a robe, looking down.*)

ALAN: Has anyone been called? The police? An ambulance?

LOREN: I don't think an ambulance would be any use.

(ALAN *goes to the study to silently phone the police as* ANDREW *comes down the stairs slowly.*)

ALICIA: I found myself holding her, then kissing her, then we were almost making love, gripping each other for purchase, holding on for dear life. It was a nourishing, replenishing experience. She said she wanted to go for a swim, and would I join her in a few minutes. She wanted to go out alone, to be alone in the night air, under the moon, to walk naked alone for a few minutes, but would I then come out and swim with her. I said I would, I went to my room and rested for a bit, perhaps I even slept. Then I put on my beach robe and went down to the beach. That's where I found you. Now it's your turn.

LOREN: My turn?

ANDREW: Tell us your story, Loren.

LOREN: It's not a story. I left you, you saw me go out to look for Billy. I found him in the dunes and we made love. Or rather he taught me how to make his kind of love. Soft and tender and very child-like. What did you say? A very replenishing experience. I've never felt like that before. I never want to feel like that again, so much in need of that that I almost fainted, I was in another world, of lost control, where I never want to be again. After a while I sensed that he was no longer there, that he'd gone off. I could hear soft voices down by the water. I walked down there. Penny was naked, and so was my Billy. They were playing by the water's edge, like two small children, splashing water and sand at each other, both completely naked, and natural, like they had almost grown up together and played like this every day. I just sat down and watched them. I don't think they even knew I was there. She said that she wanted to make love with him and he said that he would like to try, for the very first time. But then, when they embraced for a while, he cried out that he couldn't do it. He said he wanted to run back to me in the sand dunes, to make love again to me, that he only knew how to make love to his own kind. She said, Goddamn you and all of you, may you be tortured together, they were doomed together, must die together. And she had a knife.

ANDREW: She stabbed him and then killed herself?

LOREN: I think so. I thought for a moment he took the knife and did it all himself, but . . .

ALICIA: No, no, I think she must have done it. She had the knife in her room when I first went in and she was trying to cut her wrists.

ALAN: (*Now returning.*) Does it make any difference?

ANDREW: Only for the record, of course.

ALAN: Of course.

LOREN: (*Trying to wrap the bodies with the cover.*) Could we bundle them up? Could we take them outside again? Could we take them away from here?

ALICIA: Does he have any parents to notify? I thought he said he was here alone.

ALAN: He is. He was.

ALICIA: Andrew . . . ?

ANDREW: We'll leave. We'll travel on again. We'll find another house.

ALICIA: No, we must stay here. We must stop going from house to house.

ANDREW: Yes.

ALAN: Loren, help me with them. Let's take them outside to the terrace. There's blood.

(*He and* LOREN *take one and then the next body out through the following speeches.*)

ALICIA: We can stay, then?

ANDREW: Yes.

ALICIA: I can stay, then?

ANDREW: Yes.

ALICIA: You won't leave me?

ANDREW: No, Alicia, I won't leave you.

ALICIA: We can read to each other again.

ANDREW: Yes.

ALICIA: Andrew, I'm cold. Will you hold me?

(*She stands there waiting.* ANDREW *comes and embraces har perfunctorily, but it seems to be good enough for her.*)

That's good. I'll buy furniture, our very own things. I saw quite a handsome desk in a shop the other day, for you to write at. I thought you would look very good writing at it.

ANDREW: Then we must get it. And find one for you as well.

ALICIA: I don't think I should like to write anymore. I'll cook. We'll play house again. We won't need a housekeeper anymore. Or secretaries, except maybe someone part-time to type your final manuscript and do some routine accounting.

ANDREW: Loren, help your mother upstairs. In her medicine cabinet, you'll find some pink sedative pills. Give her two or three to help her rest. Tomorrow, Alicia, we'll begin again and we'll talk and be together. Would you like that?

ALICIA: Yes. Yes, I'd like that. Good night, my Andrew. (*She accepts his good-night kiss and heads upstairs with* LOREN.)

ANDREW: Good night, Alicia.

ALICIA: I love you.

ALAN: I'll go and wait for the police. And then I'll leave.

(ANDREW *grabs him and pulls him to him in a brutal motion. He takes* ALAN*'s face and sticks it to his own, kissing him harshly, as if he must suck one last breath of life and sustenance from him; then he lets the boy go.*)

ANDREW: Yes. Then, you must leave.

ALAN: I'll be outside, in front, waiting. (*Goes out the main entrance.*)

(ANDREW *moves around the room, not knowing where to rest.* LOREN *comes down.*)

LOREN: Why must Alan leave?

ANDREW: Because your mother isn't well.

LOREN: She's as well as she's ever been.

ANDREW: What do you know?

LOREN: More, much more than you think.

ANDREW: Now what is that supposed to mean?

LOREN: You will stay with her because that is the biggest agony you know how to endure. Alan isn't suffering; Alan is a toy, like I am, like Penny was. Reach out your cat's paw and watch us jump.

ANDREW: Your mother and I know each other very well.

LOREN: And the known pain is easier than the unknown.

ANDREW: At my age, yes. But not at yours.

LOREN: Billy, sweet, small Billy and I made love, just as you heard me describe. It was lovely, I told you that, but at the end, he kept calling out your name. You had made love with him, that night Alan came, and you hadn't looked at him again. It was you he wanted, not me. And he knew that you loved Alan. And he was a silly child, tasting a father for the first time, again a father he could never have, like his own father, and he was sad, reaching over and over again for something that wasn't there. So he reached for Penny, and she too wasn't there, at least so he could have her. And there was her knife. So you have wreaked a little havoc in these dark days and nights by the ocean.

ANDREW: I . . . I'm sorry to hear . . . this. I'm . . . I'm not responsible . . . I . . . I . . . didn't sleep with him . . . I slept with . . . I slept . . . I thought I slept with Alan.

LOREN: But it was dark and you were drunk and . . . how many times have you blundered into the wrong arms, stumbled onto the beach with the wrong body. Your books are full of it.

ANDREW: You must admit it is an extraordinary mistake, rather amusing. I have fallen in love with not the person I thought I slept with.

(LOREN *doesn't smile; he turns away.*)

That's why you'll never write, Loren.

LOREN: Only you wanted me to write. Only you wanted me to be an extension of yourself. Good-bye. That's what I came to tell you. And that your wife is sleeping soundly by now. (*Goes upstairs.*)

(*As* ALAN *returns.*)

ANDREW: Are they here?

ALAN: No. I don't want to sit out there with two dead bodies. They won't walk away.

ANDREW: Come sit in here with one, then.

ALAN: I suppose you're feeling very sorry for yourself now. I'm going to be going, but not because you want me to. I could talk you into letting me stay. I'm going because . . . the wrong people have been killed.

ANDREW: Then go! Get out and go!

ALAN: We never really did talk to each other. We never did pass, each to the other, something from inside of us.

ANDREW: What have you got, you little box of inbecilities? What have you got to give me? What have you got that I can use or want or can take and turn into useful commodities? Nothing. Except maybe a pain in my gut which I no longer want.

ALAN: At least that's something.

ANDREW: Is it? It's not a pain from longing. It's a pain from indigestion. I swallowed you, but you disagreed with me.

ALAN: I'm sorry for that. Maybe it'll settle after a while.

ANDREW: I'll take some Alka-Seltzer. It will go away.

ALAN: I'm sure it will.

ANDREW: You're not a fighter either. You're just like her, Alicia. One of the world's great nonfighters. Even my son, thank God, seems to be developing some spunk.

ALAN: Good for him.

ANDREW: (*Suddenly very tired.*) You disappointed me. I thought you'd . . . participate more. I would have liked that.

ALAN: Participate . . . how?

ANDREW: In the affairs of the house.

ALAN: I thought I did my share in that department.

ANDREW: As if you were one of us. I should have liked that.

ALAN: I feel great sorrow and pity, whether you want to hear this or not, because it's just come over me this evening, for you and for all of you. I can't put any of the pieces together, because they really don't fit and aren't meant to. I think your world is tormented by sex. I wish you would hurry up and die off, you and people like you—is it your entire generation?—so that my generation can carry on with how we feel.

ANDREW: A load of horseshit, that's your generation. What you call sex, I call passion, and you are strangely without it, little man. Perhaps I am disproportionately interested in bodily functions and physical things, but I am honestly so, and there is little else to be concerned with these days, except the approaching starvation of the entire world, which is not a subject which lends itself to literature, at least not yet. You . . . you won't have any literature at all. You have no . . . no longings. Go and sit with the bodies. They're your own.

ALAN: Oh, no you don't. They were here when I came. I'll take no responsibility.

ANDREW: Nor will I.

ALAN: Good-bye. (*Starts out.*)

ANDREW: Don't you have anything? Any clothes or books?

ALAN: This is how I came. (*Goes out.*)

> (ANDREW *is all alone, once again. He paces about like a caged person, wanting very much to scream out, almost in fact doing so, but then subsiding, then turning to grab some wine, then drinking from the bottle, not seeing, then ignoring his son, who has come down with his suitcase and tried to wave a good-bye to him.* ANDREW *then tries to call out to him but can't. He walks around some more, finds a box of chocolates, begins to eat them, as he proceeds to feel more caged than ever. Finally, when he can bear it no longer, he goes to his study, sits at his desk, picks up his pen, finds his piece of paper, and begins to write. The lights dim.*)

The End

Just Say No

A Comedy

My plays are like my children. I am proud of them all, but some of them have caused more heartbreak than others. I don't think I've ever written anything original that I didn't believe in passionately, and fervently want to share that passion with the world. Quite often, with my work (I guess with every writer's work), the world doesn't want to hear. Sometimes I understand why or can see that there might be reasons. Other times I just get so angry because I think the play's dismissal is unwarranted and, in the case of *Just Say No,* dismissed for reasons that have nothing to do with the play. Anyway, whatever the reasons, *Just Say No* is my big problem child. I have tried twice to get it on its feet, and both times the world has kept it from walking.

I loved researching it and writing it. I thought I had uncovered important information on why AIDS was swept under the carpet. Rehearsals for the first production, at New York's WPA Theater, were exciting. I had Kathleen Chalfant and David Margulies, two superb actors. The first readings had everyone in stitches. I rewrote like crazy to whip it into better and better (I hoped) shape (so hard that I wound up in the hospital having an emergency hernia that also revealed for the first time the extent of my deteriorating liver condition, and that I was HIV positive), and then the play was, for the most part, simply crucified. None of the critics liked my jokes or responded with any intelligence to my theses. We lasted for three weeks, mostly on subscribers. They laughed a lot, but not enough. *The New York Times* had particularly excoriated me.

I tried to answer them and my other critics by writing "The Farce in Just Saying No," my essay reprinted here.

I started out a hundred years ago wanting to be a comedy writer. I had a girlfriend, Ellen Cohn, who I thought was hysterically funny, as she did me, and I called her Ellen Comden Cohn, after Betty Comden, and I was her Adolph Green. We never actually got down to writing, but we still make each other laugh. When I moved back to New York from London, I wrote a comedy screenplay with my friend Lou Miano called *Just a Love Nest* that no one wanted to make. Then, after *Four Friends* bombed, I wrote a script called *The Big Three at Yalta,* for which my Hollywood agent said he was going to get $1 million, and didn't.

Just Say No had had no additional productions (there was some kind of staged reading in Minneapolis) when I got a call from a Chicago theater, the Bailiwick, telling me that they would like to do a benefit for Gay Pride Day. David decided we should go, as he'd never seen it. It appeared to be a success, the audience roaring away. David Zak, who runs the theater, asked if I'd mind a full production, and I found myself agreeing, even to doing some revisions. So began "the Chicago version" of *Just Say No,* which is included here. It was meant to be a little more up-to-date, a little less Ed Koch–y (people were beginning not to remember who the bastard is). I worked on the script with David Zak, who, like the original director, David Esbjornson, was a smart sounding board.

This time we had Greg Louganis, the Olympic diving champion, splendid as Ron Reagan Jr., and Alexandra Billings, a Steppenwolf actress who also happens to be transexual, positively and absolutely divine as Nancy Reagan.

Nothing helped. The Chicago critics hated it as much and for the same reasons as the New York critics. Again I was being condemned for bad taste.

Chicago Production

Just Say No was presented from May 27–July 4, 1999, at the Bailiwick Repertory Theater, David Zak, artistic director, in Chicago.

Electra Vye	Alison Halstead
Foppy Schwartz	Marc Silvia
Trudi Tunick	Amy Farrington
Gilbert Perch	Benjamin Sprunger
Junior	Greg Louganis
Mayor	David Mersault
Herman Harrod	Nathan Rankin
Mrs. Potentate	Alexandra Billings

Director	David Zak
Scenery	Jacqueline Penrod
Lighting	Eric Appleton
Costumes	Shifra Werch
Sound	Lindsay Jones
Production Stage Manager	Margot Eccles

Original Production

Just Say No was presented for a limited run October 4–November 6, 1988, at the WPA Theatre in New York City. It was produced by Kyle Renick, WPA's artistic director.

Electra Vye	Tonya Pinkins
Foppy Schwartz	David Margulies
Trudi Tunick	Julie White
Gilbert Perch	Keith Reddin
Junior	Richard Topol
Mayor	Joseph Ragno
Herman Harrod	Richard Riehle
Mrs. Potentate	Kathleen Chalfant
Director	David Esbjornson
Scenery	Edward T. Gianfrancesco
Lighting	Craig Evans
Costumes	David C. Woolard
Sound	Aural Fixation
Production Stage Manager	Paul Mills Holmes

(This version was published by St. Martin's Press but is now out of print.)

Cast of Characters

Electra Vye
Foppy Schwartz
Trudi Tunick
Gilbert Perch
Junior
Mayor
Herman Harrod
Mrs. Potentate

Setting

The town house of Foppy Schwartz in Georgetown, the capital city of the country of New Columbia.

Time

Closing in on the end of Daddy's first term.

Prologue

Electra Vye, a black woman, speaks to the audience.

ELECTRA: Listen, my children, and you shall hear
How we came to be screwed so drear
By Mommy and Daddy, who make all the rules,
And then live by other ones—making us fools.
Yet some of us have survived the worst.
We got out alive, although we are cursed
For letting them flim-flam us yet once again,
And again and again and again and again.
Someday we'll learn, that's this woman's plea.
So I tell you this story to help us all see
How we tried to fight, though given the shaft,
By their mob of the powerful, brutal, and daft.
A trivial story, Oscar once said,
But for serious people, before we are dead.

Act One

Scene: The town house of Foppy Schwartz in Georgetown, the capital city of New Columbia. It's a house of highly ornate taste. The main living area (ground floor) contains a sofa and some chairs and tables. A breakfront or bookcase with a large selection of videotapes, a TV set with VCR, and a tape recorder may or may not be seen down front, as desired. A big mirror is available for preening. The place is peppered with framed photographs of the famous. Behind one painting is a wall safe. One area has a large regal chair confronting an elaborate system of many phones, one of which is red.

On the ground floor are the following: the doorway to the Jean Genet bedroom; a grand staircase to the second floor; the door to the kitchen and Electra's quarters; the front door to the outside world; and the doorway to the Oscar Wilde bedroom. Up the staircase, on the second floor, are the door to the Marcel Proust bedroom and the door to Foppy's master bedroom. There is a small balcony that juts out above and over the front door. Under this balcony, hardly seen, is a door to a closet.

(Note: If a two-tiered set is not feasible, it's possible for all rooms to be on one level. It's also conceivable that the presentation of the play be thought of in nonrealistic terms.)

At rise: Foppy Schwartz, in a handsome dressing gown, comes down the stairway, talking on a portable phone. He goes to his table and regal chair and begins holding forth, one by one, on all phones. This area is littered with the day's newspapers, all turned to the society and gossip columns. Several elaborately wrapped gifts await his inspection.

FOPPY: Huggy Bunny, of course a woman can have a best male friend, just as a man can have a best male friend. But a woman cannot have a best woman friend because a best woman friend will do her in. Whereas I won't. Stay away from Carolina. She is evil. (*Picking up a ringing phone.*) *Momentito, cara.* Carolina! I am just telling Huggy Bunny Boo that you are evil. . . . Yes, you are. Helene came all the way from Paris to wear that hideous gown. You did not have to seat her next to me. (*Hangs up on Carolina, goes back to Huggy Bunny, while a third phone rings that he picks up and hangs up again to stop its ringing.*) Calvin got married? A fool and his mister are soon parted. (*Picking up another ringing phone.*) *Scusi, ancora.* Chesty! You smelled most peculiar last night at Nan's. Had you not time to bathe? Bunny Boo, *adios muchacha.* (*Hangs up on Huggy Bunny Boo.*) And exchange those shoes immediately. You are too old to parade your painted puckered toes. And buy some larger earrings. How many times have I beseeched you to shroud your unfortunate lobes. . . . Yes, Foppy is always in the know. Of those few things worth knowing. (*Picking up a receiver that's been lying there all along.*) Who is this? . . . Marella, I must talk to Chesty, whom I like better today. *Ciao, bella,* kiss *tutti Venezia* for Fopp. (*Kisses her, hangs up; another phone rings.*) My precious Judy! Your hair was much too large last night. Chesty, *domani, domani. Auf wiedersehn, shatzi.* (*Hangs up on Chesty.*) Yes, I had to go with *her.* Yes, Mrs. Potentate needs her taste in all areas supported. Yes, I am her jock strap. Yes, am I not the flower behind the drone!

ELECTRA: (*Entering to serve more coffee.*) *Encore café, mon plus grand Juive?*

FOPPY: *Merci, ma petite noir.* (*Picking up another ringing phone.*) Not again! Perry, Angelo, Rock, that dreadful candelabra person,

Roy ... well, we don't miss Roy. Who is it this time? It was only a question of time. Surrounded by so much ballet beauty. (*Into another ringing phone.*) *Aspetta?* Darling Suzy, you must have heard, Robert now joins Alvin as God's choreographer. (*Into another phone that's been off the hook the whole time.*) Who is this? *Dica? Dica?* Oh, Mica! (*The red phone rings. He talks into all receivers at once.*) My dears, *she* is calling! (*He hangs up on all of them. Then he picks up the red phone, which he puts on speakerphone.*) My Royal Highness! *Come stai?*

MRS. POTENTATE'S VOICE: My Foppiness!

FOPPY: My Supreme Blessedness!

MRS. POTENTATE'S VOICE: Are we alone?

FOPPY: Your bitch is my command.

MRS. POTENTATE'S VOICE: But can we talk in confidence?

FOPPY: How bad have you been?

MRS. POTENTATE'S VOICE: Herman Harrod and his bimbo Trudi Tunick have disappeared. Poof!

FOPPY: What do you mean, poof!

MRS. POTENTATE'S VOICE: They had an all-night secret sex orgy in some downtown sleazepit along with a big bunch of her bimbo broad slut friends.

FOPPY: Evidently not secret enough. How—

MRS. POTENTATE'S VOICE: And someone filmed it. Someone made a home movie of it.

FOPPY: My baroness of Baker Street, how did you discover such drastic dish?

MRS. POTENTATE'S VOICE: I must locate that movie before it goes into release. If you find out anything at all about anything at all, call Mommy.

FOPPY: Caligula has taught us that disloyalty must be flogged to death!

MRS. POTENTATE'S VOICE: She said a mouthful. (*Hangs up.*)

ELECTRA: The ideals that made our country great are more than ever turned to excrement. (*To the audience.*) That's shit.

FOPPY: They have been a good First Mommy and First Daddy.

ELECTRA: To you, white man.

(*He begins to open and model various presents. She helps him.*)

ELECTRA: I was taught if we didn't like it to speak up. There are 23,110 lobbyists in this town. There are 21,614 journalists. There are 180,234 trade reps. It is impossible to be heard from underneath the weight and volume of 224,958 other speaker-uppers.

FOPPY: You have discovered democracy's flaw. Write your chamberperson.

ELECTRA: My chamberperson received 35,836,142 letters last month. That Rifle Association sent three million telegrams in one day.

FOPPY: That is why Daddy is against gun control.

ELECTRA: His popularity was slipping. Getting shot was the best thing he ever did. Why do you always get so many presents?

FOPPY: Because I am me! First you are young, then you are middle-aged, then you are old, then you are wonderful. (*Reading a card.*) Jackie!

ELECTRA: "Good evening, Ms. Wah Wah—may I call you Bah Bah? Thank you for allowing me to commit my memoirs to TV."

FOPPY: Electra, I have warned you never ever talk to the media, not even in pretend. In our country pretend is the same thing as reality. (*Notes another gift card and rips it in pieces.*)

ELECTRA: Big bucks are paid to all those hookers who screw preachers and blow politicians. I could use a few thousand bucks.

FOPPY: I'd strangle you for talking so cheaply.

ELECTRA: "White Jew Georgetown Faggot Strangles Loyal Schvartzah for Talking Cheap." The Department of Drugs and Diseases spends . . .

FOPPY: Will you stop with your numbers!

ELECTRA: You think you're not a number? Daddy appointed an idiot to be in charge of D&D. If his IQ were any lower you'd have to water him.

FOPPY: No doubt the idiot made a generous contribution to Daddy's reelection. It is the way of the world.

ELECTRA: I should be able to retire on what I've learned in this house about the way of the world.

(*The doorbell rings.*)

You get it. (*She goes into the kitchen.*)

(FOPPY *opens the front door.* TRUDI TUNICK *stands there, lovely and nubile and wearing a hotel doorman's overcoat.*)

FOPPY: (*Preventing her entrance.*) Who are you and what are you doing here and why must it be now?

TRUDI: Please. Someone very important is meeting me here. We never fly in the same cab.

FOPPY: I cannot allow you entry on such scanty information.

TRUDI: He said you're a gentleman. He says this is a safe house.

FOPPY: Safe from what?

TRUDI: From him! He's on one of his hungry tempestuous rages. He's never satisfied.

FOPPY: I cannot bear to hear these acts. Whose are they?

TRUDI: Mine. His too, of course. Herman says we're a great team. Like Caesar and Cleopatra.

FOPPY: Herman?

TRUDI: Oh, sorry. My name is Trudi Tunick, I am Herman Harrod's mistress, and—

FOPPY: Come in, my little Red Riding Hood. Why is Herman Harrod coming here when he knows Mrs. Potentate and I are best friends to his wife, Huggy Bunny, and therefore I must loathe him and you?

TRUDI: Herman wants you to sell our sex tape to his wife.

FOPPY: Tapes as in videotapes? As one would make in the home?

FOPPY: Oh, you make them too? Isn't it great how anyone can make them? It's not like the old days when we had to schlepp around such heavy equipment.

FOPPY: Tell me about your sex tape.

TRUDI: And none of the actors have to be union members. If we did I'd have my Screen Actors Guild card by now.

FOPPY: Tell me about your sex tape.

TRUDI: I hope nothing's wrong. He finally had a checkup.

FOPPY: Tell me about your sex tape.

TRUDI: I wanted to be an actress so much.

FOPPY: My Audrey Hepburn, describe your tape.

TRUDI: Tapes of people having sex.

FOPPY: Who doing what to whom?

TRUDI: Can't we wait for Herman? I've been his mistress for twelve years.

FOPPY: My Meryl Streep, how many doing how much?

TRUDI: Herman wants to tell you himself.

FOPPY: Which acts performed by which actors, Madonna!

TRUDI: Okay. Me and the girls having sex with Herman and others.

FOPPY: Others who?

TRUDI: Others very important.

FOPPY: How important?

TRUDI: High up important.

FOPPY: How high up important? My English is being destroyed.

TRUDI: Very high.

FOPPY: The highest?

TRUDI: No. Herman says Daddy can't get it up.

FOPPY: That is classified information. Who high up?

TRUDI: Herman says only you could convince First Mommy to get Herman's wife to unfreeze his assets. Don't ever get married in California.

FOPPY: I won't. Once again. Who how high up?

TRUDI: (*Picking up a newspaper.*) You do crossword puzzles?

FOPPY: I do not do crossword puzzles!

TRUDI: What's the plural of moose?

FOPPY: (*Picking up a ringing phone.*) Mistuh Schwartz he dead. (*Hangs up the phone, then removes it from its cradle.*) Recite the entire cast of characters.

TRUDI: Don't tell Herman! They include: at least two elected Chamberpersons; at least three of Daddy's cabinet; at least four of Daddy's personal staff; at least five prominent businessmen listed on the Big Board; at least six—

FOPPY: Names! I must have names! Are we beating around the bush?

TRUDI: Oh, no, he's been faithful to his mistress longer than I've been with Herman. I can't give any more away for free.

FOPPY: How much do you have left?

(*She takes off the overcoat. She's wearing an S&M wardrobe—garter belts, hip boots, black leather zippered these and thats.*)

FOPPY: Quite a bit. (*Admiring an item.*) Oh this is nice.

TRUDI: Watergate S&M. They have them for men too.

FOPPY: Do they?

(ELECTRA *enters from kitchen with toilet plunger and Drano, wearing rubber gloves.*)

ELECTRA: (*Noticing them.*) Old saying: He who lies down with dogs gets fleas.

FOPPY: Be quiet. We are rooting out the truth.

ELECTRA: I am cleaning out your toilet. (*Goes into his bedroom.*)

FOPPY: Where is the tape?

TRUDI: Never mind.

FOPPY: You can tell me.

TRUDI: When he had his first heart attack I moved into the hospital room next door and looked after him while his wife went to all her parties with you and Mrs. Potentate.

FOPPY: Where is it?

TRUDI: Herman says if anything happens to him I'll finally have enough money if we play my tape right. It was his idea to make the movie to blackmail his wife. I'm not that smart. That's why I'm here, which is nowhere, in love with a big bazooka who has trouble keeping promises. Herman is one mighty promiser.

(ELECTRA *comes out of* FOPPY*'s room and heads back downstairs.*)

FOPPY: And one of Daddy's oldest, closest, nearest, dearest, and most trusted friends. Herman is quite correct in believing First Mommy would enjoy a private screening. Where is it?

TRUDI: Who are you?

ELECTRA: What does it look like I am? A Nubian princess down on her luck. (*Goes into the kitchen.*)

TRUDI: Daddy hasn't given Herman one single thing for all his faithfulness and valor. Not a cabinet post or being an ambassador or postmaster or head of a commission. Herman was going to make me our trade representative to Barbados. After all the money Herman collected for Daddy from all their friends in Vegas! Herman put it in a washing machine in one of those sunny places he takes me on vacation and then he gives it back all nice and clean to Daddy. Herman is one pissed-off Herman.

FOPPY: Why is this pent-up vengeance suddenly surfacing now?

TRUDI: Daddy only has a few more weeks to decide if he's running for reelection.

FOPPY: Herman only has a few more hours to decide if he's staying on earth. How much do you hope to make?

TRUDI: A million from Bob Guccione for my titties and a million from Hugh Hefner for my exclusive tell-all interview and a million from Larry Flynt for my pussy. Herman says I'll be the very first political mistress to actually make any money out of it. I'd rather be in *Vogue*. Herman says you know everybody in *Vogue*. I never seem to fall for great lookers with uncomplicated sex lives. The more fucked up everything is, the more Trudi Tunick gets involved. Mr. Schwartz . . .

FOPPY: Yes, my dear?

TRUDI: I'm very frightened.

FOPPY: Tell Uncle Foppy.

TRUDI: Marilyn murdered because she slept with Jack and Bobby and she knew too much. Daddy elected Potentate-in-Chief because of MCA and Jules, who was from Chicago, Al Capone was his friend, you know what happens in Chicago. And JFK murdered by the Mob and Lee Harvey Oswald tied into the Mob and Herman the connection between the Mob and Daddy. And Sidney and Paul and Nevada, you know what happens in Nevada. And Bill Casey's business partner was Mob, and Paul represented the Teamsters, don't forget the trucks, you can't make a move without the trucks. And Sidney's friend who worked for Jules lent Paul a fortune to buy casinos. And Howard Baker was on the board of MCA. And an important witness was murdered when Ray Donovan was under criminal investigation. And Jimmy Hoffa and Sam Giancana both murdered and Judith Exner slept with both JFK and Sam. And Leonore, whose husband owns the *Racing Form* and is Sidney's best friend and whose first two husbands were a casino operator and a bootlegger, is also Mrs. Potentate's best friend. And all the people in Daddy's Koffee Klatsch, Herman and Holmes and Walter and Joe and Earle and William, you know what happens when you drink too much coffee. And Mrs. Potentate started the Koffee Klatsch. And Bill Casey died so suddenly—did *you* see his X-rays? And all these people are Daddy's best friends! Oh, it's all connected, can't you see it's all connected, the entire network of everything in this entire world and you want to know why I'm frightened, I know too much! I don't know what to do with it! I don't know what to do period! That's why I'm frightened!

FOPPY: (*Embracing her.*) My dear, you have every right to be.

TRUDI: Herman says the greatest mystery is not only how Daddy got elected once but that it could happen twice.

(*The doorbell rings.*)

TRUDI: (*Starting for the door.*) That must be Herman.

FOPPY: (*Restraining her.*) What if it isn't Herman? My dear, trust Uncle Foppy. I must secrete you for a moment. Now I call this the Jean Genet Suite, and he was a very famous French writer. I think you will recognize most of the outré accoutrements of furbishment. Promise to stay hidden until I and only I sound the All Clear.

TRUDI: I have always trusted in the kindness of strangers.

FOPPY: You have been in error.

(TRUDI *goes into Jean Genet. The doorbell rings again.* FOPPY *rushes upstairs.*)

FOPPY: Electra, please answer that!

(ELECTRA *comes in to answer it.*)

FOPPY: If Mrs. P. calls or comes, tell her I'm having a pee. (*Goes into his bedroom.*)

(ELECTRA *opens the door.* GILBERT PERCH *runs in. He is an innocent-looking, rather ditzy young man. He carries an airline bag.*)

GILBERT: (*Looking all around.*) Are there any strange men?

ELECTRA: All men are strange.

GILBERT: He's after me again!

ELECTRA: Tell Momma.

GILBERT: You are not my mother.

ELECTRA: No shit.

GILBERT: My mother is divine. My mother is a sainted angel.

ELECTRA: Gilbert, it is unhealthy for you to worship her so excessively.

GILBERT: You remember me? I'm that memorable?

ELECTRA: Oh yes. (*Calling out.*) Mr. Foppy!

FOPPY'S VOICE: Yes!

ELECTRA: That sissy whose pants you could never get into? He's back.

(FOPPY *comes out of his room wearing another robe and runs down the stairs.* ELECTRA *goes into the kitchen.*)

FOPPY: Gilbert Perch! Darling boy, it's so good to see you again. You've kept in shape. Sort of. What are you doing here? I thought you were happily married to that pig.

GILBERT: He is after me, after my body, after my brains, after my mouth, after my life, I can't take it anymore, he is driving me nuts, he says he loves me, he says he hates me, he says he's going to eviscerate me, he says he's going to pay me off with contracts and send me to the coast, he says he's going to encase me in cement . . .

FOPPY: The Mayor still has difficulty sustaining anything . . . permanent? He is too old to be so choosy. And ugly. He's much too ugly. And mean. He's dreadfully mean.

GILBERT: I never want to see that choosy, ugly, mean old pig again!

(FOPPY *takes* GILBERT *to sit on the sofa, where he proceeds to be very touchy-feely.*)

FOPPY: Come, let us sit down and remember old times.

GILBERT: You taught me how to overcome everything except fear.

FOPPY: That is something you are born with, like impeccable taste.

GILBERT: Nevertheless.

FOPPY: My fragile petunia, what has happened since last you were in my arms?

GILBERT: I was never in your arms!

FOPPY: Alas. I could never understand why you chose him over me.

GILBERT: Because he's mayor of our largest northeastern city!

FOPPY: Ah yes, the aphrodisiac of power. You could have chosen someone who was . . . younger.

GILBERT: Younger? (*Pulls out a thick Filofax from his bag and starts thumbing through addresses.*) Rock singers.

FOPPY: A little older.

GILBERT: A little older. Olympic gold medalists.

FOPPY: A little older.

GILBERT: A little older. Stars of weekly western TV series reruns.

FOPPY: A little older.

GILBERT: Cary Grant is dead.

FOPPY: Tell me what happened.

GILBERT: You introduced us and he looked deep into my eyes and said, "I want to spend the rest of my life in your arms," and he took me to Appleberg and he found me a rent-controlled apartment and he got me a job in his Department of Sex and Germs. Just to be near him. "You won't have to do a thing, just come when I whistle," and he came every Wednesday night, we ordered in, I can't cook. . . . I had the most famous lover in the city! He told the world he loved Donny M. and then he said Donny M. was a pig and then Donny M. killed himself. He told the world he loved Stanley F. and then Stanley F. got indicted and went to prison. He told the world he loved Bessie M., but he wouldn't marry her either. And then Mario B. got indicted, and then Donny T. started saying nasty things, and then Geoffrey L. turned into a stoolie. And then Bessie M. became a shoplifter and a lesbian and said she couldn't marry him anyway. And then Herb R. and Dan W. talked to him . . .

FOPPY: Does no one walking the corridors of power retain a last name?

GILBERT: . . . and then the latest polls showed less than thirty percent want him reelected, and then he came every other Wednesday, and then he came one Wednesday a month, and then he came every other month, and then he stopped . . . paying my rent, and then in my job at Germs I learned all about the burgeoning plague and I told him and he said, "Shut up, you gonif twit, it's a secret, haven't I taught you anything about secrets," and then a huge Italian man with a big big gun came and gave me money and told me to keep my mouth shut and get out of town fast, don't even pack, or the ripple of destruction and the swirl of death would drown me in the Hudson.

FOPPY: Old man river . . .

GILBERT: And then the gay leaders discovered all about us, and they came after me to blab the truth, they are ceaseless in their tenacious fixation to destroy him for destroying them, but they're coming after me, I'm caught in the middle, so all of this—all all all of this! has brought me back to you, my first teacher, you are so good at social etiquette, can my love ever return him to the innocence of our bliss before he murders me? He's coming after me, I know too much and he knows I know too much and he knows what I know could . . . he's running for a fourth term and I moved to Appleberg to become famous, not dead!

(GILBERT *throws himself into* FOPPY'S *arms.* ELECTRA *comes in with black satin sheets and crosses the stage.*)

FOPPY: Must you always barge in unannounced! What am I paying you for?

ELECTRA: (*Climbing the stairs to Marcel Proust.*) Three hundred years of slavery. (*Goes into Proust.*)

(*The red phone starts ringing.* FOPPY *jumps up.* GILBERT *falls to the floor.*)

FOPPY: Benevolent Regina, I must ask your indulgence while I clear the hall. (*Lays the phone down and escorts Gilbert to the stairs.*) Go up to our former camping ground and rest.

GILBERT: I knew I'd be safe with you.

FOPPY: Perhaps now that you're on the market again . . .

GILBERT: You never told me he'd treat me like shit.

FOPPY: He treats everyone like shit.

(GILBERT *goes into* FOPPY'S *room.* FOPPY, *fanning himself, patting his heart now aflutter anew, picks up the phone.*)

FOPPY: *Ritorna vincitor!* Now! There is someone here . . .

MRS. POTENTATE'S VOICE: My young lawyer is there already! Is he panting with impatience?

FOPPY: Will you never rest your former habits now that you are queen.

MRS. POTENTATE'S VOICE: You do not remember anything about my former life except that it was blissful. And who is calling whom queen?

FOPPY: What becomes a legend most?

MRS. POTENTATE'S VOICE: Foppy, my body has needs!

FOPPY: Your body has what?

MRS. POTENTATE'S VOICE: One of my young lawyers is meeting me at any moment at your house.

FOPPY: I shall see that all is in readiness, my Supreme Sovereign. What is this one's name?

(*No response.*)

What does he look like?

(*No response.*)

Well, which law firm is he with?

MRS. POTENTATE'S VOICE: One of those ones full of Jews.

FOPPY: The true spirit of Bitberg. (*Locating a notebook.*) Is it Ira Pecker of Paul Weiss Rifkind?

MRS. POTENTATE'S VOICE: No.

FOPPY: Is it Pisher Slotnick at Phillips Nizer Benjamin & Krim?

MRS. POTENTATE'S VOICE: No.

FOPPY: Is it Sammy Sugarman at Schweitzer Schwartz Shagan Shafran Sheps Subotsky Stolts Sheib Schecter Saperstein Sadow Sacks & Schlem?

MRS. POTENTATE'S VOICE: All Jews sound alike.

FOPPY: Recent events in Israel have changed so many minds.

MRS. POTENTATE'S VOICE: Oh, my Foppirinia, why do I perform these dangerous acts?

FOPPY: Oh, my Challenger, How High the Moon! Now listen . . .

MRS. POTENTATE'S VOICE: Well, I'm sure I'll recognize him with his clothes off.

(*Her phone needs money.*)

FOPPY: My H&R Block, why are you calling from a pay phone? Do as Foppy instructs: Extract any silver coin from your Gucci bag and drop it into any round hole it fits into at the top. The woman has forsaken the real world.

MRS. POTENTATE'S VOICE: I'll be right there. Manny Moose is reading Daddy his antipornography report. No more dirty magazines will be allowed in 7-11s.

FOPPY: The country will turn celibate overnight. Now, *senta!*

MRS. POTENTATE'S VOICE: (*Yelling over phone noises.*) Have you found out anything about that tape?

FOPPY: I am trying to tell you . . . !

(*Dial tone is heard. She's been cut off.*)

I must always remember this is not an Age of Reason. If this were the Court of Louis XIV I would be the Duc de St. Simon. It is not, and I am Foppy Schwartz. Electra! Is her room ready?

ELECTRA'S VOICE: Which her you talking about?

(*The doorbell rings again.* FOPPY *screams in frustration.*)

You got it?

FOPPY: I got it!

(*He opens it and* JUNIOR *comes leaping in like a gazelle in a raincoat.*)

First Son!

JUNIOR: I have a terrible problem!

FOPPY: It would be uncharitable to think that you alone were spared.

JUNIOR: Uncle Foppy, you've always been the only one I can turn to.

FOPPY: Secret cosmic floodgates are opening, gushing only in my direction.

JUNIOR: Pop has discovered.

FOPPY: After so many years even his hearing aid was bound to hear it.

JUNIOR: I've never seen him so angry.

(JUNIOR *takes off his raincoat. He's wearing only a bath towel.*)

FOPPY: Does no one in this town wear clothes?

JUNIOR: (*Practices a few ballet steps in front of a mirror.*) I'm never going back. I'm making the leap. I'm going to Appleberg to find a man! I'm going to Appleberg to come out! I'm going to Appleberg to be a ballet dancer.

FOPPY: That'll do it all right. Dance! Dance! Dancers start doing it at birth.

JUNIOR: I'm a late bloomer.

FOPPY: But you don't have the bud of a Bruhn, the stem of a Serge, the petals of a Peter. All you'll have is the stigma of a sissy.

JUNIOR: I have the elevation of the son of the Potentate-in-Chief.

FOPPY: They laughed Margaret Truman off the stage.

JUNIOR: I'm not a singer, I'm a dancer.

FOPPY: What does your mother say? My God, his mother! Does she know? Does she know I know? There are numerous ballet dancers who are heterosexual men, although I can't think of any at the moment.

ELECTRA: (*Coming down the stairs.*) Hi, Junior.

JUNIOR: Hi, Electra.

ELECTRA: Tell your daddy since he took office the number of employees fighting illicit drug traffic decreased by 19,609.

JUNIOR: I told him.

FOPPY: (*Trying to get things moving faster; sotto to her.*) She's coming, she's coming . . .

ELECTRA: More than two hundred of his senior officials have been accused of illegal conduct. His administration has been the most corrupt in U.S. history. So many have been indicted or imprisoned that you can't walk twenty feet in this town without leaving the scene of a crime.

FOPPY: (*Sotto, to* ELECTRA.) You don't hear a thing I say.

JUNIOR: He doesn't hear a thing I say.

ELECTRA: Tell your ma my sister on welfare's fourth oldest son is dealing twenty thousand bucks a week. It's real hard for them to "Just say no."

JUNIOR: You tell her.

FOPPY: Yes, you tell her. (*Sotto to her.*) Someone's mother will be here any minute and you can tell her to her face. Prepare her suite!

ELECTRA: We been here before. We know what to do.

FOPPY: We've been here one at a time. We've never been here ... four at once.

ELECTRA: From personal observation "Just say no" has done for addiction what "Have a nice day" achieved for clinical depression. (*Goes into the kitchen.*)

JUNIOR: Which room is mine? I'm moving in with you.

FOPPY: Oh no, no. No, you're not. No.

JUNIOR: You always let me have overnights.

FOPPY: What happened? Tell me quickly. Give me the *Reader's Digest* version.

JUNIOR: I'm in love.

FOPPY: Give me the *Vanity Fair* version.

JUNIOR: I'm in love with both of them.

FOPPY: Give me the *National Inquirer* version.

JUNIOR: I'm in love with both my Secret Service men.

FOPPY: Two of them? We are not Mormons.

JUNIOR: The three of us were taking a shower in the Warren Harding bathtub. They're not allowed to be separated in their devotion to my safety, they can't even take their guns off. . . . And we were all naked and soaped up and Daddy suddenly yanked back the curtain. "Well, Junior, what have we here?" he said, his cheeks full of that blush that everyone thinks is makeup and which is.

FOPPY: We must not frown on a necessity for a few personal vanities. Harry Truman wore a corset to tuck in his tummy.

JUNIOR: Harry Truman didn't dye his hair.

FOPPY: Continue the tale of the tub.

JUNIOR: Randy snapped to attention. "Yes, sir! Secret Service man Randolph Pigeon of Huntington, Indiana, at your service, sir!" and his, you know . . .

FOPPY: Guns in the shower?

JUNIOR: . . . his rod firmly flapping against the pulsating force of the shower spray. "Yes, sir! Secret Service man Rich Gulliver of Tampico, Illinois, reporting for duty, sir! And his, you know . . .

FOPPY: Tushie?

JUNIOR: ... round and ready and beautiful like a perfect pumpkin. Everything was so beautiful, Foppy. Foppy, it isn't right.

FOPPY: What happened?

JUNIOR: They've both been reassigned to Lebanon.

FOPPY: Right! Right! Right is Jesse Helms and Pat Robertson and your father. We have not lived in an age of Right and Beauty since ancient Greece.

JUNIOR: After Rich and Randy were led away in handcuffs, Daddy picked up one of my ballet slippers and slapped me back and forth all over, up and down, I was still naked, and he screamed at me, "I, whose Supreme Tribunal your mother and I have packed with justices to make you null and void," slash slash slash, "I, whose court system the Shyster General and your mother and I have packed with Enforcers who know the words to 'My Way,'" slash slash slash, "I, the Potentate-in-Chief of this great country of New Columbia, have a little schmuck," slash slash slash, "fairy ballet dancer son who sucks pee-pee."

FOPPY: Such a nursery expression, pee-pee. He doth protest a wee-wee too much! Oh, the God of Jerry Falwell is cruel and merciless and unforgiving. Jimmy Swaggart did it with a hooker, but it was a female hooker. (*Comforting* JUNIOR *in his arms.*) I have always looked upon you as my son. But you must void my manse for the nonce.

JUNIOR: I can't go home again!

FOPPY: To his many other inadequacies your wretched father must now be charged with child abuse.

JUNIOR: Now be charged? You should talk to my sister.

FOPPY: How has he won the love and affection of so many millions and for so long?

JUNIOR: Beats me.

FOPPY: So you have said. Tomorrow. Come back to Tara tomorrow.

JUNIOR: Foppy, you were the first person I told I was gay. You told me I wasn't sick but to keep my mouth shut. Well, I want to open my mouth. I keep wanting to come out of the closet and you keep pushing me back in. As a public personality I have a responsibility to my people. Our people! I want to be a contender!

FOPPY: My thinner Marlon Brando, my shorter Tommy Tune, your father does not like us.

JUNIOR: But all you do is go to parties with Ma's Dragon Ladies.

FOPPY: This makes me privy to much useful information.

JUNIOR: Such as?

FOPPY: She looks good in red.

JUNIOR: She must know you're gay.

FOPPY: We do not discuss it!

JUNIOR: Why not?

FOPPY: Why not, why not, youth wants to know? Because Mommy and Daddy are rulers of over two hundred million people who look on us as freaks.

JUNIOR: You deny your true feelings.

FOPPY: Better that than she deny me all her Palace parties. One makes choices.

JUNIOR: The Supreme Tribunal makes its choice today. You want to bet we're going to be officially declared null, void, and illegal?

FOPPY: The Supreme Tribunal is voting today? Their ruling will only apply in Georgia.

JUNIOR: And in twenty-five other states where we're a felony. You can be locked up for making love in your own bedroom! I'll blackmail him. I'll tell the world about me. I am going to Appleberg to dance with Robert.

FOPPY: Robert has just died from the plague.

JUNIOR: Oh, no! (*Hug each other.*) It's getting worse and worse, and it's my own father's fault. How dare he! And you! With all you know, what are you doing to help? You have known her since she was a girl. Help me, Foppy!

FOPPY: I know nothing. That I can tell you.

JUNIOR: When Uncle Rock was in that Paris hospital and they found out with what, they wouldn't call him back.

FOPPY: She told me she called him every day. He had made too many bad movies with Jane Wyman.

JUNIOR: When you asked Mom to get your friend that experimental drug no one else could get . . .

FOPPY: She didn't help my beloved Bernie? She promised me!

JUNIOR: Foppy, you've got to wake up.

FOPPY: Your father was a cheerleader in college.

JUNIOR: A cheerleader?

FOPPY: With pom-poms. And tight sweaters. And saddle shoes. Brown and white. In his early starlet days he would emerge naked from the ocean at Santa Monica looking like an Adonis. He was always exposing his then beautiful chest. He was very popular . . . among certain sets.

JUNIOR: Pop?

FOPPY: A little diddle now and then. One had a career to father.

JUNIOR: Pop?

FOPPY: Everybody did it. Cary Grant and Randolph Scott and Tyrone Power and Errol Flynn. Well, Errol would do it with anything that moved. It was a different world then. Occasional transgressions did not require bombing Libya.

JUNIOR: So why does he hate us?

FOPPY: That is precisely why he hates us. You are too young to remember the Saturday Night Massacre.

JUNIOR: Pop killed somebody?

FOPPY: When he was Prince of Orange it was discovered that a number of his closest male staff orgied with each other at a hidden cabin. Some of these men were married. Perhaps there was a boy or two among them. Perhaps your father was even there as well. Drew Pearson of the *Georgetown Post* blabbed innuendo to the world. Your father denied it all to the press, thus commencing his lifelong tendency to do so.

JUNIOR: Are you sure this isn't only gossip?

FOPPY: Gossip! Gossip! Gossip is life! And death. Be careful with this knowledge, lest your mother be cornered into silencing her own son.

JUNIOR: So these are the facts of life. What else? What do you know about her?

FOPPY: In for a penny, in for a pound.

JUNIOR: I knew you knew more!

FOPPY: There once was a man named Benny Thau. No, I cannot. We have known each other too long. I adore her. She adores me. Why, we are so close we know each other's very thoughts.

(*The red phone rings.* FOPPY *collapses on the floor.*)

Never underestimate the power of a Queen. (*Answering.*) What do you want!

MRS. POTENTATE'S VOICE: He who hesitates must die!

FOPPY: (*Looking around to see if the house is bugged.*) On what evidence!

MRS. POTENTATE'S VOICE: Is he there yet?

FOPPY: My Lady Macbeth, what is this surprise package I hear will be unwrapped at the Supreme Tribunal?

JUNIOR: Way to go, Fopp!

MRS. POTENTATE'S VOICE: It has just happened. The vote was five to four. Tough break. You are now and still illegal.

FOPPY: But I . . . we had so hoped.

MRS. POTENTATE'S VOICE: Daddy tried his best. One of the justices was on the fence. But he fell off. Accidentally.

FOPPY: Accidentally? There are accidents at the Supreme Tribunal?

MRS. POTENTATE'S VOICE: Be careful. Friends are one thing, politics another. History is what we make it. I am only minutes away. He better be there!

FOPPY: (*Mimicking her.*) "History is what we make it." (*Hangs up on her.*)

JUNIOR: Are you beginning to get motivated?

ELECTRA: (*Carrying in milk and cookies for* JUNIOR.) Need I inform you of our unfolding saga? (*Goes back in the kitchen.*)

FOPPY: (*Pushes* JUNIOR *into Oscar Wilde.*) Go into Oscar Wilde. He was accustomed to trouble. "Yes, I am a dreamer," he said. "For a dreamer is one who can only find his way by moonlight, and his punishment is that he sees the dawn before the rest of the world." Although he did not survive it, he fought back!

JUNIOR: Then I can stay?

FOPPY: Until we die at dawn together. (*They embrace.*)

JUNIOR: I'll practice my dancing. I've got to get in shape.

FOPPY: (*Getting him into Oscar Wilde and closing its door.*) Shape! What happened to symmetry and grace? Life was meant to have grace. But she drove over a cliff. (*Starts up the stairs to his room.*) It is a far, far better world I go to . . . Herman Harrod, you are forcing me to have my rendezvous with destiny. . . . It is time for me to change into basic black. I'm ready for my close-up, Mr. De Mille. (*Goes into his room.*)

(ELECTRA *enters with an armful of sheets and towels. At the same moment,* TRUDI *comes out of Jean Genet.*)

TRUDI: That's an awful room.

ELECTRA: You're telling me. Who are you, and what are you doing in this house?

TRUDI: Does Mr. Schwartz trust you?

ELECTRA: Like a sister.

TRUDI: I've come to sell top-secret information.

ELECTRA: You know how? What's the secret?

TRUDI: Until you find the highest bidder, just say no.

ELECTRA: My sister in bondage, meet someone willing to share all her knowledge in an effort to find the highest bidder.

TRUDI: I've already used all the girls I needed.

ELECTRA: But you haven't even heard my story.

TRUDI: What is it about?

ELECTRA: Them.

TRUDI: Which them?

ELECTRA: Which them you want? This house has been witness to every major them in recent modern history. You know how Nelson Rockefeller croaked stuck in a woman, not his wife. (*Nodding to a bedroom.*) He got stuck in there first. Ike and his WAC. Lyndon grabbed a lot of ass. JFK and Judy. JFK and Emily. JFK and Sally. And Wenonah. And Ellie. And Patsy. And Marilyn. You know about Marilyn and Bobby? Right in there.

TRUDI: I was on Marilyn's bed!

ELECTRA: Did you know the CIA went into her house right after and cleared everything out? No evidence was left. Not a shard.

TRUDI: I know. I know.

ELECTRA: Dead and nothing to show for it.

TRUDI: I identify so with Marilyn. When I took acting lessons, Mr. Strasberg told me, "I see in you many of the qualities of the young Marilyn." Maybe your story added to my story . . .

ELECTRA: Would make one hell of an issue! We women of New Columbia are in one big stinking mess.

TRUDI: Could I ask you a favor? Could I give you something very important for you to lock up in a safe safe?

ELECTRA: How safe?

TRUDI: It's the only copy. (*Taking out the tape from under her coat.*) It could bring down the government.

ELECTRA: I could buy the old plantation.

TRUDI: You could buy the whole Confederacy.

ELECTRA: Our downtrodden asses could be the ruling classes. Why are you giving this to me? (*Gives it back.*)

TRUDI: I'm scared to death it will fall into the hands of men who don't understand. (*Gives it back.*)

ELECTRA: I understand. (*Gives it back.*) I thought you just said no until the highest bidder?

TRUDI: I'm afraid the highest bidder might be God. (*Gives it back.*)

TRUDI: (*Taking it.*) Oh, why were my people trained to take up the white man's burden?

(*They embrace.*)

Some women got nine lives, and I've walked through eight of them, but that doesn't mean any man can call me pussy. (*Hides the tape on her person.*)

(*The doorbell rings, then rings again.* FOPPY *rushes out from his bedroom in an extravagant robe of many blacks. He is appalled to see* TRUDI.)

FOPPY: Here only minutes and dishonored your promise! Return to incarceration!

(TRUDI *rushes back into Genet.*)

Electra, ready Mrs. Potentate's rosehip tea.

(ELECTRA *runs to the kitchen as the doorbell continues to ring and ring.*)

JUNIOR AND ELECTRA: (*Both sticking their heads out.*) Should I answer it?

FOPPY: No!

(FOPPY *rushes to the front door, checking himself in a mirror on the way. Then he opens the door. The* MAYOR *tries to come in.* FOPPY *does his best to prevent him but loses. The* MAYOR *carries a suitcase and a bag from the Gap. He walks around investigating, looking outside through the curtains, peeking in the kitchen, the basement.* FOPPY *does his best to corner him, to prevent him from opening the doors of Wilde and Genet.*)

MAYOR: They make you eat shit in this town. So I got a few municipal problems. I am not technically responsible. It's all the fault of the drug dealers. We got to murder them *before* they get into the country. That's the secret of running a big city. Hate. My people love me. All I want's a few billion. That's *bubkis.* Is he here? You got anything to eat? I only diet in Appleberg. I'm here to pig out. The Big Appleberg wants his little cherry. Where is he? I know he's here. How'm I doing?

(*He tries to open Jean Genet.* FOPPY *restrains him.*)

FOPPY: He's not in there!

MAYOR: Who's not in there! We better be alone.

FOPPY: We are all alone. It is the existential dilemma. Who are you looking for?

MAYOR: My private dick followed him to this neighborhood. But he lost him. I got to get back to Grovel Hill. I got more pricks to threaten. Fatso Kennedy. Dukakis the secret psycho. Jesse the Hymie Hater. I got to gore Gore. I'm not gay, you know.

FOPPY: If homosexuality could claim visibly all those who disclaim it, it would be the Catholic Church. You are talking to Foppy!

MAYOR: I forgot. Franny Spellman warned me. Altar boys can be trouble. But he could handle them. I miss my old friend, Franny. This new cardinal is a pain in the cassock.

FOPPY: He's just like you! He hates everybody.

MAYOR: (*Drinking* JUNIOR's *milk.*) Milk is bad for me. I'm intolerant.

FOPPY: You should have stayed with Gilbert Perch. He loved you.

MAYOR: If I ever see him again I'll blow off his pecker. There is no plague in Appleberg. I just got a lot of fairies. Nobody can see fairies.

FOPPY: As Peter Pan warned, you must never not believe in fairies.

MAYOR: Which one is my room?

FOPPY: You cannot stay in my house!

MAYOR: (*Checking out videos.*) Of course I can. I've stayed in your house ever since we were kids together in Cherry Grove.

FOPPY: You were my first.

MAYOR: Mine, too.

FOPPY: It was an unpleasant experience.

MAYOR: I'm not gay, you know.

FOPPY: Of course not, my J. Edgar Hoover.

MAYOR: Don't you find you're happier and you do a better job when you tell the truth?

FOPPY: But the truth is Appleberg stinks with scandal and corruption.

MAYOR: Are you trying to tell me I smell?

FOPPY: You smell. Your politics smell. Your administration smells. Your subways smell. Your bridges are falling down. Stepping into your ocean is like swimming in an unflushed toilet. What's come over me? Why are you letting all our boys be devoured by this horrible plague without lifting a finger?

MAYOR: You should talk! What have you done with all your fancy shiksa friends? All you do is go out with helmet-headed Barbie dolls to fress. (*Takes a video.*) God, I'm hungry. I got the best record of corruption of any major city. Any misdeeds committed by former allies now in jail, out on bail, awaiting trial, I am not technically responsible. It's all pisherdicka. Listen. I need a randy-dandy. (*Heads upstairs with his bags.*)

FOPPY: A what?

MAYOR: A shtuck in the pupick. You found me Gilbert Perch. Find me someone else! Now! (*Goes into Marcel Proust.*)

FOPPY: I won't find you anyone else!

MAYOR: (*Opening the door.*) I want a pupick! I want a randy-dandy! I'm not gay. I'm not technically responsible. How'm I doing? (*Slams the door.*)

FOPPY: (*Running to his desk.*) He denies everything like First Daddy. (*Consulting an address book.*) Tiger is busy . . . Thadd's away . . . Thor's on an overnight in Saudi Arabia . . . Thumper's with Claus von Bulow. I haven't been so nervous since Guy Burgess schtupped Dean Acheson in the poolhouse and defected to Russia.

(ELECTRA *enters.*)

FOPPY: The Mayor of Appleberg is here.

ELECTRA: What! After all he's done to all your people and mine.

FOPPY: We have to get him out of here! Maybe Junior's right. Something's got to be done. Someone's got to do something. Where is that tape? Why am I pimping for all these pimps? What have they ever done for me? Have you removed all my photographs of framed European royalty from Marcel Proust? Mrs. Potentate doesn't like to be reminded she isn't Queen for Life.

ELECTRA: How many times First Mommy come here to . . .

FOPPY: No no no don't use the F word!

ELECTRA: If that's what they're doing to all of us, why not?

FOPPY: You never get in trouble in Georgetown for lying. You only get in trouble for telling the truth.

ELECTRA: Whose truth?

FOPPY: What's happening to me? Electra, I'm tired of being a hag fag. Is this a way to live out one's life? I think it's time to change the world.

ELECTRA: What would you do with the tape if you had it?

FOPPY: I was going to give it to First Mommy.

ELECTRA: Wrong answer. After all she's done to all your people and mine.

FOPPY: You're right! You're right. What am I saying? What am I doing?

ELECTRA: You tell me. Sociologists' statistics say you're supposed to be the smart one.

FOPPY: If I am not for myself, who is for me?

ELECTRA: You tell me.

FOPPY: And if I am only for myself, what am I?

ELECTRA: A selfish pig.

FOPPY: You are correct.

ELECTRA: You are a mensch.

FOPPY: And if not now, when?

ELECTRA: I love it.

FOPPY: And if not me, who?

ELECTRA: Us! (*Hands him the tape.*)

FOPPY: We must look at it.

(*They rush to put it in the VCR.*)

FOPPY: Does our Trudi tell the truth? (*As they look at the tape.*) Our Trudi tells the truth. One, two elected Chamberpersons. One, two, three of Daddy's cabinet. One, two, three, four of Daddy's personal staff ... Ooooh. I think we have struck ...

FOPPY AND ELECTRA: Deep doo-doo.

ELECTRA: We're wasting time. Put it in the safe safe.

(*He rushes to the wall, pulls back the painting, and reveals a safe. He starts twiddling the dial, with* ELECTRA *looking over his shoulder.*)

FOPPY: What's the combination?

ELECTRA: I was hoping to refresh my memory.

FOPPY: It's up the horse's ass.

(*He runs to a small statue of a horse on a table. Gilbert comes out of* FOPPY's *bedroom, just as* JUNIOR, *wearing his dance belt, comes out of Oscar Wilde.* FOPPY *slams back the painting and sticks the tape in his robe pocket, which* ELECTRA *notes.*)

GILBERT: Fop, do you ... Oh. Hello.

JUNIOR: Hello.

FOPPY: Good-bye.

ELECTRA: This is your department. I'll be in the slave galley if you need me. (*Goes into the kitchen.*)

GILBERT: Your face is very familiar.

FOPPY: You've never seen him before in your life! (*Throwing his robe over* JUNIOR.) Clothe thy seductiveness!

JUNIOR: I'm Junior. (*Offering his hand.*)

GILBERT: I knew it. I can't tell you my name yet because I'm hiding from a powerful pig, but I'm very happy to meet you ... (*Taking his hand.*)

FOPPY: No no no no!

GILBERT: ... even though I hate your father.

FOPPY: Not as much as his father hates you.

JUNIOR: So do I.

GILBERT: You do?

(*They're still holding hands.* FOPPY *tries to break them apart, which he can't. He's also trying to either get the tape out of* JUNIOR's *robe pocket or get the robe off* JUNIOR.)

FOPPY: No no no no no no *no!* (*To* JUNIOR.) You have been incarcerated in mansions and palaces too long to make mature adult decisions. (*To* GILBERT.) You are running from a vengeful monster to play such an additional life-threatening game. (*To* JUNIOR.) This is not the moment to make such a public statement for gay rights. (*To no one.*) I am going to be electrocuted by teatime.

JUNIOR: I'm very happy to meet you, too. I have led a sheltered life. But that's all going to change.

GILBERT: I'll be happy to show you the ropes.

FOPPY: Ropes.

GILBERT: I have everyone's number.

FOPPY: I am going to be sent for dinner to Qaddafi.

GILBERT: Can I have your number?

JUNIOR: I'm staying here at present.

GILBERT: So am I! Which room is yours?

FOPPY: Mine. The one with the chair connected to electric wires and tubes of gas.

JUNIOR: Why don't you come in and we can get to know each other better?

FOPPY: Please. I shall be cut into pieces and processed into the horse-meat consumed at burger stands from coast to coast.

JUNIOR: You sound so strong and intelligent and in control.

GILBERT: I'm sorry, Foppy, but Junior is more famous. I feel it's he and I who have a future together.

FOPPY: (*Proclaimed like Lady Bracknell's "A handbag!"*) A future!

(*As they go toward and into Oscar Wilde.*)

Make your bed and go and lie in it. No, make your bed and only lie on it. No, don't lie. Think of higher things. No, don't think of any things. Out of sight, out of mind. I am out of mind.

(JUNIOR *opens the door and tosses* FOPPY *his robe, which he puts on.*)

I am an aging man trying to do good too late in life and I only have one life to give and I am about to give it. His shtuck in the pupick is randy-dandying it in the house that awaits his mother to do the same. We who are about to die pollute you.

(*The* MAYOR *comes out of Proust, holding his videotape.*)

MAYOR: Yuck. Do heteros really do this to each other?

FOPPY: You tell me. You're not gay.

MAYOR: Did you find me anybody yet? He better be safe. We don't have any disease in Appleberg. It's all out of state. (*Puts the videotape back with the others.*) The sheets are black satin. Static electricity is too . . . exciting. Change the sheets! (*Goes into the kitchen.*) Electra, here comes your favorite hozer. Piggy piggy piggy!

FOPPY: (*Screaming in frustration.*) Aiiiiiii!

TRUDI: (*Rushing out.*) Mr. Schwartz, you are so tense. Trudi knows how to relieve tense. Have you got a fever? (*Removes his robe and massages him.*)

FOPPY: I've got a fever. I've got a fever.

TRUDI: Are you having a nervous breakdown?

FOPPY: I'm having a nervous breakdown.

TRUDI: (*Sits him down on the sofa.*) I've had lot of them. I belong to a support therapy group in Malibu called the Malibu Maligned Malingerers, although you don't have to be from Malibu. But you do have to be maligned. My therapist said you have to fall completely apart before the pieces can fit back together.

FOPPY: I'm falling completely apart.

(*She massages him, and he relaxes. The doorbell rings.* FOPPY *shoots straight up.*)

FOPPY: I'm not back together!

TRUDI: I'll get it.

(*She runs to answer the door.* HERMAN HARROD, *in full leather regalia, including whip, stomps in, slamming the door. He ignores* FOPPY *and goes for* TRUDI. *She hands him* FOPPY's *robe, and* HERMAN *grabs it and puts it on. They begin fighting as if they've never stopped.*)

HERMAN: The hotel impounded my clothes because you didn't pay the bill!

TRUDI: How could I pay the bill!

HERMAN: (*To* FOPPY.) You tell our friend Mrs. Potentate that if she doesn't order her best friend, my wife, to cosign some checks . . . (*To both of them.*) . . . I'll blackmail her! (*To* TRUDI.) You got the tape someplace safe?

(*She nods. He rubs his hands together gleefully.*)

Give it to me. When I die you'll be rich.

TRUDI: I don't want you to die. I just want to be rich. (*As he snorts some coke—he will continue to snort it.*) Don't you ever get enough? What did the doctor tell you?

HERMAN: It's my money! I married her poor! She stops freezing my money because of you, or the entire world will know about you and me, Trudi and Herman and our orgy and our sex scenes and whips and chains and leather and thigh-high wading boots and rubber and masks and the rack! We've filmed it all!

(FOPPY *has been trying to get his hand into the pocket of the robe* HERMAN'*s now wearing, to get the tape.*)

HERMAN: Get out of there, you pervert!

(HERMAN *comes after* FOPPY *with the whip.* FOPPY *runs up the stairs. Trudi starts talking to get* HERMAN'*s attention back to her, and he returns.* FOPPY *stays on the stairs, listening.*)

TRUDI: You said I could have a house of my own. You said you would look after me forever. You said after I did it with the Shyster General I could stop finding girls for your White Palace friends. After twelve years with you all I've got is nothing but a dirty home movie and an autobiography that no one's even written yet.

HERMAN: It's not my fault. I helped put that lousy actor into office and what happens? He learns how to act. I screened all his applicants for high office. I chose his cabinet because he didn't know anyone to ask! I shaped his policy. I chose his issues. (*A snort each issue.*) Antiabortion. The Lord's Prayer. The Pledge of Allegiance. The sanctity of the family. The sin of perverted faggots. I made the shidduch with Jerry Falwell. I got Gary Hart into trouble. I got him millions from Vegas. And don't forget all the dirt I shoveled for her. And what thanks does Daddy give me? Dickshit. You don't exile Herman Harrod and get away with it. You got some girls we could call for a quickie?

(*He tries to get hold of her, and she keeps evading him.*)

TRUDI: Girls, girls! You're insatiable. It's just like Wall Street, pure greed. You said we could go back to kiss and cuddle. I'm not girls! I am a woman!

HERMAN: How do you know we won't kiss and cuddle? Remember how we cuddled when I called Sam Giancana? And Albert Bonnano? What a turn-on!

TRUDI: Men don't understand. Sex doesn't mean that much to most women. It's not exceptional. It's not.

HERMAN: It is! It is! You don't appreciate how good you are at it. You always shovel shit all over your good qualities.

TRUDI: It's hard finding girls who don't mind getting whomped by a strange man, even if he says he's one of the richest men in New Columbia and best friend to the Potentate-in-Chief. A whip's a whip.

HERMAN: I don't whomp hard.

TRUDI: You do, too! Unless I harness your horsepower.

HERMAN: Harness my horsepower!

TRUDI: LaWanda said at least when she's making three and a quarter an hour at Wendy's she knows she'll be alive when she goes home to get smacked by her husband.

HERMAN: Call LaWanda.

TRUDI: The Catholic Church has a lot to answer for, letting you in.

HERMAN: You leave the Church out of this! I'm real generous to the Church. I got blessed by the Pope! (*Showing his crucifix.*) Every time we have one of our orgies—oooh, come here—I go to my own personal confessor and you know it.

TRUDI: He must have cast-iron ears.

HERMAN: Don't you love me?

TRUDI: Any dream is better than no dream. I didn't know you got Gary Hart into trouble. His girlfriend Donna was a friend of mine. You've always told me what we did in private was our own business.

HERMAN: It is our business. Except when it's their business. Then it's big business.

TRUDI: You can't just blackmail Daddy and get away with it. They have all kinds of secret weapons.

HERMAN: Where's the tape? (*His hands find it in the pocket of* FOPPY'*s robe he's wearing.*) Thank you, Jesus. (*Rushes to make a phone call.*) Hello, Huggy Buggy Bunny Boo. It's your hubby wubby punkin poo. Marvin Michaelson filed suit. Trudi Tunick wants ten-million dollars palimony. Now will you sign some checks or must she tell the world!... No? Then how about this. We filmed our latest S&M orgy with some of Mommy and Daddy's closest chums. First Mommy already told you? How does she know? ... Hello? ... Hello!

(TRUDI *has managed to get the tape as* HERMAN *talks on the phone.* HERMAN *hangs up, rips off his robe, and starts chasing* TRUDI *around the room. She's running from him, and* FOPPY *is fanning himself, overcome with all the excitement.*)

TRUDI: You have that crazy look in your eyes.

HERMAN: Tell me how crazy.

TRUDI: Very crazy.

HERMAN: Ten million from the palimony and millions from the media and I shall be the Ambassador to France!

TRUDI: I love Paris!

HERMAN: Paris was made for kiss and cuddle!

TRUDI: Be careful, Herman Harrod, you're going too far.

HERMAN: Pull me back, babe, don't let me go too far.

> (*He falls on all fours and starts following her. She starts guiding him around with the whip. She sees* FOPPY *watching and whips the air that he should go away.* FOPPY *retreats into his room but keeps the door open to peek out.* TRUDI *is looking for a safe place to hide the tape. Hastily she puts it on the shelf with all the others.*)

TRUDI: Tell me how important Trudi Tunick is in your life and forever.

HERMAN: You rule my world. You're master of all passion. Don't let me go too far.

FOPPY: You go too far.

HERMAN: Tell me anything you want.

TRUDI: I already told you a million times.

HERMAN: Tell me again.

> (MRS. POTENTATE'*s red phone rings. And rings.* FOPPY *starts crawling desperately to get it.*)

HERMAN: Tell me again.

FOPPY: I cannot talk to you now!

TRUDI: I want you to take care of me forever.

HERMAN: Forever and ever.

> (HERMAN *is on his back on the floor. She unzips her skirt and sits down.*)

MRS. POTENTATE'S VOICE: What's going on that we can't talk?

HERMAN: Forever and ever?

FOPPY: We're having a dress rehearsal!

TRUDI: Forever and ever.

MRS. POTENTATE'S VOICE: A dress rehearsal?

FOPPY: Yes, what are you wearing?!

(*A sudden sound of everything suddenly stopping and becoming very quiet.*)

TRUDI: Herman. . . . Herman? . . . Herman!

(ELECTRA *wheels in a cart with the necessities for tea.*)

MRS. POTENTATE'S VOICE: What my monmy always calls my nigger red.

(*Sounds of* TRUDI *slapping* HERMAN'S *face.*)

TRUDI: Mr. Schwartz!

FOPPY: (*To* TRUDI.) Yes, my dear. (*To* MRS. POTENTATE.) Your mother?

TRUDI: I . . .

FOPPY: Yes?

TRUDI: I . . . I . . .

FOPPY: Yes yes?

MRS. POTENTATE'S VOICE: She's bored to death in Arizona and asking for you.

TRUDI: Mr. Schwartz?

FOPPY: Yes?

TRUDI: I . . . I can't . . .

MRS. POTENTATE'S VOICE: Why don't you give her a call.

FOPPY: Yes . . . Yes . . . Yes . . .

MRS. POTENTATE'S VOICE: Do you have her number?

TRUDI: I can't get off!

FOPPY: Her number . . . ?

MRS. POTENTATE'S VOICE: What is going on there?

ELECTRA: Teatime!

MRS. POTENTATE'S VOICE: A dress rehearsal for what!?

FOPPY: (*To* MRS. POTENTATE.) For what? For life itself!

ELECTRA: Time for tea!

MRS. POTENTATE'S VOICE: In Scottsdale, Arizona, you dial . . .

FOPPY: Hurry hurry hurry home to Foppy's or you'll miss it all! (*Hangs up.*)

ELECTRA: Rosehip tea and little finger sandwiches

FOPPY: Not now with the hips and fingers!

ELECTRA: There is a big black limo pulling up outside chez toi and a woman wearing a bright red Adolfo fake Chanel is rushing up our geranium-bordered walkway toward our palazzo, and in just a momentito the doorbell is going to—

(*The doorbell rings.* ELECTRA *helps* FOPPY *get* TRUDI *and* HERMAN *upright.*)

TRUDI: Why can't I get off?

ELECTRA: You have an iron in your fire.

(*They start hauling* TRUDI *and* HERMAN, *stuck in each other, maneuvering them toward Jean Genet.*)

TRUDI: Oh, Herman, you told me I don't have enough fuck-you money yet. How can I ever do it without you?

ELECTRA: So far you won't ever have to.

FOPPY: Both of you—stop beating a dead horse.

TRUDI: You're only supposed to say nice things about the dead!

FOPPY: Being hung like a horse is saying something nice.

(*The doorbell continues to ring.* JUNIOR *sticks his head out of Oscar Wilde, wearing only a towel.*)

JUNIOR: Anybody got any rubbers?

(ELECTRA *quickly puts herself between* JUNIOR *and the couple.*)

GILBERT: (*Also only in towel sticks his head out, too.*) We'd prefer Ramses Klingtite with Nonoxynol-9.

ELECTRA: You gonna have to make do with spit, your hands, and restraint. This party's strictly BYO. (*Pushes them back into Oscar Wilde.*)

MAYOR: (*Coming out of the kitchen, eating.*) Is that for me?

FOPPY: Let me inspect him first, in case he's a troll. (*Pushes the* MAYOR *back into the kitchen; sounds of a loud crash.*)

(*The doorbell ringing turns into pounding.* ELECTRA *and* FOPPY *get* HERMAN *and* TRUDI *into Genet.* FOPPY *gets into his robe, checks himself in the mirror.* ELECTRA *tidies up.*)

FOPPY: (*He's ready.*) Electra!

(*But the front door opens.* MRS. POTENTATE *enters. She has her own key. She wears a huge hat and enormous sunglasses and carries a handbag.*)

FOPPY: (*Kissing her hand.*) Mrs. Potentate, Proud Mommy, welcome once again to the House of Schwartz.

End of Act One

Act Two

The action resumes immediately. FOPPY *is kissing* MRS. POTENTATE'*s hand.* ELECTRA *closes the front door.*

FOPPY: Mrs. Potentate, Proud Mommy, welcome once again to the House of Schwartz.

MRS. POTENTATE: At last I'm here. I feel like a million, my tasteful one. No, a billion.

FOPPY: Until the budget is balanced, go for broke!

MRS. POTENTATE: Is he here?

FOPPY: You still cannot summon up a name?

MRS. POTENTATE: Who does he think he's screwing with? It's not as if I was having a slam bam with some herman in some uptown sleazepit fophouse.

FOPPY: Are you certain you have time, my Lily of France?

MRS. POTENTATE: (*To* ELECTRA.) Bring me a glass of water and a dozen aspirin.

ELECTRA: Sounds like a heavy habit, Ma'am. (*Goes into the kitchen.*)

FOPPY: With so much tape on your plate, my Wily Wedgwood, is it not best to return to service at the Palace? How is there time for—

MRS. POTENTATE: A First Lady always finds time for the important things. That's what I get laid for. Even as we talk there are so many things to take care of. Fopp, it seems ages since we dished. How's your health? How do you feel?

FOPPY: Like the man who stokes the dank at Monte Carlo. What are you taking care of?

MRS. POTENTATE: Carolina told me that you called her evil.

FOPPY: Carolina? Georgia is evil. What are you taking care of?

MRS. POTENTATE: (*Pulling some pieces of paper out of her purse.*) His doodles from his last Cabinet Meeting. How much do you think they'll fetch at Sotheby's?

FOPPY: What are you taking care of?

MRS. POTENTATE: Herman Harrod, the bimbo slut, the tape, the location, the coconspirators, punishment. That is what I have an SS for! Poof!

FOPPY: Will you stop using that word so imprecisely!

MRS. POTENTATE: And I can't decide yet whether we should run for another term. My kingdom come! (*Lays herself out on the sofa.*) Why isn't he here yet? Ooooooh.

FOPPY: My Miss Marple, how can you concentrate on so many mysteries at one fell stoop?

MRS. POTENTATE: So what if I can't think of his name. It's not his name I want. Do you think I caught Alzheimer's that time I kissed Rita Hayworth?

FOPPY: To think that I considered it meaningful to be born rich, educated at the best of schools, exposed to the most cultivated of people, and welcome in the world of power and fame. (*To her.*) Perhaps he is an Orthodox Jew and prefers to do it only after sundown.

MRS. POTENTATE: No one's as orthodox as all that.

FOPPY: You have heard about Robert?

MRS. POTENTATE: Sad. Sad. Oh, my Prince Charming of the Law.... Hurry, hurry, my young Felix Frankfurter.

FOPPY: With each minute the tally grows and grows. More and more of our dear friends are dying. Robert, your old friend Roy, my dearest old love Bernie, whom you helped so much ...

MRS. POTENTATE: (*Not remembering Bernie.*) Sad. Sad. Dearest Bernie. Sad. More than ever we must live life to the fullest. You must not dwell on a past full of old Bernies.

FOPPY: Which of us has a past that's passed, my Mommy Dearest?

MRS. POTENTATE: I am ravenous! When it gets like this I'm insatiable. Oh, Fopp, aren't I awful? (*Dialing on her portable phone.*) But you've known that forever.

FOPPY: Forever. You are awful.

MRS. POTENTATE: I'm at Uncle Foppy's. (*To* FOPPY.) Kiss kiss from Daddy. Yes, he knows you hate the faggot breath he walks on.

FOPPY: Kiss kiss back to Daddy, too.

MRS. POTENTATE: You haven't got a thing to do? Don't get depressed. Mommy will be home soon to shoot you up again. If the media calls about anything, just play dumb like you do so well on Iran. What am I doing? I'm still in there! No! Not in there! In there fighting for New Columbia! Kiss Kiss Pootie Pie. (*Disconnecting.*)

He always thinks I'm still being a naughty girl. I love it! I'm never so famished as when there's a good hot knotty steamy ... possibility. (*Slithers to the floor in ecstasy.*)

FOPPY: Will she never experience her change of life? (*Helping her off the floor and upstairs.*) Come—let us await fate in Marcel Proust. In remembrance of things past. (*Closing the door behind her.*) She would get laid during the Crucifixion.

MRS. POTENTATE: (*Coming out.*) Junior is also missing. I found a note in his wastebasket.

FOPPY: You read his basket?

MRS. POTENTATE: It said, "I'm going out into the world to dance, you bitch." What do you think it means?

FOPPY: First Mother Mary's son, Jesus, also spoke in parables.

MRS. POTENTATE: Oh, Fopp! Come help prepare me to meet my Maker. (*Pulls him into Proust.*)

MAYOR: (*Coming out of the kitchen, bruised.*) So what did he look like? (*Seeing no one is there.*) That bad, huh. (*Dialing a phone.*) Give me the latest number from Sex and Germs. . . . I don't want to know? Then don't tell me. . . . Why don't I want to know? Because it's a pooh-pooh disease. No one wants it. Breast cancer a woman gets sympathy. Parkinson's fashionable. Katharine Hepburn has it. Cystic fibrosis. Joan Rivers designs you jewelry. A faygeleh gets sick. To the lions . . . ! No, I haven't found him yet to shut him up. But I will!

(*He hangs up when* ELECTRA *comes in with the water and aspirin. The* MAYOR *grabs the aspirin and puts them in his mouth, but she keeps him from taking the water.*)

ELECTRA: Mr. Foppy says use his room temporarily.

MAYOR: (*Choking.*) Help!

ELECTRA: We got the exterminator.

MAYOR: Why? (*Drinks more of the milk.*)

ELECTRA: Rats. You should understand. (*Goes back in the kitchen.*)

MAYOR: (*Studying the choice of videos.*) On Golden Blonde. My Bare Lady. Ilse She-Wolf of the SS. Beverly Hills Copulator. (*Takes this one and starts to his room, then comes back and pops another video into his pants.*) Movies are seven bucks.

ELECTRA: (*Coming out of the kitchen with more aspirin and heading toward Proust; calling out.*) Mr. Foppy!

FOPPY: (*Coming out.*) What!

ELECTRA: I told him he had to stay in your room! (*Goes into Proust.*)

FOPPY: You must wait in your room. I sent away one ugly troll. But I've called a new one. Rob Lowe and Tom Cruise put together. Be prepared. Get ready. Go up and play with yourself.

MAYOR: I'm tired of playing with myself.

FOPPY: What good news! I must notify *The Appleberg Times.*

MAYOR: I don't have to stay here, you know. There are plenty of places in this hick town to get my doodah diddled.

FOPPY: Name one.

MAYOR: I'll stay. (*Goes into* FOPPY's *room.*)

(FOPPY *runs downstairs.* ELECTRA *comes out of* PROUST *and joins him.*)

FOPPY: (*Knocking on Genet and opening the door.*) Oh, I see you're still engaged. (*Closes the door.*)

ELECTRA: What are we planning to do since the plot got infinitely more complicated?

FOPPY: (*Running to wall safe.*) Unless you have trusted friends who don't ask questions at Frank Campbell's, I must make some calls.

ELECTRA: This is no time for you to chat with any of your cycle sluts.

FOPPY: This is precisely the time. Leave me alone to do so.

(*He opens the safe and takes out a tiny little black book. He slams the safe shut and rushes to a phone. She follows him and listens to all.*)

FOPPY: Is the Chamberperson in? Eleazer Ben Schwartz. (*To* ELECTRA.) Go unscrew her.

(ELECTRA *goes into the kitchen and immediately comes out wearing rubber gloves and carrying a large can of Crisco. She goes right into Genet.*)

FOPPY: (*On the phone.*) Big Boo, I desperately need your help. You have never heard me speak like this before. If I had the most powerful instrument of blackmail known to modern man, what would our people want? . . . What do you mean, who are our people? You are talking to Jack Lemmon in *The Apartment.* (*Listens.*) Hmmmm. Hmmm. Unh-hunh. Would Daddy ever do that? No, of course not. He hates the faggot breath we walk on. Would you help? Of course not. You do, too. Return your key immediately! (*Slams down the phone.*) I am a man possessed. I must expose their Supreme Reprehensible Hypocrisies, but I don't have the weapon in my hand yet—my instrument for her doom.

(*We suddenly hear an enormous loud sound of something going pop!*)

FOPPY: Aaaaaachhhhhh.

(*. . . followed by an enormous sigh of relief from* TRUDI. *The doors to Proust, Oscar Wilde, and* FOPPY'*s bedroom open and their inhabitants*—MRS. POTENTATE, GILBERT *and* JUNIOR, *and the* MAYOR— *stand in their respective doorways.*)

It was nothing! It was one of those thousand points of light!

(*Each returns into his or her bedroom.* ELECTRA *comes out of Jean Genet, followed by* TRUDI.)

TRUDI: How many ways do you spell relief!

MRS. POTENTATE: (*Reappearing.*) I recognize that sound!

(*She rushes out wearing a Frederick's of Hollywood lingerie outfit, her face all creamed.* ELECTRA *pushes* TRUDI *back into Genet, going in after her.*)

FOPPY: I should think you would. My Helen of Troy, go back and continue creaming!

(*But she comes down. She looks around as she rushes for a regular phone and starts dialing.*)

MRS. POTENTATE: My friend, is there any sign of danger in this afternoon's chart? . . . No, I do not plan to travel over water. To walk on it, perhaps. Any news about our running for reelection? The stars are not yet clear enough for you to see! My friend, we are the stars, and we are very very clear! (*Hangs up.*)

FOPPY: (*Sotto.*) The fault, dear Brutus, is not in our stars but in ourselves that we are underlings. (*To her.*) My Caesar's Wife, you must prepare for it. My Kitty Foyle, you are about to have it. And, my Forever Amber, to enjoy it. But my Mrs. Skeffington, you're really not quite ready. Your face is slimy. Your hair is mangy. I can see your zits. My ZaSu Pitts, you are a mess!

MRS. POTENTATE: Oh, dear. You really think so?

FOPPY: I do. And who taught you everything you know?

MRS. POTENTATE: You did.

FOPPY: I did. And may history forgive me for it.

MRS. POTENTATE: Could I exchange those two sweet little Louis XV side chairs you loaned us for the Palace for a larger size? Louis the XVI, or Louis XVII? Louis XX?

FOPPY: First Mother of Love, From Whom All Yessings flow, go back to your *chambre d'amour* and await the law.

(*He has her back in Proust. No sooner does he start down than she comes out again.*)

MRS. POTENTATE: Foppy Schwartz, answer me directly! Is Junior a confirmed fairy?

FOPPY: Confirmed in the sense of accepted into the faith? Bar mitzvahed?

MRS. POTENTATE: Answer me!

FOPPY: As Tallulah Bankhead once said, "Well, darling, he's not sucked my cock." (*As she disappears.*) Dear God, when will you give us a kinder, gentler nation?

(FOPPY *opens* Genet. TRUDI, ELECTRA, *and* FOPPY *start schlepping* HERMAN *out.*)

TRUDI: Herman, don't leave me.

ELECTRA: What are we going to do with him?

TRUDI: I want him buried with full military honors. I'll wear a beautiful black pillbox. . . .

(*She gets caught up in her fantasy, walks forward, dropping her part of* HERMAN, *who falls on the floor.*)

FOPPY: The basement.

ELECTRA: The old trunks. Like in *Arsenic and Old Lace.*

TRUDI: I locked Herman up in old trunks lots of times. Oh, Herman, how can I stand up to your wife in a palimony suit? She's a very smart lady. How can I sell a tape to the world? I couldn't even sell Mary Kay cosmetics.

(HERMAN *gets stuck.*)

Our love handcuffs!

FOPPY: My dear, so many years of such devotion to such a horrid human gives you rights. You must stand up for them and fight.

TRUDI: It's easy for you to say. You're a somebody. Courts and lawyers and the media will believe you.

FOPPY: Let us fervently hope.

TRUDI: (*To* HERMAN.) Between your wife and Mrs. Potentate, I am dead.

MRS. POTENTATE'S VOICE: Foppy!

FOPPY: Does the vampire never sleep? Yes, my Bela Lugosi!

TRUDI: I know that voice! She's found us! Boy, she doesn't waste any time.

(MRS. POTENTATE *comes out on the landing. Unseen by any save the audience,* HERMAN *opens his eyes when he hears* MRS. P.*'s voice. He is zonked, but he makes feeble reaches in her direction each time he wakes to hear her. Then he zonks out again.* ELECTRA, *not noting his movements, quickly covers him with a sheet.* TRUDI *hides by the stairs.* ELECTRA *polishes the banister with her apron, to stand between* TRUDI *and* MRS. POTENTATE.)

MRS. POTENTATE: Are you telling me Junior hasn't quite found himself yet?

FOPPY: Am I telling you that? Yes. Why not?

MRS. POTENTATE: It upsets Daddy to see him flapping around the White Palace.

FOPPY: We were flappers once. Don't you remember?

MRS. POTENTATE: I tried to explain to Junior that running a country is more important than watching a fairy dance *Swan Lake.*

FOPPY: There are no fairies in *Swan Lake.*

MRS. POTENTATE: There aren't?

FOPPY: Swans. There are swans in *Swan Lake.*

MRS. POTENTATE: Perhaps he's just going through a stage. (*Goes back into Proust.*)

(JUNIOR *and* GILBERT, *both in bath towels, and very much in love, come out of Oscar Wilde.* ELECTRA *pushes* TRUDI *into the kitchen and goes in after her.* FOPPY *runs back to the phone. Every once in a while, when no one is looking,* HERMAN's *hand reaches up toward* MRS. POTENTATE. *His body moves little by little in her direction.*)

JUNIOR: Foppy, do you think we're just going through a stage?

FOPPY: (*Looking to see who's overhearing who.*) A stage? But all the world's a stage. Oh, forget it.

GILBERT: I'm telling you, it's not time yet! There's not one single place we can live safely. And anyway, who would let you live openly and particularly with me?

JUNIOR: That bastard Mayor really destroyed your self-image.

GILBERT: He tried to pay me off with illegal contracts in Orangeberg.

JUNIOR: Nothing's illegal in Orangeberg. I have a lot of work to do on you.

GILBERT: You're willing to do a lot of work on me?

JUNIOR: You bet.

GILBERT: No one's ever said that to me before. Will it hurt?

FOPPY: (*On phone.*) Equal Fidelity Insurance. I wish to speak to your President. . . . Tell him . . . tell him Butch Ramrod. R-a-m-r-o-d.

JUNIOR: Didn't you ever have a teacher who helped you grow?

FOPPY: Big Dick, it's Butch. It's time to mobilize our members.

GILBERT: My mother loves me.

JUNIOR: That's not always a plus.

FOPPY: But you are one of the richest men in the world.

JUNIOR: I wonder if Mom would lend us her decorator.

GILBERT: To decorate what?

FOPPY: Why can't you help insure our future?

JUNIOR: We're going to live together like two men! In Appleberg!

GILBERT: I can't live in Appleberg!

JUNIOR: I can't live in Orangeberg!

FOPPY: What do you mean, since when did I become such a radical fairy! Since I started knowing twits like you, you twit! Go restore another historic home instead of your heart! (*Hangs up and dials again.*)

GILBERT: Our first fight. I knew it would happen. You famous people are all alike. Unresponsive to my genuine needs. Having your way with me.

FOPPY: Chief of Staff. . . . Foppy Schwartz. Since your daughter is, like me, a homosexual . . . (*He's hung up on.*) I don't know who else to call. Yes, I do! (*Looks for the number.*) When you're in such a big and exclusive private club, you can always find another member.

JUNIOR: The first thing we'll do when we get to Appleberg and get our first apartment is have couples therapy.

GILBERT: Can't we live on the Island?

JUNIOR: No! We are going to live right out in the open for everyone to see us! If I can help one poor kid feel better because he loves his best boyfriend, then I will have done a good deed!

FOPPY: Buffalo Studios? Give me your big, bad boss, Barry.

GILBERT: You're such an inspiration. You give me so much courage. Just be gentle.

JUNIOR: See what love can do?

FOPPY: Your friend at Dragon Pictures, dark, dapper, deceitful David, told me you have lost forty-seven friends. Then you must understand.... Understand what? That we must do something. What must we do? Well, take your pick. From Column A we could choose getting all our rich gay friends to pressure the Potentates. From Column B you could make a major motion picture at your major motion picture studio. . . . About what? About saving your life, you ungrateful penis of peril.... Hello! ... Hello!... You will not be receiving the Rock Hudson Award for Services to Your People! (*Hangs up.*)

JUNIOR: Are you all right, Uncle Foppy? You seem distraught.

FOPPY: Did either of you by some remote one-in-a-trillion chance discover a sweet little home video in a robe pocket?

GILBERT: We've been much too busy to notice anything but ourselves.

FOPPY: Perhaps it fell on the floor. (*Goes into Oscar Wilde.*)

(JUNIOR *sees* HERMAN's *head sticking out, his hand reaching up.*)

JUNIOR: Hi, Uncle Herman. Are you all right?

HERMAN: Unh.

JUNIOR: (*Gives him more coke from the tube around his neck.*) Is this better?

HERMAN: Unh.

JUNIOR: Boy, Foppy really does have a full house.

FOPPY: (*Coming out and continuing his search of the floor.*) Your debut has presented many problems.

JUNIOR: They say a lousy dress rehearsal means a hit.

FOPPY: Well, don't give up your day job. What is your day job?

JUNIOR: We're going to live together as two men in love.

FOPPY: Someone will pay you to do that? My Damian and Pythias. My David and Jonathan. My Simon and Garfunkel. Uncle Foppy would be so grateful if you would go out and take in a movie! Now!

(*They head back dewy-eyed toward Oscar Wilde.*)

Not again!

JUNIOR: You can't keep kids from fucking, 'cause it feels so good. (*Runs over to* FOPPY *and hugs him.*) Thank you for helping me find love. And for being such a warrior role model. Foppy the Great!

(JUNIOR *takes* GILBERT *into Oscar Wilde. The door closes.* HERMAN *starts to move. He even pulls himself up a stair or two.*)

FOPPY: Foppy the Late.

TRUDI: (*Coming out of the kitchen with* ELECTRA.) I really don't think I should stay here any longer. You've been very hospitable, but—I hate to say this to you—your house has bad vibes.

(MRS. POTENTATE *comes out of her room, looking ravishing, talking on a portable phone.* HERMAN *falls back down the stairs.* TRUDI *rushes back into Genet.* ELECTRA *quickly re-covers* HERMAN. MRS. P. *descends as she models for* FOPPY. ELECTRA *peeks at* HERMAN, *gives him a sniff from his inhaler.*)

MRS. POTENTATE: (*Into phone.*) Yes, Mommy will be home to dress you for tonight's performance. . . . Yes, it's a new costume. . . . Yes, the Marine Band will play you in. . . . Yes, there's a long long long red carpet. . . . Yes, you'll be on during prime time. . . . Yes, then you can play with your trains. . . . Yes, Mommy is still going to fire Uncles Ed and Donny. . . . Now don't cry. Stop it! Remember, you must say directly to the camera that you believe it is a tragic illness, but yes, you still believe they should remain illegal. And never ever say the words *AIDS* or *homosexuals*! Now you can go upstairs and watch *General Hospital.* . . . Yes, I'm still at Uncle Foppy's. . . . Yes, I already told him that. . . . No! No, listen to me! I've been a good girl since . . . I told you, I'm trying to save your . . .

ELECTRA: Evil empire.

MRS. POTENTATE: No. We can't go. I haven't a thing to wear.

FOPPY: The Smithsonian would lend you something, but you haven't returned anything since 1812.

MRS. POTENTATE: Kiss kiss Pootie Pie. (*Disconnecting.*) Oh, God, I need it. What's under that sheet?

FOPPY: The department store sent the wrong order.

MRS. POTENTATE: Which department store?

FOPPY: Harrods.

MRS. POTENTATE: You ordered all the way from London?

FOPPY: All the way. And it's not returnable.

MRS. POTENTATE: (*Sitting down and pouring herself some tea. To* ELECTRA.) Ezekial, could you get me more hot water?

ELECTRA: More hot water coming up. (*Goes into kitchen.*)

MRS. POTENTATE: Can you see how passionate I feel?

FOPPY: Yes.

MRS. POTENTATE: Do you know what it's like to really need it?

FOPPY: Oh, God, I know.

MRS. POTENTATE: The only time he really comes to life is when we stick him in front of the camera. Otherwise we hide him. Do you have any idea how desperate it is?

FOPPY: Yes.

(HERMAN's *body has turned in her direction and is inching slowly toward her.*)

MRS. POTENTATE: The latest problem is he mixes up his movies with real life. He plays with his footballs in his bathtub and wakes up in the middle of the night to see if his leg is still there. His leg! The hardest thing I've had to deal with in over thirty years of marriage is his leg!

FOPPY: That is exceedingly desperate.

MRS. POTENTATE: Every time he passes a New Columbian flag he salutes it. Do you know how many New Columbia flags are in the White Palace?

FOPPY: (*Calling.*) Electra, how many New Columbian flags are in the White Palace?

ELECTRA: (*Entering with electric teakettle with cord still attached.*) Seven hundred and twelve. (*Pours boiling water into* MRS. P.'s *cup.*)

MRS. POTENTATE: I don't know why everyone thinks this job is so much fun. Everyone thinks it's all free dishes. Everyone thinks it's all mink coats and Russian president's wives. Everyone thinks it's all Frank Sinatra for long private lunches upstairs with my door locked. Everyone thinks it's all parties, parties, parties, and balls, balls, balls. Well, it is. He said all he wants now is to live the quiet life again. Horseshit on the hacienda at our ranch high up in the middle of nowhere. Our mingy two-bedroom split-level featuring furniture from his childhood back home again in Indiana or Illinois or wherever it was. Huggy Bunny Harrod throwing it up to me on every phone call, "I have one hundred million dollars, how much do you have?" The sacrifices I've made to go into public service! But I'm making the best of it! A cup of hot tea makes you feel so brisk. (*Starts upstairs again, walking on* HERMAN.) Lady Bird planted her pansies on the highways. Eleanor Roosevelt was a lesbian with bad teeth. Mamie was a lush. Betty Ford was such a mess she opened her own cure. Rosalynn was Attila the Hun. Pat Nixon pleaded a bad heart, and she certainly had one. Who even remembers Bess Truman? All she was was just a wife and mother. I'm better than all of them! Mrs. Wilson ran the country, so can I! Why don't I get as good a press as Jackie? I dress better and my husband is faithful! Should I run for reelection? You bet your fucking ass! (*Goes into Proust and slams the door.*)

FOPPY: I know Jackie! Jackie is a friend of mine! Mrs. Potentate, you are no Jackie!

(TRUDI *rushes out and runs to the bookcase.*)

TRUDI: Mr. Schwartz, the tape is gone!

FOPPY: I know, dear. Don't you have it?

TRUDI: (*To* ELECTRA.) No, I gave it to you.

ELECTRA: (To FOPPY.) I gave it to you.

FOPPY: No one must leave the house until we find that tape.

(*They all place their hands on top of one another's, in a pact. The* MAYOR *comes out of* FOPPY's *room and heads toward Proust.*)

FOPPY: Where are you going?

(TRUDI *rushes back into Genet.*)

No, no, no, you can't go in there!

MAYOR: The exterminator's still here?

ELECTRA: Yes.

FOPPY: And it takes a long time. Electra, get our beloved Mayor some more food.

ELECTRA: He already cleaned us out.

MAYOR: (*To* ELECTRA.) You got more Charmin Plus with Lanolin? That milk gave me the runs.

(ELECTRA *goes into the kitchen. The* MAYOR *comes downstairs.* FOPPY *knocks on Proust.*)

FOPPY: My Tess of the d'Urbervilles. I am running out of things to call her.

(FOPPY *goes into Proust.* HERMAN *crawls up a few more stairs.* ELECTRA *comes out of the kitchen carrying a tray heaped with anything, plus a roll of Charmin. She starts feeding the* MAYOR *to keep his mind occupied.* HERMAN *intermittently crawls.*)

ELECTRA: Yummy yummy yummy. You want to tell me how come schools in your city so crummy?

MAYOR: Not me.

ELECTRA: Don't you want my people educated?

MAYOR: When I decide to tell you, I'll tell you. (*Notices the moving sheet, which stops moving.*) What's that sheet?

ELECTRA: Cover Up. Fawn Hall for Wamsutta. How come you got so many homeless?

MAYOR: I don't have any homeless. I just got a lot of people who like to sleep outdoors. What kind of sheets on Foppy's bed?

ELECTRA: One hundred percent cotton. Picked by slaves. How come crime and murder in your city at new historic heights?

MAYOR: You're very nosy. My people love me. They stand in line to picket me. I thought here in the South your people knew your place.

ELECTRA: My people hate you. My people are going to kill you. There are more of my people than you think.

MAYOR: Voodoo politics.

ELECTRA: When this plague hits Africa and they find out you started it, you'll find out from voodoo.

(FOPPY *comes out of Proust with the* MAYOR's *suitcase and Gap bag. He leaves them on the landing. He suddenly sits on the stairs, exhausted.*)

FOPPY: I am losing the strength to be role model to twenty-four million people.

MAYOR: I got enough bigoted whites to get me reelected. (*Looking at* HERMAN'*s covered body.*)

ELECTRA: Eighty-five percent of women and ninety-two percent of babies with AIDS are people of color.

MAYOR: Eighty-two percent and eighty-five percent. Always appear to be honest with figures. You won't succeed. But try.

(*The* MAYOR *heads straight toward her, his hand raised. She stands her ground.*)

ELECTRA: You want all faggots and schvartzehs to die!

(*But instead he walks past her toward* HERMAN'*s body.* FOPPY *jumps up and rushes down just as the* MAYOR *pulls off the sheet.*)

MAYOR: I thought so. You were right to hide him from me. He's not my type. (*Throws the sheet back over him.*) I'm going to my room. (*He takes his suitcase and the Gap bag.*)

MRS. POTENTATE'S VOICE: Foppy, can you come and look!

MAYOR: The exterminator's a woman!

ELECTRA: You bet. (*goes into the kitchen.*) How you doin'?

FOPPY: I see why Sean Connery quit. (*Goes into Proust.*)

MAYOR: (*Making another phone call.*) Give me the latest. Ten thousand new cases! Since we talked? The latest Gallup poll shows ninety percent of my people want me to disappear? *Page Six* says VIPs closest to the Potentates had a sex orgy on a home videotape. I'm glad he's in more trouble than I am. (*Hangs up.*) How long can I keep it up? Who remembers old Appleberg mayors? Impellitieri. Lindsay. Abe Beame. Are all men expected to perform endlessly and forever? Wagner and LaGuardia had three terms. I got to have four! I got to get it up one more time. (*Walking back upstairs, he passes* HERMAN *a little farther up.*) It's amazing guys your age think you can still get paid for hustling. (*Realizing.*) Hey, I was just looking at that tape! (*Runs into* FOPPY's *room.*)

(*The stage is quiet for a minute. We hear* MRS. POTENTATE *on the phone.* HERMAN *moves more.*)

MRS. POTENTATE'S VOICE: Is Prince Charles available for the First Mommy of New Columbia? . . . Well, tell him we're all so excited about his engagement and can't wait to be invited to the wedding!

(GILBERT *comes out of Oscar Wilde, still in a towel.* TRUDI, *in her overcoat, comes out of Genet at the same time as* GILBERT.)

TRUDI: Who are you?

GILBERT: Not yet. I don't have my name back yet. Someone is still after me.

TRUDI: Someone is always after you.

GILBERT: My beloved mother says all the world needs is enlightenment. But I'm discovering enlighteners have nothing but trouble.

TRUDI: Do you know how to write an autobiography?

GILBERT: I once worked in the mailroom of William Morris.

TRUDI: You smell nice. Like you've just made love.

GILBERT: (*Shyly.*) I have.

TRUDI: Did you kiss and cuddle?

GILBERT: Yeah.

TRUDI: Who with?

GILBERT: I can't tell you. You see, I'm running from an ex-lover who's high-up important.

TRUDI: How high-up important?

GILBERT: A choosy, ugly, powerful mean old pig.

TRUDI: You mean the mayor of our largest northeastern city?

GILBERT: Say, weren't you a Maligned Malingerer?

TRUDI: Malibu!

GILBERT: Manhattan! I went to one of your meetings once when they skied me out to the coast. What's your autobiography about?

TRUDI: I have secrets that could bring down governments.

GILBERT: You too! I'll show you mine if you'll show me yours.

TRUDI: I have a sex tape of Herman Harrod and some of Daddy's staff in an S&M orgy.

GILBERT: Yikes. It's just what we need. You see, I'm in love with Daddy's son.

TRUDI: You're not. Congratulations!

GILBERT: Thanks.

TRUDI: It sounds like we could be a great team, like Woodward and Bernstein. When exactly do you think we could get started?

GILBERT: With your tape . . .

TRUDI: I don't exactly have the tape. It got waylaid. It's here, in this house, somewhere.

GILBERT: We've got to find it! Then all all all of us could make enough money to live happily ever after. Do you know if there's another shower? Junior seems afraid to take a shower with anybody.

TRUDI: You can go use the one in there if you don't mind it's in a dungeon.

(*Behind them the door to Genet opens mysteriously.*)

GILBERT: I think I'll ask Electra if I can use hers. After I clean up, we can have our first story conference.

(*He exits into the kitchen.* TRUDI *starts talking to* HERMAN. HERMAN *is moving slowly, but at first she doesn't notice it.*)

TRUDI: Herman, for a minute there I didn't know what I was going to do. Now I have hope again. So don't worry, wherever you are. I started over lots of times. I can do it again. Good-bye, baby. I just wish you could tell me about the tape! . . . Herman? . . . Herman!

(*He moves some more.*)

TRUDI: This house is a trip.

(*He moves, this time unmistakably. She rushes to uncover him.*)

HERMAN: Unnnnnnhhhhh.

TRUDI: You're trying to tell me something?

HERMAN: Unnnnnh.

TRUDI: Herman, you're still alive?

HERMAN: Unnnnhhhhhhh.

TRUDI: (*Spoons him some more coke.*) To celebrate your still being alive. Next week I'm really getting you to AA.

HERMAN: Unh unh unh!

TRUDI: Oh, Herman, where is it? We're so close! To having everything that we wanted! I can hardly wait!

(*She is pacing around, looking. As she passes near the door to Genet, an arm wearing a black glove suddenly darts out, grabs her, and pulls her into Genet, closing the door.*)

HERMAN: Unnnnnnnnhhhhhhl

(JUNIOR *comes out of Oscar Wilde, still in his bath towel. He takes huge ballet leaps around the room.*)

JUNIOR: I leap over the nunnery walls! I leap out of East Berlin! Land of the free! Home of the brave! My leap is longer and higher than ever! Born free!... Uncle Herman, they still haven't found you a bed?

HERMAN: Unh.

JUNIOR: Have you seen a cute young man in a towel?

HERMAN: Unnnnnhhhhhhhh!

JUNIOR: Tough shit. I'm sorry you don't approve.

HERMAN: Unh.

JUNIOR: Well, he's the best thing that ever happened to me. You knew I was gay?

HERMAN: Unnnh.

JUNIOR: Does Mom know?

HERMAN: Unnnnnnnhhhhhhhhhh. (*Reaches toward upstairs with his arm.*)

JUNIOR: (*Giving him more coke.*) One of these days you're going to have to lick this habit. Ma should just see you now.

HERMAN: Unnnnnnnhhhhhhhhhh. (*Reaches toward upstairs with his arm.*)

JUNIOR: Yeah, she can really be a pain in the ass.

HERMAN: Unh.

JUNIOR: (*Sits down beside him.*) My sister says that's why I try to make jokes out of everything. I want everyone to think nothing's wrong. We're all a family of performers. Give us lights, camera, and a national election and we can look like we all love each other. (*Gets up.*) Well, nice talking to you. I hope you get your voice back. I have to find my fella. (*He's about to go into Jean Genet.*)

HERMAN: Unnnnnh unnnnnnh!

JUNIOR: Not this one? Upstairs? (*Runs upstairs and is about to knock on Proust.*)

HERMAN: Unnnnnnnnnnnhhhhhhhhhhhh!

JUNIOR: Definitely not this one. Thanks, Uncle Herman. I owe you one. (*Knocks on* FOPPY'*s door.*) I hope you're still all excited because I am and I can't wait. (*The door is locked.*) Sweetie—open up! Hurry up, hurry up, hurry up, hurry up! I'm in love with you.

(*The door opens and the* MAYOR, *in boxer shorts with an apple pattern, throws open his arms just as* FOPPY *comes out of Proust.*)

FOPPY: (*Pushing the* MAYOR *back in.*) He's still not the one! (*Slams the door. To* JUNIOR.) Go to your room!

(*The door to Proust opens a crack.*)

MRS. POTENTATE'S VOICE: Is he finally here?

JUNIOR: You sound just like my mother.

MRS. POTENTATE'S VOICE: Has he come yet?

FOPPY: Not yet, not yet. I am your mother.

GILBERT: (*Coming out of the kitchen, fresh from the shower. To* HERMAN.) You're Herman Harrod. I've got your number. (*Goes into Oscar Wilde.*)

MRS. POTENTATE'S VOICE: (*Singing.*) "God save our gracious Queen, God save our . . . wonderful Queen . . . God save our . . . fabulous Queen." "God save our . . ."

JUNIOR: Mom's in there!

FOPPY: On television! She's doing one of her cultural evenings with that talented Marvin Hamlisch.

JUNIOR: And that was the Mayor of our largest northeastern city. First Son must warn First Love!

(JUNIOR *makes a dash for the kitchen. The* MAYOR *comes out, carrying his suitcase and Gap bag.*)

MAYOR: I shall not remain unsatisfied inside this inept brothel one more second. I admit defeat. I can't keep it up anymore.

MRS. POTENTATE'S VOICE: "Send her victorious, happy, and . . . boisterous . . ."

MAYOR: The exterminator's British?

FOPPY: Margaret Thatcher. (*Pushing* MAYOR *into Genet.*) Go in here temporarily. (*Gets him in there* and *rushes to* HERMAN.)

MAYOR: There's a girl sleeping in there! (*Re:* HERMAN.) I told you I didn't want that one!

FOPPY: The new one will be here any minute.

MAYOR: There's a passed-out girl in there and a passed-out man out here. I do not think I should remain on these premises.

FOPPY: You must stay hidden until you hear the magic word.

MAYOR: Which is?

FOPPY: Rudolph Giuliani.

(*The* MAYOR *goes into Genet and slams the door.*)

HERMAN: Unnnnhhhh.

FOPPY: You would be alive. Is that good for me or bad? Can you possibly run outside and take the nearest subway? . . . Cat got your tongue?

HERMAN: Unnnnh.

FOPPY: Where is your goddamned tape!

HERMAN: Unnnhhhhh.

FOPPY: I do not understand "Unnnnnnh." Oh, what's the use. All you can say is "Unnnnnuh." Wait a minute. You were her dirty laundry hit man. What happened at that Saturday Night Massacre? Was Daddy actually a participant?

HERMAN: Unh.

FOPPY: What really happened with her lesbian roommate at Smith?

HERMAN: Unh unh unh unh.

FOPPY: What about that musical she was in with Mary Martin?

MRS. POTENTATE'S VOICE: (*Singing.*) "Mountain high, valley low . . ."

HERMAN: Unh.

MRS. POTENTATE'S VOICE: (*Singing.*) "Lightning fast, turtle slow . . ."

FOPPY: Where is Benny Thau?

HERMAN: Unnnnnnnhhhhhhhhunhhhhhhhhhhhunnnhhhhhnnhhhhhh!

FOPPY: Hit paydirt with that one, did we? (*Quickly finds pen and paper and sticks them in front of* HERMAN's *moving arm.*) Where is he? Where is he?

MRS. POTENTATE'S VOICE: (*Singing.*) "If you need me I will be nearby . . ."

HERMAN: Unnhunnh.

FOPPY: That does not help me. Write!

(HERMAN *starts to pass out again.*)

Oh, no you don't.

(*He spoons coke up his nose effusively and then, when* HERMAN *isn't inhaling it,* FOPPY *sits on him—up and down, up and down—like he's inflating a rubber raft, spooning in even more.*)

Wake up, little Susie!

MRS. POTENTATE'S VOICE: (*Singing.*) "Lantern gay, willow sad . . . Winter gray . . ."

FOPPY: Where is Benny Thau!

(HERMAN *wakes up with such energy that he starts writing furiously.*)

MRS. POTENTATE'S VOICE: (*Singing.*) ". . . summer glad . . ."

HERMAN: (*As he writes, he talks again.*) Benny Thau is at the Pasadena Home for Movie Old Farts. (*He immediately passes out again.*)

FOPPY: The moving finger writes and, having writ, moves on. (*Rushes to the phone and prepares a tape recorder while he talks.*) Operator, I need the number of . . . in Pasadena . . . Is there an old fart's home, folk's home, for movie old timers, you know, alter cockers. . . . My dear, thank you! Don't let anyone ever tell you again your service stinks. (*Dials as he turns on the tape recorder.*) Make way, Kitty Kelley, here comes Foppy!

(GILBERT *comes out of Oscar Wilde, dressed.*)

GILBERT: If we had Trudi's tape, we could be free and rich and live anywhere we want to.

FOPPY: Worked all that out by yourself, have you? (*On the phone.*) . . . Mr. Benny Thau, please.

GILBERT: Junior will never have to worry about Mommy and Daddy again.

FOPPY: Well, wheel his wheelchair to the phone!

(HERMAN, *awake again, tries to stand up.* GILBERT *helps him.*)

GILBERT: We could live on Fifth Avenue after all. Overlooking the park.

FOPPY: Well, don't they have phones in Intensive Care!

GILBERT: (*Propping* HERMAN *up.*) Jackie overlooks the park. And . . .

FOPPY: Well, hold the phone up to the respirator!

> (GILBERT *leaves* HERMAN *and comes to be near* FOPPY. HERMAN *starts to weave back and forth and just when it looks as if he's going to fall over, another of those black-gloved arms pulls him into Oscar Wilde.*)

GILBERT: Who are you talking to?

FOPPY: Benny, *wass machst du?* It's Foppy Schwartz, First Mommy's best friend. You remember us from the old days . . . ? I'm so glad you're still alive.

GILBERT: It sounds like you're playing a very dangerous game.

FOPPY: Will you shut up! . . . No, not you, Benny! I caught you before you're almost dead? You were on your way to meet your Maker? Well, I know you want to go and meet Him with a clear conscience. I want to ask you what you remember about First Mommy. You know, the real dish. (*Starts furiously making notes.*) I know that. Something better. . . . Not bad. A little better. . . . Now you're cooking. Now something better. Go for broke, baby. It's your last chance. . . . No fucking shit!

GILBERT: Are they going to come after Junior like the Mayor's after me? That means both of us will be on the run. Like Bonnie and Clyde.

FOPPY: Benny, I love you, Benny. . . . Yes, I know you're not a fairy. But you are, Benny. You are. You're the good fairy. (*Hangs up the phone, pops the tape out of the recorder and pockets it, and rushes up the stairs.*) Our redeemer liveth. Although he didn't sound so hot. This scene requires a change of outfit. Something more Joan Crawford. I have it. I have it! I've found my weapon. My instrument! My dick of death! (*Goes into his bedroom and slams the door.*)

GILBERT: Wow!

(*The* MAYOR *peeks out of Jean Genet, thinks the coast is clear. He is dressed in a version of what he thinks is sexually alluring: Levi's that are new and stiff and too big, a cowboy shirt and too big red bandanna around his neck, a yellow kerchief in his right hip pocket, and cowboy boots, which he wears like a young girl who can't manage her first high heels. The* MAYOR *and* GILBERT *back into each other.*)

MAYOR: (*Turning to see the back of an attractive young man.*) Howdy, True Love. You were worth waiting for. (*As* GILBERT *turns.*) You!

GILBERT: Me?

MAYOR: You wretched can of worms.

GILBERT: Me worms!

MAYOR: You torpid and fetid . . .

GILBERT: Torpid and fetid?

MAYOR: . . . lustless felsheimer.

GILBERT: I am not lustless.

MAYOR: (*Grabbing and mauling him.*) Your repellent physique disgusts me. To touch your offensive skin. And hold your obnoxious body. And strangle your precious neck. Oh my God, why why why why how how how how what what what what is happening to me? My base private parts nauseatingly worship you abhorrently. I want to kiss you kill you kiss you kill you kiss you kill you, oh Gilbert, my loathsome love . . .

(*Both kissing and mauling him.*)

I want to send you to prison. I want to take you to the moon.

GILBERT: Oh, Mayor, my Mayor . . .

MAYOR: I told you you could always call me May. How could you have left me?

GILBERT: You sent your goons to kill me!

MAYOR: That's right. I did.

GILBERT: You told me real estate interests would tear my throat out if I talked.

MAYOR: That's right. They would.

GILBERT: You said anyone working in Germs who even said the word AIDS would lose his job and rent-controlled apartment.

MAYOR: That's right. You did.

GILBERT: I could never love anyone in the closet.

MAYOR: That's right. I'm not gay. (*Starts kissing and mauling him again.*)

GILBERT: You would call me from your office sometimes four times a day.

MAYOR: Maybe three times at the most.

GILBERT: You'd say, "Why dontcha come over for a tiddy-do," and I would and we would and two seconds afterwards you would scream, "Get outta my life, I'm not gay!" But always, one, two, three, at the most four days later . . .

MAYOR: Two, three weeks.

GILBERT: . . . you'd call again and whisper, "Please come and fanky fanky," and I'd say, "But you said," and you'd say . . .

MAYOR: Never mind what I said.

GILBERT: And I'd think that was so sweet.

MAYOR: I am not sweet! Oh, Gilbert, just hearing your whiny voice, just looking into your dribbly eyes, just feeling your pasty body, I've got lover's nuts.

GILBERT: Lover. How long I've longed to hear you say that word.

MAYOR: It doesn't mean anything. It's generic. Like Kleenex and Jell-O.

GILBERT: There you go avoiding my needs again. My shrink said your bite is worse than your bark.

MAYOR: You told a shrink! I'll enter the psychiatric literature. You feel so rancid and good and putrid and good, and I love you hate you love you hate you . . .

GILBERT: He said you were a very confused and mixed-up person. And I am a conflicted young man in pain.

MAYOR: I was just waiting for you, waiting to tear you limb from limb into pieces of itty bitty flesh, oh flesh, oh flesh. Oh oh oh oh flesh.

GILBERT: Did I misunderstand you, May? (*Noting the* MAYOR'*s hard crotch.*) Oh, May, you've grown!

MAYOR: Let's get to a bed, we got to get to a bed . . .

GILBERT: You never were this big and hard. Did you send away for that kit?

MAYOR: . . . we must get somewhere fast pronto schnell . . .

GILBERT: Will you promise me that you'll call *The Appleberg Times* and announce a plague emergency?

MAYOR: We got to lie down on something or it will be toooooooo . . . late. I mussed my . . . Thank God I wore four pairs of underpants.

GILBERT: And then call the Potentate and ask for emergency help?

MAYOR: I will not be blackmailed. I will not do anything to rid your fairy community of your filthy disease and to all your habits and desires I say feh! I am not gay!

GILBERT: (*Still investigating his hard crotch.*) But the Surgeon General says this is going to happen to everybody. You're still hard.

MAYOR: The Surgeon General! It's so unattractive when an older man becomes so obsessed with sex.

GILBERT: A tisket, a tasket, I found a bigger basket . . . (*Extracts the tape from the* MAYOR's *crotch and holds it at arm's length, delicately.*)

MAYOR: (*Starts chasing* GILBERT.) Give me that tape! I could become Potentate-in-Chief. Give it to me! I could expose this awful canker in Daddy's asshole and become a national hero and take its place.

GILBERT: But I could become Mrs. Junior Potentate.

MAYOR: Will my life never be free of faggots trying to be free! You are low and the wretched scum of the earth, and in order never to see you again I will see that you are sent to the top of the World Trade Center and, like a bird turd, dropped.

(*He's caught him again and they're gyrating again, and* JUNIOR *comes in from the kitchen.*)

JUNIOR: I never want to see you again!

GILBERT: I was only trying to grab his powerful tape!

JUNIOR: But you are in his arms! My true love is in another's arms.

GILBERT: You're much more powerful to me!

MAYOR: My God, you are First Son! Can a dapper, wiser, older, powerful man offer guidance and assistance?

GILBERT: May . . . ! Junior . . . !

(*The doorway to Proust opens.*)

MRS. POTENTATE'S VOICE: Foppy . . .

FOPPY'S VOICE: Yes?

MRS. POTENTATE'S VOICE: I am tired of vamping till ready.

JUNIOR: Ma is here!

MAYOR: The exterminator is the First Lady!

(JUNIOR, GILBERT, *and the* MAYOR *rush to go into rooms to hide. But the doorways to Gide and Wilde are locked. They run into the closet under the balcony.* MRS. POTENTATE *starts down the stairs, fully dressed as when she arrived.* ELECTRA *comes out of the kitchen.*)

MRS. POTENTATE: This must be remembered as my Golden Age.

FOPPY: (*Coming out of his bedroom wearing his most dramatic robe yet.*) This must be remembered as my Golden Age. Electra, prepare for high tea.

ELECTRA: Mr. Foppy, there is nothing left to eat in this entire house.

FOPPY: Then she shall eat cake.

(JUNIOR, GILBERT, *and the* MAYOR *tumble out of the closet, gasping for breath.*)

GILBERT: How am I supposed to breathe?

(FOPPY *pushes them back in.*)

ELECTRA: You're not.

MRS. POTENTATE: Whoever the traitor is who betrayed me, off with his head when he presents it. I don't like going back to the Palace, so . . .

FOPPY: So coitus interruptus.

MRS. POTENTATE: So coitus not-even-startus.

FOPPY: Serve tea. Hot tea, iced tea, Mister T, serve anything! Hurry!

ELECTRA: Just remember that women get meaner when they thought they were going to get it and didn't.

MRS. POTENTATE: Amen.

FOPPY: That is not a characteristic exclusive to your sex. Hurry!

ELECTRA: Go give her one for the Gipper. (*Goes into the kitchen.*)

MRS. POTENTATE: If it's not one hole to plug up, it's another. I wonder what my dearest friend, Queen Elizabeth, would have done if Mr. Profumo and his friends were all available on home video-tapes. Do you think anybody even remembers the Profumo affair?

(ELECTRA *rushes back in from the kitchen with a tray on a stand, with an assortment of any old things, including a large bottle of instant tea.*)

ELECTRA: A sex scandal that brought down the British government.

MRS. POTENTATE: No. Nobody remembers the Profumo affair.

ELECTRA: An innocent man was sacrificed and a guilty man protected because he had the right connections.

FOPPY: No, nobody remembers that it was two bimbo sluts who brought down Betty Windsor's government.

MRS. POTENTATE: Two bimbo sluts?

ELECTRA: (*Offering tea.*) Earl Grey. Prince of Wales . . .

MRS. POTENTATE: Thank you, Electrolux.

ELECTRA: Princess Electra's Hemlock.

(ELECTRA *plops all the instant tea into a cup, causing clouds, and hands the overflowing mess to* MRS. POTENTATE. FOPPY *motions to* ELECTRA *to leave, which she does. During the following confrontation,* ELECTRA'*s face can be seen peeking through the kitchen door and* JUNIOR'*s head sticking out of the closet—to try to hear all.*)

FOPPY: My Capital Concubine . . .

MRS. POTENTATE: Yes, my oldest friend, First Fop . . .

FOPPY: . . . you have always surrounded yourself with the sensitive, the gifted, the amusing . . . You have even allowed yours truly to be among your most trusted confidants . . . You do remember all your dear mother's dear lesbian friends who were so helpful to you? Your godmother, the queen of the Hollywood dykes. Your Broadway career—such as it was . . .

MRS. POTENTATE: Such as it was?

FOPPY: Such as it was, and due to lesbian stars.

MRS. POTENTATE: I am beginning to feel less friendly. (*Singing.*) "I'm gonna wash that man right outa my hair . . ."

FOPPY: Oh, my Supreme Arbiter, my Dictator of Right and Wrong, our Omnipotent Excalibur, New Columbia's only ruling goddess, I have been thinking of how happy we were in those old days, when we were young and carefree, swinging along Hollywood and Vine, gallivanting at homes and studios, with powerful moguls like Benny Thau . . .

MRS. POTENTATE: Benny Thau?

FOPPY: MGM's studio head has nominated yours as the best blow job he ever had.

MRS. POTENTATE: My Beatrice Lillie, will there be fairies at the bottom of my garden?

FOPPY: You were a very ambitious starlet, my Eve Harrington.

MRS. POTENTATE: "Were," my Addison De Wittless?

FOPPY: Ah, I taught you well. Yes, it's always been mandatory for you to get ahead. Soon perhaps historians will have the balls to fill in the bank with: whose.

MRS. POTENTATE: You are treading on very tender toes.

FOPPY: You were kneeling on the sorest knees.

MRS. POTENTATE: Since when have you become so interested in the politics of power, my Benedict Arnold?

FOPPY: Since you became so interested in fucking my people, my Linda Lovelace.

MRS. POTENTATE: Then be careful that you don't go too far, my Alger Hiss.

FOPPY: I go too far? From your very first screen test—was it not with Spencer Tracy *and* Clark Gable—you gave new meaning to your party's slogan: "Life is better under the Republicans."

MRS. POTENTATE: Spencer Tracy was a drunk who could never get it up.

FOPPY: As was said of your own husband and why he married you.

MRS. POTENTATE: Oh, you silly poofter faggot queen, now you go too far!

FOPPY: Why? First Daddy's First Wife said, "He was about as good in bed as he was on the screen."

MRS. POTENTATE: Do you know the penalty for exposing official secrets about an official?

FOPPY: Does it not depend on whether the secrets are about Betsy Ross or Betsy Bloomingdale?

MRS. POTENTATE: What else do you think you know, sweet Betsy from Kike?

FOPPY: My Ilse Koch, I have located dear Benny. (*Displays the tape of their conversation.*)

MRS. POTENTATE: You, too, are into tapes, my Tricky Dicky. Georgetown is afflicted with a plague of tapeworm.

FOPPY: A plague, to be sure. Let us try not to allow history to punish us too much, my Barbara Tuchman.

MRS. POTENTATE: Do I sense a negotiation about to transpire?

FOPPY: You do.

MRS. POTENTATE: It is a tawdry one.

FOPPY: Filled with junk bonds, my Drexel Burnham. Daddy has ignored all action on AIDS. Why, it appears he cannot even form the word with his lips. With three official reports on this deadly matter, is it not time you taught him not only how to read them but how to say our name out loud? Indeed, with your own son at such peril . . .

MRS. POTENTATE: So you are going to tell the world about Junior?

JUNIOR: (*Jumping out.*) Junior is going to tell the world about Junior!

MRS. POTENTATE: You are naked.

JUNIOR: For all the world to see.

MRS. POTENTATE: So everybody knows.

JUNIOR: Aw, come on, Ma. Everybody knows. And I was born this way.

MRS. POTENTATE: You were not born this way! You were just too young when I took you to see *The Red Shoes*.

FOPPY: Oh, come now, dear. A mother always knows.

JUNIOR: Why did you lock me up in my room all those years? Because you were ashamed of me or so you could blow your wild oats?

FOPPY: Now. I also want Daddy to propose legislation prohibiting discrimination on the basis of sexual orientation. . . .

JUNIOR: And don't forget: Men are going to marry men!

ELECTRA: (*Sticking her head out.*) And women are going to marry women!

(*Everyone looks at her.*)

FOPPY: (*To audience.*) Who knew?

MRS. POTENTATE: (*To* FOPPY.) So this is your price?

JUNIOR: Hey, Ma, it's not such a high price.

FOPPY: And as long as we are negotiating, my Sandra Day O'Connor, Daddy must also petition the Supreme Tribunal to rehear that wretched wrongful case that has made your own son illegal.

JUNIOR: Oh, Uncle Foppy, I'm so proud of you! I can't thank you enough. Our brothers . . .

ELECTRA: . . . and sisters . . .

JUNIOR: . . . can't thank you enough!

MRS. POTENTATE: (*Not understanding.*) Your brothers and sisters?

FOPPY: I am overdue for Kennedy Center honors.

MRS. POTENTATE: Is it too late to marry him off to an understanding older woman or a dyke? In the old days all the dykes made movies. Now they play tennis. Your mother will buy you a tennis player!

(JUNIOR *goes and pulls* GILBERT *out of the closet.*)

JUNIOR: Mom—I want you to meet your new Billie Jean.

GILBERT: Junior, I'm sorry about our fight, and I love you and I'll live anywhere with you, even Appleberg, but be careful, not all beasts are men.

MRS. POTENTATE: Enunciate your name with clarity.

GILBERT: Oh, ma'am. I don't know what to say. I'm so honored. I love your son.

MRS. POTENTATE: How do you wish to die?

GILBERT: I just loved your husband's first wife in *Johnny Belinda.*

MRS. POTENTATE: I repeat my question.

GILBERT: But she won an Oscar!

MRS. POTENTATE: For playing deaf and dumb.

JUNIOR: Mom—why are you such a hypocrite? (*Adjusts an article of her clothing gone askew.*) You can have your privacy if we can have our equality.

FOPPY: Why does familiarity breed such contempt?

JUNIOR: If you don't let me live with Gilbert I'm going to tell the world that the First Family has the worst family life since the Addams Family, and not John Quincy, Charles.

ELECTRA: (*Entering with champagne and glasses.*) It sounds like mother-fucking time to me.

MRS. POTENTATE: Beware!

ELECTRA: You have the highest disapproval rating of any First Mommy ever. I'm not afraid of you.

MRS. POTENTATE: You should be. I'll take your drugs away.

ELECTRA: Oh, thank you, thank you, glory hallelujah, it's about time!

MRS. POTENTATE: Oh, not those drugs. Take all those drugs you want. I mean health care, medicine, education—that's a drug for you people—and abortion! I've already taken away all your abortions. So you can never get out of your filthy rut, with your voracious appetite for sex, and children, and sex, and more children, and more sex . . .

FOPPY: Really, my Mad Scene from *Lucia!*

JUNIOR: Maybe it's time for you to go home and talk all this out with Daddy.

FOPPY: Before you steal home, we must settle our grand design for our new history, my Clare Loose Tooth.

MRS. POTENTATE: Home! Home! I've swallowed enough. What do faggots know of home? You don't have any children. We won't let you have any children. We won't let you get married. Unless you marry one of us and have our children. You call yourselves gay, but you're not really happy. How could you be happy with all the laws we pass to make certain that you can't be. (*To* JUNIOR.) Tell the world? You think the world cares? You think the world wants to know that my son is gay? That my daughter is a drugged-out hippie? That my husband's children by another marriage are of little interest to us? That Benny Thau blabs how many times I got down on my knees and opened my mouth?

(And he should know.) All my people care about is that I'm a married woman and a mother who not only faithfully reads but regularly appears in *People* magazine. Only normal people read *People* magazine. Everyone normal is married. So you're not normal. Daddy is the most powerful potentate since Jesus. No one wants to know anything juicy about Jesus!

FOPPY: Dishonor is the bitter part of squalor. But I have yet to play my ace. (*Runs to the front door, throws it open, rushes out, and screams to the neighborhood.*) Media! Are you there, media! Can you hear me? Max Frankel! Tom Brokaw! Dan Rather! Ted Koppel! Peter Jennings! Baa Baa Wah Wah!

(*Somewhere above, the sound of sirens has appeared and increased in closeness and volume.* FOPPY *gets bathed in a searchlight. Two arms hold up rifles to either side of* FOPPY's *temple. He is forced to come back in.*)

MAYOR: (*Entering.*) This place is noisier than Appleberg, to which I must now immediately return.

MRS. POTENTATE: The Potentate has indicated to me he might look with favor upon Appleberg's request for emergency bubkis . . . millions.

GILBERT: Where's Trudi?

MRS. POTENTATE: There's her room.

GILBERT: Trudi, I've got the tape. We can be rich together!

(GILBERT *runs to Genet. The door is no longer locked. He goes in and comes back out holding a baseball bat.*)

FOPPY: You've got the tape? You put your own personal greed above the greater good of our movement?

GILBERT: Trudi's dead.

FOPPY: Trudi's dead?

MRS. POTENTATE: She has been clobbered to death with a Louisville Slugger.

FOPPY: All is becoming too unsavory to the aesthete's eye.

MRS. POTENTATE: And where is the film's director, Herman Harrod?

(*Everyone looks around.*)

Herman Harrod will be found in St. John's Hospital. Dead. From a heart attack. He will be buried in the ground at dawn tomorrow before anyone sees him.

FOPPY: My Holy Mother . . .

MRS. POTENTATE: I'm not ready for you yet. (*To* GILBERT.) Do you play baseball?

JUNIOR: Of course he doesn't play baseball. He's gay.

MRS. POTENTATE: Of course you play baseball. Are you a good boy who loves your mother more than life itself?

GILBERT: Trudi's been murdered.

MRS. POTENTATE: Of course you love your mother more than life itself. Does she live in the luxury you wish and dream for her?

GILBERT: She lives a humble life in a rent-controlled apartment in Greenwich Village.

MAYOR: I thought I evicted you from that apartment.

MRS. POTENTATE: While you are in prison for the murder of Trudi Tunick your beloved mother will receive great sums of money.

JUNIOR: You can't do this!

FOPPY: She would perform any act to get ahead. Now she's going down on history.

MRS. POTENTATE: You amateur. Me a supporting player? You are playing opposite a star! Gilbert Perch, you were found with the body of Trudi Tunick, holding that baseball bat, which can be identified definitely as the murder weapon. (*With a handkerchief, takes the baseball bat.*) And with this filthy dirty vile putrid disgusting sex tape. (*Takes the tape.*) Poof! All gone! (*Separating* JUNIOR *and* GILBERT.) Poofs! All gone!

JUNIOR: You can't do this!

FOPPY: She just did.

MAYOR: (*To* MRS. POTENTATE.) If after you leave the White Palace you might consider running for Chamberperson from Appleberg... (*Presents her his card.*) Gilbert Perch, you have betrayed my trust in you. (*Taking out a document.*) I have a warrant for your arrest for soliciting illegal contracts in Orangeberg.

GILBERT: Help me, Junior ... I need your strength. . . .

JUNIOR: I love him! And our love is good and pure and eternal and everlasting and forever and ever ...

MRS. POTENTATE: No, you won't tell the world. No, you won't become a dancer. And you will get married. To a woman. Or you'll never dance on *Saturday Night Live* alive. And your people will be quarantined, put into camps, after mandatory testing, with no research, or treatments, or insurance, or jobs, and allowed to die. . . .

FOPPY: The song is ended.

MRS. POTENTATE: You think New Columbia has time for you or your people . . . ?

JUNIOR: But soon there will be . . . (*Seeking help from* ELECTRA.)

ELECTRA: One billion . . .

JUNIOR: . . . . people all over the world infected.

MRS. POTENTATE: . . . or their problems.

FOPPY: But the melody lingers on.

JUNIOR: Mommy, please don't do this to us. To me! I don't want to pretend forever.

MRS. POTENTATE: Why not? I have. After a while you can't tell the difference.

JUNIOR: I will never speak to you again.

MRS. POTENTATE: I have to get us reelected! I have to untangle Iran! I have to win the cold war! I have to end the arms race! I don't have time to end your filthy plague! You think the world cares if I sucked every dick in America? Amused, perhaps. But the American People know that a person's sex life is his own business and in no way affects his job. I have a man to run! I have a country to rule!

ELECTRA: Old Georgetown saying: If you dig grave for enemy, dig two—one for self.

MRS. POTENTATE: And darling, Fopp, who will invite you to any parties? Not Carolina, or Chessy, or Mica, or Pat, or Marella, or Nan, or Louise, or Estee, or Ann, or Judy, or Slim, or Betsy, or Jackie, or Me . . .

ELECTRA: (*To audience.*) Another old Georgetown saying: If you haven't got anything good to say about anyone, come sit with me.

MRS. POTENTATE: (*On her portable phone.*) Sheilasuellen, inform all media that writing about any of this is a grossly punishable no-no. And call Huggy Bunny Harrod and tell her we're celebrating tomorrow after Herman's secret burial. I'll wear my new Galanos and she must wear her old Blass. And call Jean, and Virginia, and Marion, and Martha, and Leonore, and Harriet, and Mary Jane, and tell them to join us at Le Cirque. (*To* FOPPY.) How much do you love me? (*Holds out her hand to him.*)

FOPPY: How deep is the ocean? (*Hands her* BENNY THAU*'s tape.*)

MRS. POTENTATE: (*Still on phone.*) No. Not Mr. Schwartz. Mr. Schwartz regrets he's unable to lunch . . . today (*Dials another number.*) Pootie Pie, it's all done. I've saved our reign for history. Now you can announce we're running for our second term. (*Hangs up.*) Daddy's on TV.

(*The* MAYOR *rushes to turn on the TV. Everyone goes to watch. Lights down.*)

FOPPY: So now I am all alone. What I always feared the most. From glamorous and powerful to forgotten and . . . forgotten. To have lived so long for this. (*Picks up a telephone; then another; then a third. He speaks into all of them.*) Listen to me! We know that lives like mine are lived unendingly because we continue to pay the price.

Hello? How much was squandered! Hello? The power we still don't have! Are you there? Is anyone there? What are you doing tonight? This weekend? This life? Hello? Hello? Hello? We who had to lie for so long know that because of it our lives were lived differently! Hello . . .

(*Lights down.*)

ELECTRA: Gilbert Perch confessed to the murder of Trudi Tunick. He died in the prison nuthouse from AIDS. I hope Junior's health is okay. And his wife's. No, the police didn't come inside to investigate the deaths. It's Marilyn all over again. The Mayor didn't get reelected to his fourth term. But he's on TV so much he might as well have. Junior and his parents still don't speak. First Daddy's sick now, from a slow, messy, humiliating, intractable, incurable disease, which I guess is what you call ironic. Somewhere in some vault where innocent men are locked up and from which the guilty are set free, the tape is resting. Along with the tapes of Bill and Monica and Kathleen and Paula and Susan . . . and the plague, of course, is worse than ever all over the world. It is the world's most deadly and widespread infectious disease. Mr. Foppy and me—we're still together. Nobody would buy our story. I'm afraid now. Now I know too much, too. Now, so do you. Now, what are you going to do?

The End

Speech to the nation announcing Reagan's candidacy for reelection, January 29, 1984:

"My fellow Americans. It's been nearly three years since I first spoke to you from this room. Together we've faced many difficult problems and I've come to feel a special bond of kinship with each one of you. Tonight I'm here for a different reason. I've come to a difficult personal decision as to whether or not I should seek reelection. Vice President Bush and I would like to have your continued support and cooperation in completing what we began three years ago. I am therefore announcing that I am a candidate and will seek reelection to the office I presently hold. Thank you for the trust you've placed in me. God bless you, and good night."

—From *Ronald Reagan: the Great Speeches,* volume II

On Speechworks Records
P.O. Box 4608
Rolling Bay, WA 98061-0608
www. Soundworks.net

(*Used with exit music for the Chicago production.*)

Reading List

If you would like to read about the characters and events of *Just Say No*, you will find very interesting things in each of the following:

Dark Victory: Ronald Reagan, MCA, and the Mob by Dan E. Moldea, 1986. A classic study of doo-doo in high places. Be sure and read all the footnotes and between the lines. Not an easy read.

Nancy Reagan: The Unauthorized Biography by Kitty Kelley, 1991. An exceedingly valuable and underappreciated work.

Nancy by Nancy Reagan, with Bill Libby, 1980. Poo.

My Turn, The Memoirs of Nancy Reagan by Nancy Reagan, with William Novak, 1989. Poo-poo.

Vicki: The True Story of Vicki Morgan and Alfred Bloomingdale by Joyce Milton and Ann Louise Bardach, 1986. Riveting and heartbreaking and the sex tape makes Bill and Monica look like tots.

Early Reagan: The Rise to Power by Anne Edwards, 1987. A good history of the early years.

The Way I See It by Patti Davis, 1992. A daughter's autobiography. Very sad.

Nazimova by Gavin Lambert, 1997. A biography of the legendary lesbian actress Alla Nazimova, Nancy's godmother and the great chum of Chicago's own Edith (Mrs. Loyal) Davis, Nancy's mother.

The Peter Lawford Story by Patricia Seaton Lawford, with Ted Schwarz, 1988. Early blow jobs' first mention in print. (See also *Playboy*, September 1993 issue.)

Make-Believe, The Story of Nancy & Ronald Reagan by Laurence Leamer, 1983. (Hilariously and terrifyingly reviewed by Gore Vidal in his essay "Ronnie and Nancy: A Life in Pictures," which is included in *The Essential Gore Vidal*, 1999.)

Reagan's America by Garry Wills, 1988. The great Professor of American Culture at Northwestern's great book about his great thesis: that Reaganland was Disneyland.

Many of these titles are out of print, but all are available from secondhand stores or Internet sites.

A two-part article about Ronny and Nancy by Bob Colacello in the July and August 1998 issues of *Vanity Fair* is also worth a look.

Yes, it all really happened.

The Farce in Just Saying No

You've got to have rocks in your head to write a play.

You must be a masochist to work in the theater and a sadist to succeed on its stages.

And you must be retarded to believe you can support yourself.

These tenets apply to any and all playwrights. But particularly to those who have anything important to say.

Playwrights, of course, are nuts anyway. I think it's ten times harder to write a play that works than a novel, and a hundred times harder to write a play than a screenplay. Screenwriting is craft, not art (and group craft at that), and novelists have all the time and pages in the world through which to leisurely maneuver their investigations.

Playwrights have two or three acts, two and a little more hours, and about a hundred pages to create an entire world containing a certain kind of truth, to peel away the pain within the pain within the pain and hit the jugular.

What makes a good play? Oh, there are lots of theories. A strong clothesline that keeps pulling an audience along while it unconsciously asks, and the writer quite consciously answers: "What next?" "Now what?" Tension. What goes on between the lines. The tension in relationships between characters. The tension between characters and events. The tension between the characters and their actions, and the audience. The tension between what the playwright tells you and what he or she doesn't tell you. The tension between what you are told and what you are thinking. The tension between ideas and actuality. The tension between right and wrong.

Conflict. All of drama is fights. Fights between conflicting needs, desires, ideas.

I don't think there's any playwright who sits down and consciously applies all these pretentious formulas I've just listed. Though that's what possibly comes out, we sit down and write because we simply want to say something.

That's much easier to deal with, isn't it? I want to say something. I want to tell you about my mother and father. I want to tell you about my childhood. I want to tell you this story I heard. I want to tell you about this unusual character. I want to tell you the world is awful—or wonderful—or funny—or sad. I want to tell you what I think about something. I want to tell you what it's like to be gay. (Did you want to hear that one?)

And I believe the resolution of all this must be moral. Very unfashionable, morals. Very out of season, morality.

Most of what today's critics acclaim as good plays bores me greatly. These plays are thin, trendy, banal, plain, pointless. They bear little relevance to the life I am living or have lived. I don't respond to the tensions and the conflicts and the what nexts. I find few characters challenged—at least in the way I understand challenge. I don't leave the theater enlightened. Or angry because I've been forced to confront something I don't want to think about but should. These plays are about people I don't want to know. These characters and the world they inhabit not only bear little relation to my life or my dreams, they don't even arouse my curiosity. And I am a pretty curious guy.

And the writers of these plays rarely present a point of view or a resolution—or a moral—that isn't banal. These plays add nothing important to life and to the world. Why should I waste my time attending them?

Until recently, good plays were also about language. They weren't composed in words of one syllable. Or in dialogue so aching to be street-smart accurate (or Jewish suburban or minority ghetto—though black playwriting of late often has been more interesting than white playwriting) that a heritage that includes Aeschylus, Sophocles, Shakespeare, Shaw, and Williams might never have existed. Once upon a time, heightened language reached for the same stars as big themes and noble conflicts. Until Beckett and Pinter and their bastard offspring came along and diminished what was said. Why do we now settle for so little? Beckett didn't destroy the theater of language; that was done by the critics who so slavered over his work that it became unfashionable to pursue other possibilities. That is, if you wanted a good review and desired to be included in college curricula. Critics like to be trendy, like everyone else. And God knows Americans—and particularly New Yorkers— like to be trendies.

It seems to me that the more a play is *about* something—an opinion, a philosophy, a specific point of view—the more the critic feels bound to attack it. The modern play, to be "artistically correct," must not take sides, ruffle feathers, churn up waters, make you think. It must also not be about "others," because that makes the trendies uncomfortable, unless it is about the poor or downtrodden, which allows trendies to condescend. It definitely must not be critical of the status quo—that is, the trendies themselves; we are not a nation good at either criticizing or laughing at ourselves. Once upon a time, Gustave Flaubert (with Joyce, the altar trendy critics worship at in the world of Novelty, as they kiss poor Beckett's ass in the world of Play) maintained that a writer must be careful not to intrude too personally into his characters' lives, action, and thoughts. *Ne pas conclure* ("Draw no conclusions") was his motto, and "You should write more coldly" was his advice. These somehow became the definitions, the highest goals, the boundaries of modern writing. Distance. Objectivity. Observation without authorial intrusion. Well, if you read Flaubert, you will find that he is just as intrusive and opinionated and selective and manipulative and emotional an author as the many great ones who preceded him. But because critics have said *"Ne pas couclure"* and "You should write more coldly," It Must Be So, and writers have been pulverizing their brains and their talent ever since, as, with determination, they actually extract their juices from their work. Imagine writers trying to make their writing less interesting! But that is exactly what is considered good writing today. The word and deed flattened, lest they be too orotund.

It is no different in the theater. Thirty-five years ago, Walter Kerr wrote a book, *How Not to Write a Play,* which pleaded (obviously to no avail) for a return to heightened and poetic theater—language and ideas and challenge. Shaw, Ibsen, Chekov, Aeschylus, Sophocles, Shakespeare: remember them? They would probably be out of work if writing today. TV and tabloid critics would bemoan "wordiness" and "length" and "author's message" and "too complicated plot" or "lack of action." Meanwhile raving about plays where characters have no opinions, take no sides, give and/or lose nothing of import. Where there is no conflict, only petty obstructions. Where nothing of life and death is at stake. Where there is no *drama.*

Might as well stay home, thee and me. Which most audiences now do. And watch TV.

Theater should astonish, amaze, frighten, shock, purge, touch, and move. (Here I go again.) Make you angry. Make you cry. Make you laugh. Help you learn. Inspire. All of the above. That's what it used to do. That's what it started out to do. Intentionally.

Once upon a time the theater was the home of opinion and anger. (Not only drama, but tragedy, farce, and comedy can be very angry.) It was actually meant—can you believe it?—to rouse the public and create discussion and change the world. Sophocles and Shakespeare and Marlowe and Pirandello and Racine even dared to criticize rulers and kings. Aeschylus actually dared to question the gods. What's the last American play where our "rulers" were taken to task? Or a religion challenged? Congreve and Wycherly and Goldsmith and Sheridan and Marivaux and Wilde dared to satirize the ruling classes. What's the last American play you saw that dared to do that?

American theater reflects an inordinate inability to laugh at ourselves, to criticize any powers-that-be. How exceptionally boring. And polite.

Theater today is polite and boring. Compared with what's available everywhere else—movies, television, fiction, nonfiction, rock videos, magazines, street corners, Central Park, even journalism and daily newspapers—theater is terribly polite and boring. No wonder audiences stay away in droves.

When something comes along that is offensive, and is meant to be offensive—actually aggressively affronting current thinking; actually struggling with determination to crash through a brick wall of apathy or denial or ignorance—today's theater of boring politesse is now so entrenched, and the critics now say "You must write more coldly" so automatically that what should be the true nature of the playwright's calling is not only overlooked, *it* is found to be offensive. The playwright's true task is now viewed, by critics and their desperate-to-be-led-into-trendiness audiences alike, as a different kind of breach: a breach of taste, of the status quo, of politesse—the very tepid qualities the playwright, if he or she is any good, should be trying to blast off an audience's shoulders like the leaden, scurvy dandruff it is.

The last time the American theater was healthy—through the 1920s and 1930s and 1940s (and don't give me that hoary argument that now there's TV and all sorts of other distractions for our leisure time: people inherently love to go out)—plays were about issues and ideas and interesting people and danger and conflict and *the world* (as against the contemplation of the playwright's navel). These are some of the people who wrote plays then: Lillian Hellman, Robert E. Sherwood, Clifford Odets, George S. Kaufman, Moss Hart, Edna Ferber, Maxwell Anderson, Elmer Rice, Eugene O'Neill, Arthur Miller, Philip Barry, Sidney Howard, Sidney Kingsley, William Saroyan, Paul Osborne, S. N. Behrman, George Abbott, Ben Hecht, Charles MacArthur, the Marx Brothers, John Steinbeck, P. G. Wodehouse, Thornton Wilder. And I'm not even touching the musical, or foreign writers whose work was produced here, such as Sartre, Anouilh, Coward, Maugham, Shaw, Pinero, Priestly, O'Casey. Sort of makes you realize how stinking the paucity is now, doesn't it?

The opinionated play published herein is *about* something. About something that may murder millions of people, that is murdering tens of thousands of my fellow gay men, and is possibly set to murder me. I was not surprised when a number of New York critics slaughtered me. I'm accustomed to that by now. By now I have learned that I rarely get good reviews and that critics don't review what Larry Kramer writes or says, they review what Larry Kramer is, which is a homosexual. And they review what they think of homosexuality—they don't like it—or what they think homosexuality should be—they don't like it the way it is—and they aren't very interested in hearing what I, or any other gay writer, has to say about it. When Neil Simon writes an autobiographical play, they don't review his life or his heterosexuality; they review his play; but that's because critics are heterosexual, too, or maintain they are. So they don't have to confront anything. Or be challenged. Or lead the way. They can just sit back on their politesse.

Wouldn't it be the most boring world if everything and everyone were alike? And if everyone wrote the same play?

The theater now is the most boring place in the world. And everybody *is* writing the same play.

What I was most surprised by in the reviews for *Just Say No* was the amazement a number of critics registered that I really thought plays could change people's minds, *accomplish something.* Help change the world for the better. How dare I have harbored such a thought! And written such a play!

But I do believe this. Oh, I do believe it so.

And so should the critics.

That's what art started out to do. Once upon a time. Back in those once upon a times when criticism, too, was considered an art, and to serve art.

I am certainly not the first nor will I be the last writer to complain bitterly that bad critics destroy creativity and understand little about it. I get angry that reputedly comprehensive heterosexual publications have yet to give me—or most other gay writers—really good reviews. By "good" I mean thoughtful. Considered and considerate of what we are trying to say. We don't mind being criticized; we do mind being blindly attacked by bigots, or relegated to thumbnail assessments in the back pages, or—most likely—totally ignored and unreviewed at all.

There are many fine openly gay writers writing about gay subjects now. Our novelists include Andrew Holleran, David Leavitt, Christopher Bram, Paul Monette, Gary Indiana, Rita Mae Brown, Sarah Schulman, Gary Glickman, Edmund White, John Rechy, Dorothy Allison, Brad Gooch, Dennis Cooper, Michael Nava, May Sarton, James Purdy, Gene Horowitz, Krandall Kraus, James McCourt, Armistead Maupin, George Baxt, Allan Garganus, Paul Bowles. Our playwrights writing about gay subjects include Victor Bumbalo, William Hoffman, Terrence McNally, Harvey Fierstein, Doric Wilson, Robert Patrick, Charles Busch, Craig Lucas, Tony Kushner, Martin Sherman, Albert Innaurato, Robert Chesley, Joseph Pintauro, Lanford Wilson, Arthur Laurents. How many of them have you read or seen? How many of them have you tried to understand? If you find depiction of gay life, particularly gay sex, foreign, does it ever occur to you that we often find depictions of straight sex and heterosexuality foreign?

It is exceedingly painful to face the fact that, over the years, I know that such treatment has taken its toll on me and on every other gay writer. (And, for that matter, on every "minority" writer.) And that I would have been a more productive artist if I didn't have to withstand all the diatribes hurled at me, because few critics, and the publications they write for, have empathy or interest in homosexuality and what it's like to be gay in this world. It rankles to see all the second-rate straight white males who churn out dreck year after year get all the recognition, the best-seller lists, the Broadway hits, the Tonys and Pulitzers and National Book Awards, the movie sales, when I know I and other gay writers are better writers and thinkers than a lot of them and we are treated so dismissively, if we are noted at all. Such positioning also turns many of us to other endeavors completely, or into bitter men and women, from either fighting a fight that seems never to be over or—even more debilitating—ceasing the struggle altogether.

Sour grapes, you say? Well, as my best friend fielded my fear that this entire essay might be construed as filled with nothing but: "Those folks tried to kill you, honey; you're due a few sour grapes."

The New Yorker does not consider gay literature a category worthy of discussion. Nor does *Esquire.* Or any of the literary quarterlies—the *Paris Review, Antaeus, Grand Street,* and their like. *The New York Review of Books* does not appear to believe that such a thing as homosexuality even exists. *Vanity Fair,* despite the existence on its staff of many gays, seems to me to be so homophobic as to often come close to actually breaking laws against slander. The same can be said of *The Nation.* The *Village Voice* rarely reviews gay books and plays. *Time* never and *Newsweek* infrequently. And for publications located outside of New York, gay writing simply does not exist.

The New York Times does occasionally nod our way. But it is a condescending nod: reviewers are rarely equipped for the task. Would you give a book on electrical engineering to a florist to review? Would a feminist manifesto be fairly treated at the hands of a misogynist? The *Times* often appears to go out of its way to locate a reviewer ludicrously removed from a sensitivity toward gay subjects. My recent nonfiction book on AIDS was reviewed by someone completely unfamiliar with this epidemic and its effects on my community. But then I have never had a considered review in *The New York Times.* Yes, I am still sucking on a few sour grapes.

But gay artists try not to. We try to reason with ourselves that it is the creation first and foremost that is most important—not its reception by a world. Perhaps there will be acceptance after death—now much closer for too many of us. Because of a growing network of gay bookstores and an increase in the number of gay community theaters, our work does reach an audience that supports us, financially and emotionally, little by little and more and more. My family may think, from reading and viewing what they read and view, that everything I've written is a flop; but in the gay world I have made a certain higher mark.

But there is no writer who can accept relegation to a ghetto happily. Like any other writer, we want to be universally heard. We want you to try to understand what we are trying to say to you. If we are widely panned and even more widely ignored, how are we to get our message out? We want gay playwrights chronicling our history to reach the acceptance of, say, August Wilson.

Gay writers try hard to avoid the paranoid scenario: the straight world does not want us to get our message out. Stomp us into oblivion and there will be no gay literature to attend to. At its worst, we have come to see this attitude exemplified in our government's inattention to AIDS. Perhaps it will go away, or perhaps they will go away, we now know to be the subtext of what's going on. Harvey Fierstein spends twelve years trying to get *Torch Song Trilogy* produced, before finally putting it on himself. David Leavitt gets clobbered, in *Vanity Fair,* not for what he's written but for what he hasn't written, because the homosexuality he's writing about differs from the homosexuality the critic James Wolcott wants to read about. Every second-rate heterosexual playwright and filmmaker gets invited to the Eugene O'Neill Theater Center or Robert Redford's Sundance Institute, but not openly gay ones dealing with openly gay subject matter. Every major New York play agent—fourteen of them—turned down my play about AIDS, *The Normal Heart.*

By the time the AIDS epidemic came along and I knew I had to write about it, I'd learned many of the above lessons. AIDS was not being, and has not been, attended to because it occurs in populations the majority isn't interested in and finds expendable. Just as the media had, traditionally, brutally treated gay artists and their work, so had the media shown a remarkable lack of interest in covering this devouring epidemic.

I've come to realize that most critics, reporters, and journalists (there is often very little difference among the three) are, along with what they write, and whom they write it for, painfully conservative in bias. So here comes AIDS—a medical mystery so complicated as to make it very difficult to make comprehensible in sound bites, in short paragraphs, and certainly not without first carrying out a great deal of digging, research, and homework. The press has been very reluctant to do this research and homework. Consequently, most of the many AIDS scandals just aren't written about.

And our ideas of what is truly scandalous unfortunately often involve the heterosexual majority. If some think AIDS was allowed to fester and grow unattended in New York because they believe its Mayor is a closeted homosexual terrified of being revealed as such if he be found too attentive to the demands of the city's gay population, how in the world do you get the straight press to report this suspicion? If some think AIDS was allowed to further fester and grow unattended on a national level because they believe our former President and his First Lady were fearful lest various sexual scandals and proclivities in their own pasts and their own family be revealed, how in the world do you get the straight press to report these suspicions? These are valid suspicions—that sexual hypocrisies have more to do with the conduct of the affairs of state than historians allow. But "straight" leaders "protect" themselves by erecting unwritten codes of decorum—if you will, politesse—that an increasing number of gays do not support. There is no actual law that prohibits naming a public official as homosexual or that constrains a press from revealing a boisterous heterosexual life—no law, that is, except the unwritten ones: it is considered by heterosexuals as bad taste.

But gay people do not consider it bad taste to be identified as gay. In fact, huge numbers of us consider it exceedingly prideful. And exceedingly, tragically, unhealthy to conceal it. This has become brutally apparent as such hypocrisy allows so many of us to be so casually put to death.

Such, indeed, is the message, the moral, of *Just Say No*.

And such, indeed, is the continuing unwillingness of the heterosexual world to hear a message so unpleasant to them that they will do everything in their power—including their continuing ignoble attempts—to stifle our creative voices in any and every way they can.

In 1973, my first play, *Sissies' Scrapbook,* was produced. In those days, Playwrights Horizons was not so handsomely ensconced in its Forty-second Street home; rather, it shared space with a dance company at the old YWCA on Eighth Avenue and Fifty-third Street, and all its plays were put on in an old gym, with bleachers for seats. The entire budget for the five performances (extended to eight) allowed by Actors Equity (because nobody got paid anything) could not have been more than several hundred dollars. I had a wonderful cast, the audiences were exceptionally responsive, I felt my play was appreciated and my message understood. Critics did not review these "showcase" productions in those days; though I wrote to Clive Barnes, then a *Times* critic, he did not respond or come to see it. When the play closed, there seemed no hope for further productions. Since I then supported myself primarily as a screenwriter, I went back to the movies.

But I was hooked. I kept remembering: I had moved people. I'd made them cry. *Something I had written* had been able to touch the audience. After each performance, I could see them leave the theater crying. Some of them would seek me out, still in tears. I had made people feel what I had felt, for my characters, for their stories, for what had happened to them. Heady stuff. No movie I had ever written had provided me with that experience. (Anyway, movies don't work in the same way. Movie actors don't create their performances from interaction and tension with an audience. That doesn't lessen their effectiveness or usefulness—as entertainment. But it's a hard medium through which to convey *ideas,* and as I have said, I think good plays should contain a large dollop of good ideas. And it's ideas that change the world, not entertainment.)

A year later a producer appeared who offered to produce *Sissies' Scrapbook* commercially off Broadway. During two weeks of previews, again people were moved: I saw them crying. Despite a production inferior to the first one, and despite my inability to solve to my satisfaction a structural defect, something was still working. The play was about four men who had been best friends since their days together at Yale. The producer objected to the original title, and *Four Friends,* an inadequate substitute, was used. But the play was still about cowardice and the inability of some men to grow up, leave the emotional bondage of male collegiate camaraderie, and assume adult responsibilities. Three of the men were straight and one of them was gay. They all were cripples in one way or another and one of the straight ones did indeed become actually crippled in Act Two.

This was to be my first experience of extending to the straight world—and straight men—messages they did not wish to hear. I received a brutal clobbering from the *Times.* Clive Barnes, who arrived half an hour late, began his review with: "With friends like these you don't need enemies." Despite other and more encouraging reviews, the producer closed the play on opening night. "The *Times* closed it," the producer said to me. "You can't beat the *Times.*"

We now come to an unfortunate fact of life with which I've been told even the *Times* itself is uncomfortable—the disproportionate influence of a *Times* review on the run of a play. Although they had also disliked the film of D. H. Lawrence's *Women in Love,* which I'd scripted and produced, and they were to be vitriolic toward my novel, *Faggots,* which came out in 1978, a movie and a novel can eventually outrace bad reviews: the former because film companies spend fortunes in advertising to dispel all bad words, and the latter by the very fact that a small volume of printed pages can somehow stay around for a long time and find its own audience. But a play rarely survives a bad *Times* review, particularly without an enterprising and/or rich producer. This kind of producer is now exceptionally rare. And foolish, because by now the public, those trendies, has handed over responsibility to the *Times* for making theatrical judgments for them. A bad review more than not elicits the reaction: thank goodness—another play I don't have to see.

I did not suffer my failure well. I had witnessed the slaughter of my child, and it hurt too much. And back in the movie business, I was confronted once again by another painful obstacle: Movies are not interested in what I am interested in. Increasingly aware of my gay identity, I wanted to write about that. Film companies are even more homophobic than theater critics. To this day there has never been a good American film financed by a major studio about homosexuality, despite the fact that every studio has more than its share of gay executives, producers, stars, and writers—even, in some cases, the very studio heads themselves.

When I knew I had to write about AIDS, I found I had no choice but to return to the play form, for several reasons. I knew no film company would finance such a movie. It had taken me three years to write my novel, and I was obsessed with the notion that my AIDS message had to get into the world quickly. It also seemed to me that only the play form could provide the sense of *immediacy* I felt essential.

I also thought the play form was the best way to get matters attended to. Ed Koch and Ronald Reagan would have no choice but to pay attention to AIDS after the opening night of *The Normal Heart.* Yes, I conceived of the theater as a means of achieving something politically. I was going after Koch, and Reagan, and—courageous me—*The New York Times.* My soapbox was planted firmly on the ground of Joe Papp's Public Theater and Joe Papp is as good a producer and attention getter as there is. And although I might suffer critical clobberings again, I knew Joe guaranteed us an eight-week run.

Why was I going after *The New York Times?* Because, along with Koch and Reagan, they shared an ignoble disdain for AIDS. Their early reporting was rare and grudging. In the first nineteen months of the epidemic, as the number of cases rose from 41 to 958, they allowed only seven articles into its pages, and never on page one. During the three months of the Tylenol scare, in 1982, the *Times* wrote about it a total of fifty-four times. Four of these articles appeared on the front page. The total number of Tylenol deaths: seven.

I cannot tell you if the *Times* critic Frank Rich liked *The Normal Heart.* I think he was conflicted. On the one hand, my play criticized the hell out of his employer. On the other hand, my play was about dying young men. Even he wasn't that cruel as to totally crucify a play about dying young men. The day after he came to see it, the *Times* called for two tickets for that evening's preview. In those seats sat William Honan, their cultural affairs editor, and a lawyer with a flashlight. Every time the *Times* was mentioned in the play, the flashlight would go on and the lawyer would write down the line. When Rich's review appeared, appended to it was a short announcement from the editors denying the charges I'd made. To my knowledge, such an editorial appendage to a critic's review was an historic first.

Rich did throw a couple of great quotes into his review, I guess to hedge his bets. And Joseph Papp is that rare producer who is also a courageous promoter. He read us Rich's review immediately after the opening night's performance. And he vowed that he would keep the play running. And he kept his promise. To this day, *The Normal Heart* holds the record of being the longest-running play at his Public Theater.

Did *The Normal Heart* change the world? Of course not. But it did accomplish more than a little something here and there. It has been produced all over America and all over the world, including such unlikely places as South Africa, Russia, and Poland (and Poland is a land where there is such homophobia that gay people often commit suicide). In Lafayette, Louisiana, a town where they beat up gay people in the streets, the play was done by an amateur group, in a run that was extended twice and then repeated a year later; local straights joined the few local gays who were out of the closet to form an AIDS service organization. And, in Baton Rouge, the local drama critic came out of the closet in his review.

And I'd estimate a few hundred thousand people have seen what I wanted them to see—including two men actually kissing each other and in love and caring for each other and one of them dying in the other's arms. Human beings, just like those watching them.

And I did shame *The New York Times*. Though I still bitch at them continuously, their AIDS coverage is now better than it was.

And Joe Papp and Joe Papp's lawyers joined with me in offering on a stage the dramatic argument: AIDS was originally allowed to grow and grow and grow because the Mayor of New York is a closeted homosexual so terrified of being uncovered that he would rather allow an epidemic. This argument has now entered the general discourse on the history of AIDS. And all future historians will have no choice but to take note. I'm proud of that. I'm proud that I've been able to help gays realize that we who are proud do not have to be victimized by one of our own who is ashamed. Yes, plays can help change history. If you can keep the damn things running.

Going after a Mayor is one thing. Going after a First Family is evidently quite another. It looks as though the world will not see *Just Say No* as it has seen *The Normal Heart.* Even my mother thinks *Just Say No* was a flop because the *Times* review was so hateful. It doesn't occur to her to ask: Why did Mel Gussow scream at me so much? As with *Four Friends,* the producer did not have the resources to surmount a wretched *Times* review, and he closed the show.

Gussow accused *Just Say No* of being in the worst possible taste. Is it bad taste to let a country be destroyed by a plague? Is it bad taste for a Mayor to sell out his city? Is it bad taste for a mother and father to hypocritically sell their son and their gay friends down the river? Gussow, and others, didn't like it that my characters lampooned real people. I don't like it that those real people—and their actions and their attitudes and their secrets, their politesse—are killing me and mine. And I have a moral right to present my case. It's bad taste that the critic for New York's most important newspaper doesn't even try to understand my message or convey it to his readers. Just because my truth is light-years away from Mel Gussow's truth doesn't make my truth in bad taste.

I have seen nothing but bad taste in the last nine years since AIDS came into my life. On the part of this city, on the part of this state, on the part of the federal government, on the part of not just the *Times* but every major publication and network. Why is it bad taste for me to point it out? To point out the venal and crass hypocrisy that became the hallmark of the Reagan years—and looks to be continuing during these years in the Bush—seems to me not to be bad taste at all, but a way of maintaining some sort of spiritual health. And the gay audiences who saw *Just Say No* know exactly what I meant and mean. And, God bless them, they were able to laugh. Perhaps it takes being pushed almost over the edge day after day for nine years to make you see a certain kind of truth.

But gay truths are different from straight truths. And most of the straight world does not wish to hear gay truths. Because, as all truth should, it often contains hurts enough for everyone.

But the trendy heterosexual world of politesse is stronger than we are.

And we are all dying for it.

November 1989